THE

FABLE OF THE BEES

THE

FABLE OF THE BEES

or Private Vices, Publick Benefits

Newly Edited, with an Introduction by

IRWIN PRIMER

DEPARTMENT OF ENGLISH, RUTGERS UNIVERSITY

CAPRICORN BOOKS, NEW YORK

CONTENTS

CONTENTS

THE

FABLE OF THE BEES

INTRODUCTION

AMONG THE MASTERWORKS of Augustan England few can be said to anticipate our dilemmas of individual, social, economic and political morality more ably than Bernard Mandeville's *Fable of the Bees.* Much misunderstood by his Augustan contemporaries, many of whom declared his book pernicious, Mandeville turned his physician's eye upon his society's health, and found that it thrived everywhere upon individual corruptions. His analyses of the role of social ideals and personal impulses in human motivation are as stimulating today as they were in his time, and those who believe that the political morality of Machiavelli is still alive today cannot ignore the pungent social criticism of Mandeville, his kindred spirit.

Born either in Dort or Rotterdam in 1670, Mandeville attended the University of Leyden and in 1691 took the degree of Doctor of Medicine, following in his father's footsteps. He later went to England to learn the language, married there in 1699, and lived in England until his death in 1733. In 1703 and 1704 he published some fables in the manner of La Fontaine, and a subsequent fable, *The Grumbling Hive: or, Knaves Turn'd Honest* (1705), achieved popularity enough to be pirated. Some years later Mandeville called this poem "a story told in doggerel." Had it not been retained as the nucleus of *The Fable of the Bees,* it would never have achieved the fame which it earned as part of the amplified edition.

The fable of *The Grumbling Hive* is quite transparent. The bees lived like men and performed all our actions "in small." The hive was naturally full of vice, "Yet the whole mass" was "a Paradise." Millions endeavored "to supply / Each other's lust and vanity"— and hence the affluent society of Mandeville's time, and ours. The worst cheats in the hive were those who most vociferously complained of the dishonesty and fraud which infested their nation: ". . . all the rogues cry'd brazenly, / Good gods, had we but honesty!" Jove, indignant, angrily rid the hive of fraud, but with remarkable results. The reign of honesty in the complex society of the hive turned out to be disastrous. As honesty triumphed over the common vices, pride and envy and all incentives to social and political emulation waned. The need for dozens of luxuries to gratify one's palate and passions diminished; hence industry and trade declined, and what was once a flourishing society founded upon a healthy and natural human selfishness soon became vulnerable to its enemies. Finally, after being decimated in battle, the remaining bees retreated into a hollow tree to lead temperate, frugal lives "Blest with content and honesty." Surrendering their vices, the bees also surrendered their progress in civilization. The moral of the story is quite explicit: do not indulge the utopian longing for a flourishing society free of vice; ". . . fools only strive / To make a great an honest hive."

When Mandeville's poem was republished as the basis of *The Fable of the Bees: or, Private Vices, Publick Benefits* (1714), he explained in his Preface that the purpose of his amplified edition was to correct the misapprehensions of several readers who "either wilfully or ignorantly" misunderstood his poem and who imagined that it was a satire upon virtue and morality, composed entirely "for the encouragement of vice." The much-argued question of the purpose and intention of Mandeville's *Fable* plays a major part in the controversy which grew out of his repeated attacks upon the ethical benevolism of the third Earl of Shaftesbury. This controversy remained active throughout the eighteenth century and concerned not only the purpose but the very meaning of his doctrines.

The 1714 edition of the *Fable* contained an important preface, the original poem, an essay entitled *An Enquiry into the Origin of Moral Virtue,* and twenty *Remarks*—some of them full essays—

which were prose expansions and interpretations of various lines in the poem. This edition seems not to have excited any public furor; that came when a later edition appeared in 1723, containing two further essays, *An Essay on Charity and Charity-Schools* and *A Search into the Nature of Society.* Mandeville's earlier editions certainly revealed his distaste for orthodox clerical opinion, but only with the 1723 edition, in which he disparaged the vulnerable institution of charity schools, did he elicit strong public disapproval from William Law and others. The Grand Jury of Middlesex, in fact, branded his book as a public nuisance. While Mandeville was earning his notorious reputation in the 1720's, he was busy composing the second volume of the *Fable,* consisting of a preface of six dialogues which further amplify and buttress his unorthodox views. This 1728 edition in two volumes is substantially the complete *Fable* as it has come down to us.

Mandeville's doctrine is deceptively simple, and hence the unsuspecting reader who merely browses through the *Fable* might conclude that Mandeville's *leitmotif*—private vices, public benefits —sanctions indulgence in vice on the ground that such indulgence is, after all, unavoidable and socially useful. In the 1720's incensed moralists such as the anonymous author of "An Abusive Letter to Lord C." (which Mandeville reprinted in his *Vindication* at the close of volume I of the *Fable*) agreed that this ostensible *carte blanche* for the pursuit of vice was intolerable:

> . . . this profligate author of the Fable . . . has taken upon him to tear up the very foundations of moral virtue, and establish vice in its room. The best physician in the world did never labour more, to purge the natural body of bad qualities, than this bumble-bee has done to purge the body-politic of good ones.

It is to Mandeville's credit that while he stood up to such charges and retaliated, he did so rarely and never descended to the name-calling or coarser modes of controversy common in his times.

Mandeville, in fact, took pains to reiterate his adherence to virtue and morality, to revelation, and to the Church of England. Morally respectable passages such as the following can be found throughout his writings: "I lay down as a first principle, that in all societies, great or small, it is the duty of every member of it to be good, that virtue ought to be encouraged, vice discountenanced, the laws obeyed, and transgressors punished." Is this not straight-forward? Seen from another point of view, however, Mandeville's professed faith in revelation and Christian ethics is supremely ironic. We cannot imagine him believing in a faith the ideals of which he so dexterously undermined. Professor F. B. Kaye, our ablest interpreter of Mandeville, admirably emphasizes this point:

> Mandeville's *feeling* is throughout anti-ascetic. He *rejoices* in destroying the ideals of those who imagine that there is in the world any real exemplification of the transcendent morality which he formally preaches. He is delighted to find that the rigoristic creed which he has adopted is an absolutely imprac-ticable one.

Mandeville, then, dons the mask of irony, but he does not main-tain his pose consistently, as does Swift in his *Modest Proposal*. Modern writers on Mandeville, though generally suspicious of his sincerity in maintaining contradictory positions on morality and religion, regard his views on economics, psychology, and sociology as being more straightforward and literal.

The reader who expects that Mandeville will always put his cards on the table and be honest or sincere is simply ignoring the fact that had Mandeville published his opinions without any hedg-ing whatever, he might not have avoided the prosecution and imprisonment to which freethinkers in his time were still subject. Discretion, for Mandeville, was indeed the better part of valor; he had no intention of suffering martyrdom of any sort for his cause. Bruno and Vanini, he remarked, "were both executed for openly professing and teaching of atheism." Shall we praise them for having the courage of their convictions? for being martyrs in the caues of freedom of speech? According to Mandeville, their self-sacrifice is merely an index of their pride: "There is no pitch of self-denial that a man of pride and constitution cannot reach, nor any passion so violent but he'll sacrifice it to another which is superior to it. . . ."

One explanation for Mandeville's retreat behind irony, then, might be prudence, or his unwillingness to purchase his freedom of speech at the price of his liberty in society. Another explanation does Mandeville much more credit: to oppose the official morality derived from revelation is one thing, but to oppose that morality while simultaneously professing to believe it is a maneuver that would attract far more attention and provoke many a complacent conscience. His oblique and paradoxical remarks are thus both defensive and offensive, and are employed mischievously. He criticized the English clergy savagely for their worldliness, but always maintained his allegiance to the Church of England. Today, when parson-baiting is no longer a fashionable cause to the intellectual, we are less shocked at his open disrespect, or we may indeed enjoy it.

As the immediacy of Mandeville's moralizing has waned, his literary vitality has come to be properly appreciated. The writer who was once regarded as a national menace is now praised in our literary histories as one of the more vigorous satirists of the age which produced Pope, Swift, Gay and "Martinus Scriblerus." Furthermore, Mandeville has also made his way into histories of philosophy, psychology, sociology and economics. His anticipations of some modern ideas and approaches in the social sciences are striking, but before we turn to them let us first consider such difficulties of interpreting Mandeville's thesis as would trouble most readers.

The difficulties in establishing what Mandeville meant begin in the very title of the *Fable*. He not only hides his intention and meaning in the contradictory halves of a paradox, but also renders them yet more elusive through intentional ambiguity. What relationship actually exists between "private vices" and "public benefits"? The reader of the second edition in 1714 could not be censured for believing that Mandeville wished, for the benefit of society, to replace the virtues with the vices. If we judge from the title page of that edition, this is precisely the bait that we find: *The Fable of the Bees: or, Private Vices Publick Benefits. Containing Several Discourses, to demonstrate, That Human Frailties, during the degeneracy of Mankind, may be turn'd to the Advantage of the Civil Society, and made to supply the Place of Moral Virtues.* At the end of his *Search into the Nature of Society* (1723), Mandeville more cautiously concluded that "private vices, by the dexterous management of a skilful politician, may be turned into public benefits." This is a relatively guarded assertion, for Mandeville surely realized that most readers would tend to insert "are" between "private vices" and "public benefits."

Commenting further on the meaning of his paradox, Mandeville noted that if his reading of the paradox were unacceptable, then

> . . . the worst construction that can be put upon the words is, that they are an epitome of what I have labored to prove throughout the book, that luxury and the vices of man, under the regulations and restrictions laid down in the *Fable of the Bees,* are subservient to, and even inseparable from the earthly felicity of the civil society; I mean what is commonly called temporal happiness, and esteemed to be such.
>   —*A Letter to Dion* (1732), p. 37.

It is characteristic of Mandeville that only a page later he asserted that his "true reason" for citing the paradox in his title—indeed, the only reason—was to increase the sale of his book by stimulating the reader's curiosity! Mandeville's ambiguity led his contemporary Francis Hutcheson to distinguish five ways in which Mandeville meant and applied his paradox: (1) "private vices are themselves public benefits," (2) "private vices naturally tend, as the direct and necessary means, to produce public happiness," (3) "private vices by dexterous management of governors may be made to tend to public happiness," (4) "private vices natively and necessarily flow from public happiness," and (5) "private vices will probably flow from public happiness through the present corruption of men." A careful study of the *Fable* will convince one that Mandeville in fact actually uses all of these readings of his paradox, and perhaps a few others as well.

As the omission of a specific verb in his paradox occasioned much criticism, so did his use of particular words, especially the words *vice, virtue,* and *public benefit.* Like many strict interpreters of religious morality, Mandeville reasoned that there can be no middle ground of neutral or indifferent acts. Whatever is not clearly virtuous is to be considered vicious, and nothing can be considered virtuous if it is in any way motivated by our self-regard. Kaye has named this ethical position "rigorism," and a few quotations will amply illustrate Mandeville's rigorism. In the *Enquiry into the Origin of Moral Virtue* we learn that "skilful politicians" agreed with their community to regard as vice "everything which, without regard to the public, man should commit to gratify any of his appetites"; and they gave the name of virtue "to every performance by which man, contrary to the impulse of nature, should endeavor the benefit of others or the conquest of his own passions out of a rational ambition of being good." In 1732 Mandeville wrote that he had always "strenuously insisted . . . that no practice, no action or good quality, how useful or beneficial soever they may be in themselves, can ever deserve the name of virtue, strictly speaking, where there is not a palpable self-denial to be seen." And further on in his *Origin of Honour,* "There is no virtue that has a name, but it curbs, regulates, or subdues some passion that is peculiar to human nature. . . ." Mandeville has obviously chosen an ethical standard to which only true ascetics can conform. Once this is recognized, the destructive power of his rigorous definition of virtue becomes clear. Virtue then becomes the property of the saintly, and Mandeville can exult in having shown how the generality of men live and act under the dominion of vice. By his strict interpretation of virtue, he denies not the existence, but merely the *presence* of virtue in the lives of most men. Consequently, he is able to add to the catalogue of vices many moral traits that are commonly regarded as virtues. Chastity and humility, for instance, become "vicious" to the extent that they bloat one's pride or self-esteem. Even charity, any benevolent public service whatever, could be traced to man's desire to think well of himself.

In such instances Mandeville's paradox amounts to a denigration of what most of us regard as virtuous behavior. But when he discusses the traditional or the "real" vices, he does not waste his words to convince us that they are indeed vicious; his aim on such occasions is to demonstrate that the vices, without exception, yield public benefits. Thus prostitution is beneficial to the public in that it diminishes the threat of the predatory male to the honor of chaste wives and maidens. In a separate essay entitled *A Modest Defence of Publick Stews* (1724), Mandeville used this argument to defend government-regulated prostitution. The fallacy of such reasoning is obvious, and Mandeville often admitted that in a great many instances the enormity of the crime or vice far exceeded the social benefit it produced. His strategy in such cases was to insist upon the truism that *some* social good was the inevitable derivative of even the most heinous of crimes: "The worst of all the multitude/Did something for the common good."

The latter half of his paradox is construed more easily. By *public benefits* Mandeville meant any goods or good acts which are pleasurable or useful to any member of the public, apart from the individual agent. He was careful to point out, in his *Letter to Dion,* that he used these words in the sense which was current among most ordinary men: not the advantages of the City of God, not the salvation of souls in the afterlife, but all temporal and terrestrial goods or advantages whatever. In thus limiting his notion of public benefits, Mandeville was clearly answering the contention of the orthodox that the true public benefit awaits man in the afterlife. In the later nineteenth century J. M. Robertson, the editor of Shaftesbury's *Characteristicks* and author of a fine appreciation of Mandeville, subjected Mandeville's idea of public benefits to further attack, though from a position far removed from the religious orthodoxy of most of Mandeville's contemporary critics:

> For us to-day, the fallacy of Mandeville's thesis, in so far as that is expressed by his sub-title, lies not in the definition of vice, for which he was not specially responsible, but in his implied definition of "public benefits." What he really does is to show that the "vices" of some people work good to some other people: what he fails to define, and what he ought to define, is "public benefit." Everything there depends on what you understand by "public," and our answer to Mandeville may be stated very simply thus: That no benefit is a public benefit which involves the degradation of any. So long, of course, as we do not feel as a personal grievance the hardship of others, we shall tend to find Mandeville's demonstration either satisfactory or perplexing according as we are unprejudiced or biassed in favour of a transcendental ethic; but as soon as we attain the sense of the solidarity of society, and reason out the nature of the social interdependences, Mandeville's case becomes an exposure of social evil and a proof of the need for a reconstruction. We do not deny that such "vices" involve such "benefit"; we say we want to have our benefits of a different kind.

> —*Essays towards a Critical Method*
> (London, 1889), pp. 217-18.

Mandeville's reply to this would probably have been conciliatory: we do indeed want to have our benefits of a different kind; but (he would have added) I am merely pointing to those goods which most people daily regard as benefits. In his own way Robertson seems to have been driving toward a rigorous egalitarian view of public benefit, much as Mandeville maintains a rigorous view of virtue. Yet Mandeville's theory of public benefit does deserve criticism, as Robertson and others felt. The point lies not, however, in his notion of the benefits but in his idea of the public. Mandeville's public, far from being democratic and egalitarian, was rigidly hierarchical. One's class or position in the state was directly related to the kind and degree of public benefit to which one had access, or to which he was entitled. When Robertson objected that we want our benefits to be of a different kind, he ought to have added that we also want our public to be different.

Much of the strength of Mandeville's argument lies in the fact that he repeatedly claims to be dealing with the facts. In the fifth dialogue (*Fable,* Part II) Cleomenes, who defends the *Fable* and speaks for Mandeville, observes that "as all our knowledge comes *a posteriori,* it is imprudent to reason otherwise than from the facts." Throughout his *Treatise of the Hypochondriack and Hysterick Passions* (1711) Mandeville recommends close and steady observation as the best means for diagnosing and treating a patient. In his *Fable* he diagnoses the fundamental evils of society with zest, but refrains from offering major or drastic cures for the simple reason that society is in a sufficiently flourishing and healthy state. True, he did urge reforms of specific evils, as in his *Enquiry into the Causes of the Frequent Executions at Tyburn* (1725). In this work Mandeville attempted to improve the condition—the *spiritual* condition—of the imprisoned; he also recommended in behalf of the medical profession that the corpses of the executed be donated to the advancement of science. He was not a sweeping reformer, not a sentimental humanitarian of the later-eighteenth-century kind.

The foundation of Mandeville's critique of society is his view of human nature. Introducing the prose commentary upon his poem, he candidly asserts that ". . . without any compliment to the courteous reader, or myself, I believe man (besides skin, flesh, bones, &c. that are obvious to the eye) to be a compound of various passions; that all of them, as they are provoked and come uppermost, govern him by turns, whether he will or no." Human nature, then, is founded initially on man's instinctive self-regard. We either indulge our passions directly or we skillfully disguise them, but our behavior is fundamentally based upon our overt or latent self-regard. Mandeville sharply limits the role of reason in determining or governing human behavior. Reason he regards as intimately allied with virtue; both provide the power of individual restraint and self-control. Mandeville would have agreed with Pope that

> Two Principles in human nature reign;
> Self-love to urge, and Reason, to restrain;

but Pope did not ridicule man's pride in his reason as consistently as did Mandeville. Mandeville, in fact, came as close as any writer in the eighteenth century to anticipating the psychoanalytical devaluation of the rational in human conduct. Like our depth psychologists, he was expert in recognizing such common "defense mechanisms" as rationalization and repression. In writing about the "hypochondriack" and "hysterick" passions—he later referred to them as "diseases"—he was clearly dealing with the neurotic personality of his time. He believed strongly that the gratification of our libidinal impulses is more beneficial to society than ascetic denial and self-mortification—that is, whenever he was not paying lip-service to orthodoxy.

His views on human psychology consist mainly in specific analyses of pride, shame, fear, envy, jealousy, avarice, prodigality, ambition, courage and other passions. Such cataloguing and description in Mandeville seem to follow lines set down by Montaigne, Hobbes, Locke, Bayle and La Rochefoucauld, among others. What is new in Mandeville, or at least singularly accented, is his sense of a slowly developing, evolutionary social psychology. The student of Mandeville should be aware that his two major "historical" accounts of the origin of morals and society—*An Enquiry into the Origin of Moral Virtue* and the *Fifth Dialogue* in the *Fable, II*—are separated by a span of fourteen years and differ considerably. Mandeville begins the earlier account with the selfish savage in the primitive state of nature, and relates that he could not be made "tractable" (*i.e.,* sociable and capable of self-improvement) unless he could be made to subordinate his private desires to the public interest. Unlike the social-contract theories of the origin of society, Mandeville's theory attributes the initial step in the socialization of man to the egoistic impulses of "skilful politicians" who encouraged social intercourse not through any selfless love of their fellow creatures, but merely as a means to fulfill their selfish desires. Since it would have been impossible to reward the social behavior of the savage with a concrete gift for each virtuous act, they internalized the reward by flattering man upon the rationality of his soul and by inculcating the notions of honor as the highest good and shame as the worst of evils. By urging man's superiority to the animals and the indignity of gratifying his brutish lusts, they established through flattery a code of ethical ideals which made social progress possible. Mandeville summarized this "process" in his much-quoted remark that "the moral virtues are the political offspring which flattery begot upon pride."

Though many of Mandeville's critics took this sketch of the origin of moral virtue as a *bona fide* historical account, it is certainly wiser to read this sketch not literally but as an allegory of the moral structure of civilized society. The speculations on the slow and gradual evolution of society which we find in the second volume of the *Fable* seem to have been designed to fulfill the expectation of a historical explanation of society, an expectation which had been raised in the editions prior to 1728. The history we are offered in the later dialogues is not chronological in the sense that specific dates are made available, but is rather of the kind of hypothetical or conjectural history of early society such as became increasingly popular later in that century. Mandeville tried to reconstruct the story of prehistoric society in accordance with empirical probability, as against revelation; his nearest approach to chronology is no more than a series of three major "steps to society," followed by other important developments. The first stage occurred when savages were compelled by necessity to band together in mutual defense against animals. "The second step to society," says Cleomenes, "is the danger men are in from one another: for which we are beholden to that staunch principle of pride and ambition that all men are born with." And "the third and last step to society is the invention of letters," by which means laws would remain stable and trustworthy, rather than subject to the errors of oral tradition. Speech, of course, preceded the inven-

tion of letters. Mandeville's account of the gradual evolution of
spoken language as a process in which the savage gropingly sought
to supplement his insufficient gestures has been highly praised as
one of the earliest empirical explanations of the origins of language. For reasons of prudence he does not deny the "inspira-
tional" theory of language origins which divines demonstrated in
Genesis; he merely offers his theory as an adjunct, as one of the
ways in which language might have been rediscovered by the
"fallen" savages.

Other milestones of social evolution cited by Mandeville are
the invention of weapons and tools, the use of iron, the division
of labor, and the use of money. In the later seventeenth century
these stages of development had been widely discussed and evalu-
ated by all participants in the battle of the Ancients and the Moderns. In Mandeville's account they are set within a context that
repeatedly stresses a slow, uncertain, not-quite-fortuitous evolution of society during innumerable ages. When asked "how many
ages do you think it would require to have a well-civilized nation
from such a savage pair as yours?" Cleomenes replies, "That is
very uncertain; and I believe it impossible to determine anything
about it." In the mid-eighteenth century Buffon allegorized the
six days of the Creation into an account of the procession of geological ages, and later naturalists came to rely further on Nature
as a reliable recorder of time. Lacking their insights into geological
time, Mandeville was nevertheless more acutely aware than were
his contemporaries of the immense stretches of time involved in
the emergence of modern society.

His later versions of the socialization of man did not cancel out
but rather incorporated his earlier myth of the "skilful politicians."
The later account is especially commendable for his reliance upon
realistic "empirical" guesswork. He here regards society not as
something that men agreed upon, a social contract, nor as a condition into which men were flattered by politicians. Society, rather,
was forced upon them through various exigencies; it was their
response to a challenge. Were we to add that society is hence one
more *natural* occurrence in the stream of time, we would be com-
plicating Mandeville's use of the terms "nature" and "natural."
For Mandeville, society is an artifice through which men learned,
and still learn, to regulate their impulses and instincts. The "natu-

ral" man is that bundle of irrational passions—instincts, drives, desires, impulses and so forth—which are innate in all men, everywhere and in all ages. Mandeville's natural man, we might say, is very much of a piece with the Freudian *id,* and whatever causes natural man to restrain his impulses, to deny the demands of his *nature,* is an "unnatural" or artificial socializing and "rationalizing" of man. Only after the natural man was driven by necessity into social behavior did the crafty politicians encourage society in order to exploit it to their advantage. Mandeville did not want to surrender his earlier myth, but it is clearly unessential in his revised account of social origins. Mandeville is more generally accurate when he reasons that the restraints upon natural man (*i.e.,* upon the passions) are tolerable only because man learns that they insure a higher return of ease and happiness than he could attain without them.

Mandeville's views on the growth of society reveal that he maintained, as his contemporaries generally did, the conviction that the course of human history has been in the main progressive, the revolutions and declines of empire notwithstanding. But his attachment to progress was far removed from the quasi-religious sentiment or inebriation which the idea of progress often inspired later in his century. The Godwins and Condorcets at the close of the century professed a "salvationist" faith in secular progress and desired, in Carl Becker's terms, the heavenly city of the eighteenth-century philosophers. Their naive faith in the infinite perfectibility of man, a faith which even the optimists in Mandeville's day lacked, he would have thoroughly disparaged. And as for the possibility of man's returning to a purer existence, Mandeville relegated all such tendencies toward primitivistic regression to the poets; no one in his right mind would be so foolish as to surrender the obvious advantages of present-day society.

While speaking of the "salvationism" he disliked, let us also note that Mandeville's thought is often of the same mold as the Christianity he subverted. In order to discredit Christian ideals he tried to demonstrate that for all practical purposes they are ineffective and even unreal. At the root of his evolutionary humanism, however, his Hobbesian image of natural man reminds us very much of the Calvinist image of depraved, fallen mankind. We can also find in Mandeville's social thought the idea of social predestination. In various passages Mandeville urges that the poor should remain poor, and that they ought not to be educated and thereby encouraged to transcend the class into which they were born. A complex society, he reasons, is necessarily dependent upon a class of poor workers who will relieve their betters of all menial tasks and drudgery. Nowhere does Mandeville entertain any belief in the natural equality of men.

Such views were quite common in his time. On the question of ameliorating the lives of the poor as a class, Mandeville was merely taking a well-known conservative position which could be defended by the orthodox and the freethinkers alike. In a double-edged argument he asserts that the poor could be made very tractable and docile if only their governors saw to it that they were well-instructed in religious faith. This tongue-in-cheek reasoning is but one more example of his early belief that religion is a political instrument that was managed by politicians for their own ends.

Mandeville's unsentimental desire that the poor be kept in their condition of servitude, a condition he regarded as a prerequisite for a flourishing society, might suggest to us that he believed in a strongly regimented if not totalitarian state. But his preference in government is quite clear: he valued the English Settlement of 1688 highly. The society of Augustan England he regarded as the best workable social system improvised by man, and for that reason he was a thorough conservative and reactionary on questions of major social or political revision. From his conviction that human reason could not devise a better *practicable* society we are well prepared to understand his preference for a *laissez-faire* economy over a state-regulated or mercantilist economy. While he did not discard the notion that the economic health of a nation was dependent upon a favorable balance of trade, he liked to believe that commerce would develop best and be most advantageous when it was free to follow its own lines of interest, adjusting supply and demand as well as it could. "As things are managed with us," he wrote, "it would be preposterous to have as many brewers as there are bakers, or as many woolen-drapers as there are shoemakers. This proportion as to numbers, in every trade, finds itself and is never better kept than when nobody meddles or interferes with it."

Mandeville not only anticipated the shift to *laissez-faire* economics which culminated in Adam Smith's *Wealth of Nations* (1776), but also maintained a criterion of value—public *utility, whatever contributes to the general happiness*—which became the foundation of Benthamite Utilitarianism in the later eighteenth century. Bentham credited Joseph Priestley with the utilitarian principle of the greatest happiness for the greatest number, but it has also been found in an earlier writer, Francis Hutcheson. Though in his general social thought Mandeville thinks of good as "public benefit," he does not really accept the greatest-happiness principle of the later utilitarians. Mandeville might have accepted a principle which read: the greatest happiness for the greatest number, *in their degree or station.* If his opinions on the poor sound harsh to us, we ought to recall that he was partially concerned to expose the numerous discrepancies between what public morality professed and how people in fact behaved. When we examine Hogarth's striking depictions of the disreputable poor, as in his "Gin Lane," or Mandeville's description of the uncouth mobs who accompanied the condemned to Tyburn, we can understand somewhat better the sentiments of aversion and disgust that the "mobility" inspired among the polite and educated.

Of course, we admire Mandeville's candor, but we regret his inability, or his unwillingness, to think better of common humanity. The view of human nature which he expressed in his *Grumbling Hive* he held consistently for the next three decades. As the implications of *The Grumbling Hive* became clearer to him, he realized that his polemic had to be directed not only against the clergy but also against the ethical philosophy of Anthony Ashley Cooper, the third Earl of Shaftesbury. Though we have not elaborated upon this aspect of Mandeville's thought, we must note that had Mandeville no other claim to our attention, he would still retain historical importance as a major critic of Shaftesbury. Shaftesbury's principal work, his *Characteristicks of Men, Manners, Opinions, Times, etc.* (1711) was, like Mandeville's *Fable,* a miscellany some parts of which had been published earlier. It is not unlikely that in the six dialogues of Part II of the *Fable* Mandeville might have been emulating the elegance of Shaftesbury's dialogues. But there, except for some common assumptions they shared with their times, the resemblance ends.

While Mandeville had to withstand a volley of criticisms in the 1720's, Shaftesbury's system was taken up by deists such as Hutcheson and, among the poets, especially by James Thomson, whose *Seasons* spread Shaftesbury's benevolism and nature philosophy to wherever English was read. Mandeville began to oppose Shaftesbury in the 1723 edition of the *Fable* and devoted much effort in the dialogues of the 1728 edition to further refutation. Horatio in these dialogues is a Shaftesburian whom Cleomenes, Mandeville's spokesman, converts to Mandeville's creed. The parting note of the *Fable* is Mandeville's summary evaluation of the case against Shaftesbury:

> . . . as, on the one hand, it must be confessed that his sentiments on liberty and humanity are noble and sublime, and that there is nothing trite or vulgar in the *Characteristicks,* so, on the other, it cannot be denied that the ideas he had formed of the goodness and excellency of our nature were as romantic and chimerical as they are beautiful and amiable. . . .

What Mandeville disliked most in Shaftesbury's thought is its underlying and pervading faith in the natural goodness of man and in the ultimate goodness of the universe. He rejected Shaftesbury's view that harmonious, orderly society *is* the state of nature, a norm or terminal state into which the child develops. Shaftesbury's vaguely platonic transcendentalism; his faith in the platonic trinity of truth, beauty, and goodness; his belief that we have a "moral sense" by which we can intuitively or spontaneously distinguish good from evil, just as we distinguish between the beautiful and the ugly; his belief that virtue is its own reward and that (as Pope put it) "true Self-Love and Social are the same": these and many other tenets in Shaftesbury's system were all targets for Mandeville.

Their works and reputations gradually came to symbolize two fairly distinct ethical atmospheres. Shaftesbury's views, somewhat lofty or angelic, are directed toward an otherworldly Divine Mind; Mandeville's, rather earth-bound, perhaps demonic, are dedicated to the preservation and aggrandizement of national wealth and glory. Neither provides us with an ethic at once satisfying and practicable, but the moral predilections of each are still essentially vital, and conflicting, in our time.

Modern scholars have been much more attentive to Shaftesbury than to Mandeville, because Shaftesbury's *Characteristicks* exerted widespread European influence not only in morals, but also in aesthetics and in the nature-philosophies of the later eighteenth and early nineteenth centuries. Shaftesbury certainly deserves this attention, but if Mandeville has generated less discussion, we ought not to conclude that he is far less interesting to scholars or general readers. Mandeville is actually the much livelier and more stimulating of the two. Shaftesbury's appeal to the academician is real enough, but turning to Mandeville from a reading of Shaftesbury is somewhat like meeting Rabelais after a session with Plato. Mandeville's sense of humor is not his least recommendation to the modern reader:

Cleomenes: Set before your eyes a robust warrior that, having lost a limb in battle, is afterwards trampled upon by twenty horses; and tell me, pray, whether you think that lying thus helpless with most of his ribs broke and a fractured skull, in the agony of death for several hours, he suffers less than if a lion had dispatched him?

Horatio: They are both very bad.

We do, of course, agree, but we cannot help smiling at the understatement: an experience which the reader may often expect in Mandeville's company.

—Irwin Primer
Newark College of Rutgers University

A NOTE ON THIS EDITION

THE TEXT OF THIS edition is based upon that of the one-volume edition of the *Fable* which appeared in 1795. While spelling and punctuation have occasionally been altered for the needs of the general reader, the order of the words—with a few exceptions that have been silently corrected—remains unchanged. When particularly involved sentences resisted modernization, they were left in their original form in order to save their precise meaning. Those who wish to study Mandeville more thoroughly must certainly turn first to Professor F. B. Kaye's monumental edition of the *Fable* (two vols., Oxford, 1924; reprinted in 1957), which has been invaluable in the preparation of this popular edition.

I here wish to thank my colleague Professor G. S. Alleman for his valuable criticism and advice relating to this edition.

SUGGESTED READINGS

Paul B. Anderson, "Bernard Mandeville on Gin," *PMLA*, LIV (1934), 775-84.

Bonamy Dobrée, *Variety of Ways: Discussions of Six Authors*, Oxford, 1932.

———, (ed.), *A Letter to Dion*, by Bernard Mandeville, Liverpool, 1954; another edition, ed. by Jacob Viner, Augustan Reprint Society, Ann Arbor, 1953.

F. B. Kaye, "Mandeville on the Origin of Language," *Modern Language Notes*, XXXIX (1924), 136-142.

———, "The Influence of Bernard Mandeville," *Studies in Philology*, XIX (1922), 83-108 (reprinted in *Studies in the Literature of the Augustan Age*, ed. by R. C. Boys, Ann Arbor, 1952).

———, "The Writings of Bernard Mandeville: A Bibliographical Survey," *Journal of English and Germanic Philology*, XX (Oct., 1921), 419-467.

———, "The Mandeville Canon: A Supplement," *Notes and Queries*, III, (May, 1924).

Sterling P. Lamprecht, "The Fable of the Bees," *Journal of Philosophy*, XXIII (1926), 561-579.

Arthur O. Lovejoy, *Reflections on Human Nature*, Baltimore, 1961.

J. C. Maxwell, "Ethics and Politics in Mandeville," *Philosophy*, XXVI (1951).

J. M. Robertson, *Pioneer Humanists*, London, 1907. (His essay on Mandeville was revised from its earlier form in his *Essays towards a Critical Method*, London, 1889.)

A. K. Rogers, "The Ethics of Mandeville," *International Journal of Ethics*, XXXVI (1925), 1-17.

LeRoy W. Smith, "Fielding and Mandeville: the 'War Against Virtue,'" *Criticism*, III, 1 (Winter, 1961), 7-15.

Sir Leslie Stephen, *History of English Thought in the Eighteenth Century*, 1876; 3rd ed., 1902 (reprinted, N.Y., 1949), vol. II.

N. Wilde, "Mandeville's Place in English Thought," *Mind*, VII (1898), 219-232.

Basil Willey, *The Eighteenth Century Background: Studies on the Idea of Nature in the Thought of the Period*, London, 1940, pp. 95-100. (A paperback reprint of this work has been issued recently by the Beacon Press.)

James D. Young, "Mandeville: A Popularizer of Hobbes," *Modern Language Notes*, LXXIV, 1 (Jan., 1959), 10-13.

PREFACE

LAWS AND GOVERNMENT are to the political bodies of civil societies what the vital spirits and life itself are to the natural bodies of animated creatures; and as those that study the anatomy of dead carcasses may see that the chief organs and nicest springs more immediately required to continue the motion of our machine are not hard bones, strong muscles and nerves, nor the smooth white skin that so beautifully covers them, but small trifling films and little pipes that are either overlooked or else seem inconsiderable to vulgar eyes; so they that examine into the nature of man, abstract from art and education, may observe that what renders him a sociable animal consists not in his desire of company, good nature, pity, affability, and other graces of a fair outside; but that his vilest and most hateful qualities are the most necessary accomplishments to fit him for the largest, and, according to the world, the happiest and most flourishing societies.

The following Fable, in which what I have said is set forth at large, was printed above eight years ago* in a six penny pamphlet called The Grumbling Hive, or Knaves turn'd Honest; and being soon after pirated, cried about the streets in a halfpenny sheet. Since the first publishing of it, I have met with several that, either willfully or ignorantly mistaking the design, would have it that the scope of it was a satire upon virtue and morality and the whole wrote for the encouragement of vice. This made me resolve, whenever it should be reprinted, some way or other to inform the

---

*[In 1705].

21

reader of the real intent this little poem was wrote with. I do not
dignify these few loose lines with the name of Poem, that I would
have the reader expect any poetry in them, but barely because they
are rhyme, and I am in reality puzzled what name to give them;
for they are neither heroic nor pastoral, satire, burlesque, nor
heroi-comic; to be a tale they want probability, and the whole
is rather too long for a fable. All I can say of them is that they
are a story told in doggerel, which, without the least design of
being witty, I have endeavoured to do in as easy and familiar a
manner as I was able: the reader shall be welcome to call them
what he pleases. It was said of Montaigne that he was pretty well
versed in the defects of mankind, but unacquainted with the excellencies of human nature: if I fare no worse, I shall think myself
well used.

What country soever in the universe is to be understood by the
Bee-Hive represented here, it is evident, from what is said of the
laws and constitution of it, the glory, wealth, power, and industry
of its inhabitants, that it must be a large, rich and warlike nation,
that is happily governed by a limited monarchy. The satire, therefore, to be met with in the following lines upon the several professions and callings and almost every degree and station of people
was not made to injure and point to particular persons, but only
to show the vileness of the ingredients that altogether compose
the wholesome mixture of a well-ordered society; in order to extol
the wonderful power of political wisdom, by the help of which so
beautiful a machine is raised from the most contemptible branches.
For the main design of the Fable (as it is briefly explained in the
Moral) is to show the impossibility of enjoying all the most elegant
comforts of life that are to be met with in an industrious, wealthy
and powerful nation, and at the same time, be blessed with all
the virtue and innocence that can be wished for in a golden age;
from thence to expose the unreasonableness and folly of those,
that desirous of being an opulent and flourishing people and wonderfully greedy after all the benefits they can receive as such, are
yet always murmuring at and exclaiming against those vices and
inconveniences that from the beginning of the world to this present
day have been inseparable from all kingdoms and states that ever
were famed for strength, riches, and politeness, at the same time.

To do this, I first slightly touch upon some of the faults and corruptions the several professions and callings are generally charged with. After that I show that those very vices of every particular person, by skillful management, were made subservient to the grandeur and worldly happiness of the whole. Lastly, by setting forth what of necessity must be the consequence of general honesty and virtue, and national temperance, innocence and content, I demonstrate that if mankind could be cured of the failings they are naturally guilty of, they would cease to be capable of being raised into such vast potent and polite societies, as they have been under the several great commonwealths and monarchies that have flourished since the creation.

If you ask me why I have done all this, *cui bono?* and what good these notions will produce? truly, besides the reader's diversion, I believe none at all; but if I was asked what naturally ought to be expected from them, I would answer that, in the first place, the people who continually find fault with others, by reading them, would be taught to look at home, and examining their own consciences, be made ashamed of always railing at what they are more or less guilty of themselves; and that, in the next, those who are so fond of the ease and comforts and reap all the benefits that are the consequence of a great and flourishing nation would learn more patiently to submit to those inconveniences, which no government upon earth can remedy, when they should see the impossibility of enjoying any great share of the first, without partaking likewise of the latter.

This, I say, ought naturally to be expected from the publishing of these notions, if people were to be made better by any thing that could be said to them; but mankind having for so many ages remained still the same, notwithstanding the many instructive and elaborate writings by which their amendment has been endeavoured, I am not so vain as to hope for better success from so inconsiderable a trifle.

Having allowed the small advantage this little whim is likely to produce, I think myself obliged to show that it cannot be prejudicial to any; for what is published, if it does no good, ought at least to do no harm: in order to this, I have made some explanatory notes, to which the reader will find himself referred in those passages that seem to be most liable to exceptions.

The censorious, that never saw the Grumbling Hive, will tell me that whatever I may talk of the Fable, it not taking up a tenth part of the book, was only contrived to introduce the Remarks; that instead of clearing up the doubtful or obscure places, I have only pitched upon such as I had a mind to expatiate upon; and that far from striving to extenuate the errors committed before, I have made bad worse, and shown myself a more barefaced champion for vice in the rambling digressions than I had done in the Fable itself.

I shall spend no time in answering these accusations: where men are prejudiced, the best apologies are lost; and I know that those who think it criminal to suppose a necessity of vice in any case whatever will never be reconciled to any part of the performance; but if this be thoroughly examined, all the offence it can give must result from the wrong inferences that may perhaps be drawn from it, and which I desire nobody to make. When I assert that vices are inseparable from great and potent societies, and that it is impossible their wealth and grandeur should subsist without, I do not say that the particular members of them who are guilty of any should not be continually reproved or not be punished for them when they grow into crimes.

There are, I believe, few people in London, of those that are at any time forced to go a-foot, but what could wish the streets of it much cleaner than generally they are, while they regard nothing but their own clothes and private convenience; but when once they come to consider that what offends them is the result of the plenty, great traffic, and opulency of that mighty city, if they have any concern in its welfare, they will hardly ever wish to see the streets of it less dirty. For if we mind the materials of all sorts that must supply such an infinite number of trades and handicrafts as are always going forward; the vast quantity of victuals, drink, and fuel that are daily consumed in it; the waste and superfluities that must be produced from them; the multitudes of horses and other cattle that are always dawbing the streets; the carts, coaches, and more heavy carriages that are perpetually wearing and breaking the pavement of them; and, above all, the numberless swarms of people that are continually harassing and trampling through every part of them: If, I say, we mind all these, we shall find that every moment must produce new filth; and, considering how far distant the great streets are from the river side, what cost and care soever be bestowed to remove the nastiness almost as fast as it is made, it is impossible London should be more cleanly before it is less flourishing. Now would I ask, if a good citizen, in consideration of what has been said, might not assert, that dirty streets are a necessary evil, inseparable from the felicity of London, without being the least hinderance to the cleaning of shoes, or sweeping of streets, and consequently without any prejudice either to the blackguard or the scavingers.

But if, without any regard to the interest or happiness of the city, the question was put, What place I thought most pleasant to walk in? Nobody can doubt, but before the stinking streets of London, I would esteem a fragrant garden or a shady grove in the country. In the same manner, if laying aside all worldly greatness and vain glory, I should be asked where I thought it was most probable that men might enjoy true happiness, I would prefer a small peaceable society, in which men, neither envied nor esteemed by neighbours, should be contented to live upon the natural product of the spot they inhabit, to a vast multitude abounding in wealth and power that should always be conquering others by their arms abroad and debauching themselves by foreign luxury at home.

Thus much I had said to the reader in the first edition and have added nothing by way of preface in the second. But since that, a violent outcry has been made against the book, exactly answering the expectation I always had of the justice, the wisdom, the charity, and fair dealing of those whose good will I despaired of. It has been presented by the Grand Jury and condemned by thousands who never saw a word of it. It has been preached against before my Lord Mayor; and an utter refutation of it is daily expected from a reverend divine, who has called me names in the advertisements and threatened to answer me in two months time for above five months together. What I have to say for myself, the reader will see in my Vindication at the end of the book, where he will likewise find the Grand Jury's Presentment and a letter to the Right Honourable Lord C.* which is very rhetorical beyond argument or connection. The author shows a fine talent for invectives and great sagacity in discovering atheism, where others can

---

*Not in this edition.

find none. He is zealous against wicked books, points at the Fable of the Bees, and is very angry with the author. He bestows four strong epithets on the enormity of his guilt, and by several elegant innuendos to the multitude, as the danger there is in suffering such authors to live and the vengeance of Heaven upon a whole nation, very charitably recommends him to their care.

Considering the length of this epistle and that it is not wholly levelled at me only, I thought at first to have made some extracts from it of what related to myself; but finding, on a nearer inquiry, that what concerned me was so blended and interwoven with what did not, I was obliged to trouble the reader with it entire, not without hopes that, prolix as it is, the extravagancy of it will be entertaining to those who have perused the treatise it condemns with so much horror.

[1705]

THE

GRUMBLING HIVE:

OR,

KNAVES TURN'D HONEST.

A spacious hive well stock'd with bees,
That liv'd in luxury and ease;
And yet as fam'd for laws and arms,
As yielding large and early swarms;
Was counted the great nursery
Of sciences and industry.
No bees had better government,
More fickleness, or less content:
They were not slaves to tyranny,
Nor rul'd by wild democracy;   10
But kings, that could not wrong, because
Their power was circumscrib'd by laws.
   These insects liv'd like men, and all
Our actions they perform'd in small:
They did whatever's done in town,
And what belongs to sword or gown;
Though th' artful works, by nimble slight
Of minute limbs, 'scap'd human sight;
Yet we've no engines, labourers,
Ships, castles, arms, artificers,   20
Craft, science, shop, or instrument,
But they had an equivalent:
Which, since their language is unknown,

Must be call'd, as we do our own.
As grant, that among other things,
They wanted dice, yet they had kings;
And those had guards; from whence we may
Justly conclude, they had some play;
Unless a regiment be shown
Of soldiers, that make use of none.　　　　　　　30

　　Vast numbers throng'd the fruitful hive;
Yet those vast numbers made 'em thrive;
Millions endeavouring to supply
Each other's lust and vanity;
While other millions were employ'd,
To see their handy-works destroy'd;
They furnish'd half the universe;
Yet had more work than labourers.
Some with vast stocks, and little pains,
Jump'd into business of great gains;　　　　　　　40
And some were damn'd to scythes and spades,
And all those hard laborious trades;
Where willing wretches daily sweat,
And wear out strength and limbs to eat:
While others follow'd mysteries,
To which few folks binds 'prentices;
That want no stock, but that of brass,
And may set up without a cross;
As sharpers, parasites, pimps, players,
Pickpockets, coiners, quacks, southsayers,　　　　　　50
And all those, that in enmity,
With downright working, cunningly
Convert to their own use the labour
Of their good-natur'd heedless neighbour.
These were call'd Knaves, but bar the name,
The grave industrious were the same:
All trades and places knew some cheat,
No calling was without deceit.

　　The lawyers, of whose art the basis
Was raising feuds and splitting cases,　　　　　　60
Oppos'd all registers, that cheats
Might make more work with dipt estates;

As were't unlawful, that one's own,
Without a law-suit, should be known.
They kept off hearings wilfully,
To finger the refreshing fee;
And to defend a wicked cause,
Examin'd and survey'd the laws,
As burglars shops and houses do,
To find out where they'd best break through.   70
    Physicians valu'd fame and wealth
Above the drooping patient's health,
Or their own skill: the greatest part
Study'd, instead of rules of art,
Grave pensive looks and dull behaviour,
To gain th' apothecary's favour;
The praise of midwives, priests, and all
That serv'd at birth or funeral.
To bear with th' ever-talking tribe,
And hear my lady's aunt prescribe;   80
With formal smile, and kind how d'ye,
To fawn on all the family;
And, which of all the greatest curse is,
T' endure th' impertinence of nurses.
    Among the many priests of Jove,
Hir'd to draw blessings from above,
Some few were learn'd and eloquent,
But thousands hot and ignorant:
Yet all pass'd muster that could hide
Their sloth, lust, avarice and pride;   90
For which they were as fam'd as tailors
For cabbage, or for brandy sailors,
Some, meagre-look'd, and meanly clad,
Would mystically pray for bread,
Meaning by that an ample store,
Yet lit'rally received no more;
And, while these holy drudges starv'd,
The lazy ones, for which they serv'd,
Indulg'd their ease, with all the graces
Of health and plenty in their faces.   100
    The soldiers, that were forc'd to fight.

If they surviv'd, got honour by't;
Though some, that shunn'd the bloody fray,
Had limbs shot off, that ran away:
Some valiant gen'rals fought the foe;
Others took bribes to let them go:
Some ventur'd always where 'twas warm,
Lost now a leg, and then an arm;
Till quite disabled, and put by,
They liv'd on half their salary;   110
While others never came in play,
And staid at home for double pay.

   Their kings were serv'd, but knavishly,
Cheated by their own ministry;
Many, that for their welfare slaved,
Robbing the very crown they saved:
Pensions were small, and they liv'd high,
Yet boasted of their honesty.
Calling, whene'er they strain'd their right,
The slipp'ry trick a perquisite;   120
And when folks understood their cant,
They chang'd that for emolument;
Unwilling to be short or plain,
In any thing concerning gain;
For their was not a bee but would
Get more, I won't say, than he should;
But than he dar'd to let them know,
That pay'd for't; as your gamesters do,
That, though at fair play, ne'er will own
Before the losers that they've won.   130

   But who can all their frauds repeat?
The very stuff which in the street
They sold for dirt t' enrich the ground,
Was often by the buyers found
Sophisticated with a quarter
Of good-for-nothing stones and mortar;
Though Flail had little cause to mutter,
Who sold the other salt for butter.

   Justice herself, fam'd for fair dealing,
By blindness had not lost her feeling;   140

Her left hand, which the scales should hold,
Had often dropt 'em, brib'd with gold;
And, though she seem'd impartial,
Where punishment was corporal,
Pretended to a reg'lar course,
In murder, and all crimes of force;
Though some first pillory'd for cheating,
Were hang'd in hemp of their own beating;
Yet, it was thought, the sword she bore
Check'd but the desp'rate and the poor;   150
That, urg'd by mere necessity,
Were ty'd up to the wretched tree
For crimes, which not deserv'd that fate,
But to secure the rich and great.

    Thus every part was full of vice,
Yet the whole mass a paradise;
Flatter'd in peace, and fear'd in wars
They were th' esteem of foreigners,
And lavish of their wealth and lives,
The balance of all other hives.   160
Such were the blessings of that state;
Their crimes conspir'd to make them great:
And virtue, who from politics
Has learn'd a thousand cunning tricks,
Was, by their happy influence,
Made friends with vice: And ever since,
The worst of all the multitude
Did something for the common good.

    This was the state's craft, that maintain'd
The whole of which each part complain'd: 170
This, as in music harmony
Made jarrings in the main agree,
Parties directly opposite,
Assist each other, as 'twere for spite;
And temp'rance with sobriety,
Serve drunkenness and gluttony.

    The root of evil, avarice,
That dam'd ill-natur'd baneful vice,
Was slave to prodigality,

That noble sin; whilst luxury   180
Employ'd a million of the poor,
And odious pride a million more:
Envy itself, and vanity,
Were ministers of industry;
Their darling folly, fickleness,
In diet, furniture, and dress,
That strange ridic'lous vice, was made
The very wheel that turn'd the trade.
Their laws and clothes were equally
Objects of mutability!   190
For, what was well done for a time,
In half a year became a crime;
Yet while they alter'd thus their laws,
Still finding and correcting flaws,
They mended by inconstancy
Faults, which no prudence could foresee.
   Thus vice nurs'd ingenuity,
Which join'd with time and industry,
Had carry'd life's conveniences,
Its real pleasures, comforts, ease,   200
To such a height, the very poor
Liv'd better than the rich before.
And nothing could be added more.
   How vain is mortal happiness!
Had they but known the bounds of bliss;
And that perfection here below
Is more than gods can well bestow;
The grumbling brutes had been content
With ministers and government.
But they, at every ill success,   210
Like creatures lost without redress,
Curs'd politicians, armies, fleets;
While every one cry'd, damn the cheats,
And would, though conscious of his own,
In others barb'rously bear none.
   One, that had got a princely store,
By cheating master, king, and poor,
Dar'd cry aloud, the land must sink

For all its fraud; and whom d'ye think
The sermonizing rascal chid? 220
A glover that sold lamb for kid.
    The least thing was not done amiss,
Or cross'd the public business;
But all the rogues cry'd brazenly,
Good gods, had we but honesty!
Merc'ry smil'd at th' impudence,
And others call'd it want of sense,
Always to rail at what they lov'd:
But Jove with indignation mov'd,
At last in anger swore, he'd rid 230
The bawling hive of fraud; and did.
The very moment it departs,
And honesty fills all their hearts;
There shows 'em, like th' instructive tree,
Those crimes which they're asham'd to see;
Which now in silence they confess,
By blushing at their ugliness:
Like children, that would hide their faults,
And by their colour own their thoughts:
Imag'ning, when they're look'd upon, 240
That others see what they have done.
    But, O ye gods! what consternation,
How vast and sudden was th' alteration!
In half an hour, the nation round,
Meat fell a penny in the pound.
The mask hypocrisy's flung down,
From the great stateman to the clown:
And some in borrow'd looks well known,
Appear'd like strangers in their own.
The bar was silent from that day; 250
For now the willing debtors pay,
Ev'n what's by creditors forgot;
Who quitted them that had it not.
Those that were in the wrong, stood mute,
And dropt the patch'd vexatious suit:
On which since nothing less can thrive,
Than lawyers in an honest hive,

All, except those that got enough,
With inkhorns by their sides troop'd off.
    Justice hang'd some, set others free;   260
And after gaol delivery,
Her presence being no more requir'd,
With all her train and pomp retir'd.
First march'd some smiths with locks and grates,
Fetters, and doors with iron plates:
Next gaolers, turnkeys and assistants:
Before the goddess, at some distance,
Her chief and faithful minister,
'Squire Catch,* the law's great finisher,
Bore not th' imaginary sword,   270
But his own tools, an ax and cord:
Then on a cloud the hood-wink'd fair,
Justice herself was push'd by air:
About her chariot, and behind,
Were serjeants, bums† of every kind,
Tip-staffs, and all those officers,
That squeeze a living out of tears.
    Though physic liv'd, while folks were ill,
None would prescribe, but bees of skill,
Which through the hive dispers'd so wide,   280
That none of them had need to ride;
Wav'd vain disputes, and strove to free
The patients of their misery;
Left drugs in cheating countries grown,
And us'd the product of their own;
Knowing the gods sent no disease,
To nations without remedies.
    Their clergy rous'd from laziness,
Laid not their charge on journey-bees;
But serv'd themselves, exempt from vice,   290
The gods with pray'r and sacrifice;
All those, that were unfit, or knew,
Their service might be spar'd, withdrew:

---

*Jack Ketch, the generic nickname for the hangman.
†bums—bumbailiffs, officers of the lowest degree.

Nor was here business for so many,
(If th' honest stand in need of any,)
Few only with the high-priest staid,
To whom the rest obedience paid:
Himself employ'd in holy cares,
Resign'd to others state-affairs.
He chas'd no starv'ling from his door,   300
Nor pinch'd the wages of the poor:
But at his house the hungry's fed,
The hireling finds unmeasur'd bread,
The needy trav'ller board and bed.
    Among the king's great ministers,
And all th' inferior officers,
The change was great; for frugally
They now liv'd on their salary:
That a poor bee should ten times come
To ask his due, a trifling sum,   310
And by some well-hir'd clerk be made
To give a crown, or ne'er be paid,
Would now be call'd a downright cheat,
Though formerly a perquisite.
All places manag'd first by three,
Who watch'd each other's knavery
And often for a fellow-feeling,
Promoted one another's stealing,
Are happily supply'd by one,
By which some thousands more are gone.   320
    No honour now could be content,
To live and owe for what was spent;
Liv'ries in brokers shops are hung,
They part with coaches for a song;
Sell stately horses by whole sets;
And country-houses, to pay debts.
    Vain cost is shunn'd as much as fraud;
They have no forces kept abroad;
Laugh at th' esteem of foreigners,
And empty glory got by wars;   330
They fight but for their country's sake,
When right or liberty's at stake.

Now mind the glorious hive, and see
How honesty and trade agree.
The show is gone, it thins apace;
And looks with quite another face.
For 'twas not only that they went,
By whom vast sums were yearly spent;
But multitudes that liv'd on them,
Were daily forc'd to do the same.   340
In vain to other trades they'd fly;
All were o'er-stock'd accordingly.

    The price of land and houses falls;
Mirac'lous palaces, whose walls,
Like those of Thebes, were rais'd by play,‡
Are to be let; while the once gay,
Well-seated household gods would be
More pleas'd to expire in flames, than see
The mean inscription on the door
Smile at the lofty ones they bore.   350
The building trade is quite destroy'd,
Artificers are not employ'd;
No limner for his art is fam'd,
Stone-cutters, carvers are not nam'd.

    Those, that remain'd, grown temp'rate, strive
Not how to spend, but how to live;
And, when they paid their tavern score,
Resolv'd to enter it no more:
No vintner's jilt in all the hive
Could wear now cloth of gold, and thrive;   360
Nor Torcol* such vast sums advance,
For Burgundy and Ortolans;
The courtier's gone that with his miss
Supp'd at his house on Christmas peas;

---

‡An allusion to the legend that the walls of the Thebes arose to the music of Amphion. This passage suggests that *play* refers not only to music, but also to gambling.

Torcol—a character in Edward Ravenscroft's Restoration comedy, *The English Lawyer* (1678), based upon George Ruggle's famous Latin comedy, *Ignoramus,* which had been performed before King James I in 1615.

Spending as much in two hours stay,
As keeps a troop of horse a day.
    The haughty Chloe, to live great,
Had made her husband rob the state:
But now she sells her furniture,
Which th' Indies had been ransack'd for;   370
Contracts th' expensive bill of fare,
And wears her strong suit a whole year:
The slight and fickle age is past;
And clothes, as well as fashions, last.
Weavers, that join'd rich silk with plate,
And all the trades subordinate,
Are gone; still peace and plenty reign,
And every thing is cheap, though plain:
Kind nature, free from gard'ners force,
Allows all fruits in her own course;   380
But rarities cannot be had,
Where pains to get them are not paid.
    As pride and luxury decrease,
So by degrees they leave the seas.
Not merchants now, but companies
Remove whole manufactories.
All arts and crafts neglected lie;
Content, the bane of industry,
Makes 'em admire their homely store,
And neither seek nor covet more.   390
    So few in the vast hive remain,
The hundredth part they can't maintain
Against th' insults of numerous foes;
Whom yet they valiantly oppose:
'Till some well fenc'd retreat is found,
And here they die or stand their ground.
•No hireling in their army's known;
But bravely fighting for their own,
Their courage and integrity
At last were crown'd with victory.   400
    They triumph'd not without their cost,
For many thousand bees were lost.
Harden'd with toils and exercise,

They counted ease itself a vice;
Which so improv'd their temperance;
That, to avoid extravagance,
They flew into a hollow tree,
Blest with content and honesty.

THE MORAL.

Then leave complaints: fools only strive
To make a great an honest hive.   410
T' enjoy the world's conveniences,
Be fam'd in war, yet live in ease,
Without great vices, is a vain
Eutopia seated in the brain.
Fraud, luxury, and pride must live,
While we the benefits receive:
Hunger's a dreadful plague, no doubt,
Yet who digests or thrives without?
Do we not owe the growth of wine
To the dry shabby crooked vine?   420
Which, while its shoots neglected stood,
Chok'd other plants, and ran to wood;
But blest us with its noble fruit,
As soon as it was ty'd and cut:
So vice is beneficial found,
When it's by justice lopp'd and bound;
Nay, where the people would be great,
As necessary to the state,
As hunger is to make 'em eat.
Bare virtue can't make nations live   430
In splendor; they, that would revive
A golden age, must be as free,
For acorns as for honesty.

THE

INTRODUCTION.

ONE OF THE GREATEST reasons why so few people understand themselves, is, that most writers are always teaching men what they should be, and hardly ever trouble their heads with telling them what they really are. As for my part, without any compliment to the courteous reader, or myself, I believe man (besides skin, flesh, bones, &c. that are obvious to the eye) to be a compound of various passions; that all of them, as they are provoked and come uppermost, govern him by turns, whether he will or no. To show that these qualifications, which we all pretend to be ashamed of, are the great support of a flourishing society, has been the subject of the foregoing poem. But there being some passages in it seemingly paradoxical, I have in the preface promised some explanatory remarks on it; which, to render more useful, I have thought fit to inquire, how man, no better qualified, might yet by his own imperfections be taught to distinguish between virture and vice: and here I must desire the reader once for all to take notice, that when I say men, I mean neither Jews nor Christians; but mere man, in the state of nature and ignorance of the true Deity.

[1714]

AN

INQUIRY

INTO THE

ORIGIN OF MORAL VIRTUE.

All untaught animals are only solicitous of pleasing themselves and naturally follow the bent of their own inclinations, without considering the good or harm that, from their being pleased, will accrue to others. This is the reason that, in the wild state of nature, those creatures are fittest to live peaceably together in great numbers, that discover the least of understanding and have the fewest appetites to gratify; and consequently no species of animals is, without the curb of government, less capable of agreeing long together in multitudes than that of man; yet such are his qualities, whether good or bad I shall not determine, that no creature besides himself can ever be made sociable: but being an extraordinary selfish and headstrong, as well as cunning animal, however he may be subdued by superior strength, it is impossible by force alone to make him tractable, and receive the improvements he is capable of.

The chief thing, therefore, which lawgivers and other wise men that have laboured for the establishment of society have endeavoured, has been to make the people they were to govern believe that it was more beneficial for everybody to conquer than indulge his appetites, and much better to mind the public than what seemed his private interest. As this has always been a very difficult task, so no wit or eloquence has been left untried to compass it; and the moralists and philosophers of all ages employed their utmost skill to prove the truth of so useful an assertion. But whether mankind would have ever believed it or not, it is not likely that anybody could have persuaded them to disapprove of their natural inclinations or prefer the good of others to their own, if, at the same time, he had not showed them an equivalent to be enjoyed as a reward for the violence, which, by so doing, they of necessity must commit upon themselves. Those that have undertaken to civilize mankind were not ignorant of this; but being unable to give so many real rewards as would satisfy all persons for every individual action, they were forced to contrive an imaginary one, that, as a general equivalent for the trouble of self-denial, should serve on all occasions, and without costing any thing either to themselves or others, be yet a most acceptable recompense to the receivers.

They thoroughly examined all the strength and frailities of our nature, and observing that none were either so savage as not to be charmed with praise, or so despicable as patiently to bear contempt, justly concluded that flattery must be the most powerful argument that could be used to human creatures. Making use of this bewitching engine, they extolled the excellency of our nature above other animals, and setting forth with unbounded praises the wonders of our sagacity and vastness of understanding, bestowed a thousand encomiums on the rationality of our souls, by the help of which we were capable of performing the most noble achievements. Having, by this artful way of flattery, insinuated themselves into the hearts of men, they began to instruct them in the notions of honour and shame; representing the one as the worst of all evils, and the other as the highest good to which mortals could aspire: which being done, they laid before them how unbecoming it was the dignity of such sublime creatures to be solicitous about gratifying their appetites, which they had in common with brutes, and at the same time unmindful of those higher qualities that gave them the preeminence over all visible beings. They indeed confessed, that those impulses of nature were very pressing; that it was troublesome to resist, and very difficult wholly to subdue them. But this they only used as an argument to demonstrate how glorious the conquest of them was on the one hand and how scandalous on the other not to attempt it.

To introduce, moreover, an emulation amongst men, they divided the whole species into two classes, vastly differing from one another: the one consisted of abject, low-minded people, that always hunting after immediate enjoyment, were wholly incapable of self-denial, and without regard to the good of others, had no higher aim than their private advantage; such as being enslaved by voluptuousness, yielded without resistance to every gross desire, and made no use of their rational faculties but to heighten their sensual pleasure. These wild grovelling wretches, they said, were the dross of their kind, and having only the shape of men, differed from brutes in nothing but their outward figure. But the other class was made up of lofty high-spirited creatures, that free from sordid selfishness, esteemed the improvements of the mind to be their fairest possessions; and, setting a true value upon themselves, took no delight but in embellishing that part in which their excellency consisted; such as despising whatever they had in common with irrational creatures, opposed by the help of reason their most violent inclinations; and making a continual war with themselves, to promote the peace of others, aimed at no less than the public welfare and the conquest of their own passion.

> Fortior est qui se quam qui fortissima Vincit
> Moenia . . .*

These they called the true representatives of their sublime species, exceeding in worth the first class by more degrees than that itself was superior to the beasts of the field.

As in all animals that are not too imperfect to discover pride, we find that the finest and such as are the most beautiful and valuable of their kind have generally the greatest share of it; so in man, the most perfect of animals, it is so inseparable from his very essence (how cunningly soever some may learn to hide or disguise it) that without it the compound he is made of would want one of the chiefest ingredients; which, if we consider, it is hardly

---

*Stronger is the man who conquers himself than he who conquers the strongest cities. Mandeville's Latin closely resembles that in the Vulgate text of *Proverbs,* 16:32.

to be doubted but lessons and remonstrances, so skilfully adapted to the good opinion man has of himself as those I have mentioned, must, if scattered amongst a multitude, not only gain the assent of most of them as to the speculative part, but likewise induce several, especially the fiercest, most resolute, and best among them to endure a thousand inconveniences and undergo as many hardships, that they may have the pleasure of counting themselves men of the second class and consequently appropriating to themselves all the excellencies they have heard of it.

From what has been said, we ought to expect, in the first place, that the heroes who took such extraordinary pains to master some of their natural appetites and preferred the good of others to any visible interest of their own would not recede an inch from the fine notions they had received concerning the dignity of rational creatures; and having ever the authority of the government on their side, with all imaginable vigour assert the esteem that was due to those of the second class, as well as their superiority over the rest of their kind. In the second, that those who wanted a sufficient stock of either pride or resolution to buoy them up in mortifying of what was dearest to them, followed the sensual dictates of nature, would yet be ashamed of confessing themselves to be those despicable wretches that belonged to the inferior class and were generally reckoned to be so little removed from brutes; and that therefore, in their own defence, they would say as others did, and hiding their own imperfections as well as they could, cry up self-denial and public spiritedness as much as any: for it is highly probable, that some of them, convinced by the real proofs of fortitude and self-conquest they had seen, would admire in others what they found wanting in themselves, others be afraid of the resolution and prowess of those of the second class, and that all of them were kept in awe by the power of their rulers; wherefore it is reasonable to think, that none of them (whatever they thought in themselves) would dare openly contradict what by everybody else was thought criminal to doubt of.

This was (or at least might have been) the manner after which savage man was broke; from whence it is evident, that the first rudiments of morality broached by skilful politicians to render men useful to each other, as well as tractable, were chiefly contrived, that the ambitious might reap the more benefit from and govern vast numbers of them with the greater ease and security. This foundation of politics being once laid, it is impossible that man should long remain uncivilized: for even those who only strove to gratify their appetites, being continually crossed by others of the same stamp, could not but observe, that whenever they checked their inclinations or but followed them with more circumspection, they avoided a world of troubles and often escaped many of the calamities that generally attended the too eager pursuit after pleasure.

First, they received, as well as others, the benefit of those actions that were done for the good of the whole society and consequently could not forbear wishing well to those of the superior class that performed them. Secondly, the more intent they were in seeking their own advantage, without regard to others, the more they were hourly convinced that none stood so much in their way as those that were most like themselves.

It being the interest then of the very worst of them, more than any, to preach up public-spiritedness, that they might reap the fruits of the labour and self-denial of others, and at the same time indulge their own appetites with less disturbance, they agreed with the rest to call everything, which, without regard to the public, man should commit to gratify any of his appetites, VICE; if in that action there could be observed the least prospect that it might either be injurious to any of the society or ever render himself less serviceable to others: and to give the name of VIRTUE to every performance, by which man, contrary to the impulse of nature, should endeavour the benefit of others or the conquest of his own passions out of a rational ambition of being good.

It shall be objected that no society was ever any ways civilized before the major part had agreed upon some worship or other of an over-ruling power and consequently that the notions of good and evil and the distinction between virtue and vice were never the contrivance of politicians, but the pure effect of religion. Before I answer this objection, I must repeat what I have said already, that in this inquiry into the origin of moral virtue, I speak neither of Jews or Christians, but man in his state of nature and ignorance of the true Deity; and then I affirm, that the idolatrous superstitions of all other nations and the pitiful notions they had of the Supreme Being, were incapable of exciting man to virtue and good for nothing but to awe and amuse a rude and unthinking multitude. It is evident from history that in all considerable societies, how stupid or ridiculous soever people's received notions have been as to the deities they worshipped, human nature has ever exerted itself in all its branches and that there is no earthly wisdom or moral virtue, but at one time or other men have excelled in it in all monarchies and commonwealths, that for riches and power have been any ways remarkable.

The Egyptians, not satisfied with having deified all the ugly monsters they could think on, were so silly as to adore the onions of their own sowing; yet at the same time their country was the most famous nursery of arts and sciences in the world and themselves more eminently skilled in the deepest mysteries of nature than any nation has been since.

No states or kingdoms under heaven have yielded more or greater patterns in all sorts of moral virtues than the Greek and Roman empires, more especially the latter; and yet how loose, absurd and ridiculous were their sentiments as to sacred matters? For without reflecting on the extravagant number of their deities, if we only consider the infamous stories they fathered upon them, it is not to be denied but that their religion, far from teaching men the conquest of their passions and the way to virtue, seemed rather contrived to justify their appetites and encourage their vices. But if we would know what made them excel in fortitude, courage, and magnanimity, we must cast our eyes on the pomp of their triumphs, the magnificence of their monuments and arches; their trophies, statues, and inscriptions; the variety of their military crowns, their honours decreed to the dead, public encomiums on the living, and other imaginary rewards they bestowed on men of merit; and we shall find that what carried so many of them to the utmost pitch of self-denial was nothing but their policy in making use of the most effectual means that human pride could be flattered with.

It is visible, then, that it was not any heathen religion or other idolatrous superstition that first put man upon crossing his appetites and subduing his dearest inclinations, but the skilful management of wary politicians; and the nearer we search into human nature, the more we shall be convinced that the moral virtues are the political offspring which flattery begot upon pride.

There is no man, of what capacity or penetration soever, that is wholly proof against the witchcraft of flattery, if artfully performed and suited to his abilities. Children and fools will swallow personal praise, but those that are more cunning, must be managed with much greater circumspection; and the more general the flattery is, the less it is suspected by those it is levelled at. What you say in commendation of a whole town is received with pleasure by all the inhabitants: speak in commendation of letters in general, and every man of learning will think himself in particular obliged to you. You may safely praise the employment a man is of or the country he was born in because you give him an opportunity of screening the joy he feels upon his own account under the esteem which he pretends to have for others.

It is common among cunning men that understand the power which flattery has upon pride, when they are afraid they shall be imposed upon, to enlarge, though much against their conscience, upon the honour, fair dealing, and integrity of the family, country, or sometimes the profession of him they suspect; because they know that men often will change their resolution and act against their inclination, that they may have the pleasure of continuing to appear in the opinion of some what they are conscious not to be in reality. Thus sagacious moralists draw men like angels, in hopes that the pride at least of some will put them upon copying after the beautiful originals which they are represented to be.

When the incomparable Sir Richard Steele, in the usual elegance of his easy style, dwells on the praises of his sublime species, and with all the embellishments of rhetoric sets forth the excellency of human nature, it is impossible not to be charmed with his happy turns of thought and the politeness of his expressions. But though I have been often moved by the force of his eloquence and ready to swallow the ingenious sophistry with pleasure, yet I could never be so serious, but, reflecting on his artful encomiums, I thought on the tricks made use of by the women that would teach children to be mannerly. When an awkward girl before she can either speak or go begins after many entreaties to make the first rude essays of curtesying, the nurse falls in an ecstacy of praise; "There is a delicate curtesy! O fine Miss! there is a pretty lady! Mama! Miss can make a better curtsey than her sister Molly!" The same is echoed over by the maids, whilst Mama almost hugs the child to pieces; only Miss Molly, who being four years older, knows how to make a very handsome curtesy, wonders at the perverseness of their judgment, and swelling with indignation, is ready to cry at the injustice that is done her, till, being whispered in the ear that it is only to please the baby and that she is a woman, she grows proud at being let into the secret, and rejoicing at the superiority of her understanding, repeats what has been said with large additions and insults over the weakness of her sister, whom all this while she fancies to be the only bubble among them. These extravagant praises would by anyone above the capacity of an infant be called fulsome flatteries, and, if you will, abominable lies; yet experience teaches us that by the help of such gross encomiums young misses will be brought to make pretty curtesies and behave themselves womanly much sooner, and with less trouble, than they would without them. It is the same with boys, whom they will strive to persuade that all fine gentlemen do as they are bid and that none but beggar boys are rude or dirty their clothes; nay, as soon as the wild brat with his untaught fist begins to fumble for his hat, the mother, to make him pull it off, tells him before he is two years old that he is a man; and if he repeats that action when she desires him, he is presently a captain, a lord mayor, a king, or something higher if she can think of it, till egged on by the force of praise, the little urchin endeavors to imitate man as well as he can and strains all his faculties to appear what his shallow noddle imagines he is believed to be.

The meanest wretch puts an inestimable value upon himself, and the highest wish of the ambitious man is to have all the world, as to that particular, of his opinion: so that the most insatiable thirst after fame that ever hero was inspired with was never more than an ungovernable greediness to engross the esteem and admiration of others in future ages as well as his own; and (what mortification soever this truth might be to the second thoughts of an Alexander or a Caesar) the great recompense in view, for which the most exalted minds have with so much alacrity sacrificed their quiet, health, sensual pleasures, and every inch of themselves, has never been anything else but the breath of man, the aerial coin of praise. Who can forbear laughing when he thinks on all the great men that have been so serious on the subject of that Macedonian madman, his capacious soul, that mighty heart, in one corner of which, according to Lorenzo Gratian, the world was so commodiously lodged that in the whole there was room for six more? Who can forbear laughing, I say, when he compares the fine things that have been said of Alexander with the end he proposed to himself from his vast exploits to be proved from his own mouth; when the vast pains he took to pass the Hydaspes forced him to cry out, Oh ye Athenians, could you believe what dangers I expose myself to, to be praised by you! To define then the reward of glory in the amplest manner, the most that can be said of it is that it consists in a superlative felicity which a man, who is conscious of having performed a noble action, enjoys in self-love, whilst he is thinking on the applause he expects of others.

But here I shall be told that besides the noisy toils of war and public bustle of the ambitious there are noble and generous actions that are performed in silence; that virtue being its own reward, those who are really good have a satisfaction in their consciousness of being so, which is all the recompense they expect from the most worthy performances; that among the heathens there have been men, who, when they did good to others, were so far from coveting thanks and applause, that they took all imaginable care to be forever concealed from those on whom they bestowed their benefits, and consequently that pride has no hand in spurring man on to the highest pitch of self-denial.

In answer to this I say that it is impossible to judge of a man's performance, unless we are thoroughly acquainted with the principle and motive from which he acts. Pity, though it is the most gentle and the least mischievous of all our passions, is yet as much a frailty of our nature as anger, pride, or fear. The weakest minds have generally the greatest share of it, for which reason none are more compassionate than women and children. It must be owned that of all our weaknesses, it is the most amiable and bears the greatest resemblance to virtue; nay, without a considerable mixture of it, the society could hardly subsist: but as it is an impulse of nature that consults neither the public interest nor our own reason, it may produce evil as well as good. It has helped to destroy the honour of virgins and corrupted the integrity of judges; and whoever acts from it as a principle, what good soever he may bring to the society, has nothing to boast of, but that he has indulged a passion that has happened to be beneficial to the public. There is no merit in saving an innocent babe ready to drop into the fire: the action is neither good nor bad, and what benefit soever the infant received, we only obliged ourselves; for to have seen it fall, and not strove to hinder it, would have caused a pain, which self-preservation compelled us to prevent: Nor has a rich prodigal, that happens to be of a commiserating temper and loves to gratify his passions, greater virtue to boast of when he relieves an object of compassion with what to himself is a trifle.

But such men, as without complying with any weakness of their own, can part from what they value themselves and from no other motive but their love to goodness perform a worthy action in silence: such men, I confess, have acquired more refined notions of virtue than those I have hitherto spoke of; yet even in these (with which the world has yet never swarmed) we may discover no small symptoms of pride, and the humblest man alive must confess that the reward of a virtuous action, which is the satisfaction that ensues upon it, consists in a certain pleasure he procures to himself by contemplating on his own worth: which pleasure, together with the occasion of it, are as certain signs of pride as looking pale and trembling at any imminent danger are the symptoms of fear.

If the too scrupulous reader should at first view condemn these notions concerning the origin of moral virtue and think them perhaps offensive to Christianity, I hope he will forbear his censures when he shall consider that nothing can render the unsearchable depth of the Divine Wisdom more conspicuous than that man, whom Providence had designed for society, should not only by his own frailties and imperfections be led into the road to temporal happiness, but likewise receive, from a seeming necessity of natural causes, a tincture of that knowledge, in which he was afterwards to be made perfect by the true religion, to his eternal welfare.

REMARKS.

[Notes on individual sections of *The Grumbling Hive*]

Line 101. The soldiers that were forc'd to fight,
If they surviv'd got honour by't.

So UNACCOUNTABLE is the desire to be thought
well of in men, that though they are dragged into the war against
their will, and some of them for their crimes, and are compelled to
fight with threats and often blows, yet they would be esteemed for
what they would have avoided if it had been in their power:
whereas, if reason in man was of equal weight with his pride, he
could never be pleased with praises, which he is conscious he does
not deserve.

By honour, in its proper and genuine signification, we mean
nothing else but the good opinion of others, which is counted
more or less substantial, the more or less noise or bustle there
is made about the demonstration of it; and when we say the
sovereign is the fountain of honour, it signifies that he has the
power, by titles or ceremonies, or both together, to stamp a mark
upon whom he pleases that shall be as current as his coin and
procure the owner the good opinion of everybody, whether he
deserves it or not.

The reverse of honour is dishonour, or ignominy, which consists in the bad opinion and contempt of others; and as the first
is counted a reward for good actions, so this is esteemed a punishment for bad ones; and the more or less public or heinous the
manner is in which this contempt of others is shown, the more
or less the person so suffering is degraded by it. This ignominy is
likewise called shame from the effect it produces; for though the
good and evil of honour and dishonour are imaginary, yet there
is a reality in shame, as it signifies a passion, that has its proper
symptoms, over-rules our reason, and requires as much labour and

self-denial to be subdued as any of the rest; and since the most important actions of life often are regulated according to the influence this passion has upon us, a thorough understanding of it must help to illustrate the notions the world has of honour and ignominy. I shall therefore describe it at large.

First, to define the passion of shame, I think it may be called a sorrowful reflection on our own unworthiness, proceeding from an apprehension that others either do, or might, if they knew all, deservedly despise us. The only objection of weight that can be raised against this definition is that innocent virgins are often ashamed and blush when they are guilty of no crime and can give no manner of reason for this frailty: and that men are often ashamed for others for, or with whom, they have neither friendship or affinity, and consequently that there may be a thousand instances of shame given, to which the words of the definition are not applicable. To answer this, I would have it first considered that the modesty of women is the result of custom and education, by which all unfashionable denudations and fifthy expressions are rendered frightful and abominable to them, and that notwithstanding this, the most virtuous young woman alive will often, in spite of her teeth, have thoughts and confused ideas of things arise in her imagination, which she would not reveal to some people for a thousand worlds. Then, I say that when obscene words are spoken in the presence of an unexperienced virgin, she is afraid that some body will reckon her to understand what they mean, and consequently that she understands this and that and several things which she desires to be thought ignorant of. The reflecting on this, and that thoughts are forming to her disadvantage, brings upon her that passion which we call shame; and whatever can sting her, though never so remote from lewdness, upon that set of thoughts I hinted and which she thinks criminal, will have the same effect, especially before men, as long as her modesty lasts.

To try the truth of this, let them talk as much bawdy as they please in the room next to the same virtuous young woman, where she is sure that she is undiscovered, and she will hear, if not hearken to it, without blushing at all, because then she looks upon herself as no party concerned; and if the discourse should stain her cheeks with red, whatever her innocence may imagine, it is certain that what occasions her colour is a passion not half so mortifying as that of shame; but if, in the same place, she hears something said of herself that must tend to her disgrace, or anything is named of which she is secretly guilty, then it is ten to one but she will be ashamed and blush, though nobody sees her; because she has room to fear that she is, or, if all was known, should be thought of contemptibly.

That we are often ashamed and blush for others, which was the second part of the objection, is nothing else but that sometimes we make the case of others too nearly our own; so people shriek out when they see others in danger: Whilst we are reflecting with too much earnest on the effect which such a blameable action, if it was ours, would produce in us, the spirits, and consequently the blood, are insensibly moved, after the same manner as if the action was our own, and so the same symptoms must appear.

The shame that raw, ignorant, and ill-bred people, though seemingly without a cause, discover before their betters, is always accompanied with and proceeds from a consciousness of their weakness and inabilities; and the most modest man, how virtuous, knowing, and accomplished soever he might be, was never yet ashamed without some guilt or diffidence. Such as out of rusticity and want of education are unreasonably subject to and at every turn overcome by this passion, we call bashful; and those who out of disrespect to others and a false opinion of their own sufficiency have learned not to be affected with it when they should be, are called impudent or shameless. What strange contradictions man is made of! The reverse of shame is pride, (see Remark on 1. 182 [pp. 86 ff.]) yet nobody can be touched with the first that never felt anything of the latter; for that we have such an extraordinary concern in what others think of us can proceed from nothing but the vast esteem we have of ourselves.

That these two passions, in which the seeds of most virtues are contained, are realities in our frame, and not imaginary qualities, is demonstrable from the plain and different effects that, in spite of our reason, are produced in us as soon as we are affected with either.

When a man is overwhelmed with shame, he observes a sinking of the spirits; the heart feels cold and condensed, and the blood flies from it to the circumference of the body; the face glows, the neck and part of the breast partake of the fire: he is heavy as lead; the head is hung down, and the eyes through a mist of confusion are fixed on the ground: no injuries can move him; he is weary of his being, and heartily wishes he could make himself invisible: but when, gratifying his vanity, he exults in his pride, he discovers quite contrary symptoms; his spirits swell and fan the arterial blood; a more than ordinary warmth strengthens and dilates the heart; the extremities are cool; he feels light to himself and imagines he could tread on air; his head is held up, his eyes rolled about with sprightliness; he rejoices at his being, is prone to anger, and would be glad that all the world could take notice of him.

It is incredible how necessary an ingredient shame is to make us sociable; it is a frailty in our nature; all the world, whenever it affects them, submit to it with regret and would prevent it if they could; yet the happiness of conversation depends upon it, and no society could be polished if the generality of mankind were not subject to it. As, therefore, the sense of shame is troublesome, and all creatures are ever labouring for their own defence, it is probable that man striving to avoid this uneasiness would, in a great measure, conquer his shame by that he was grown up; but this would be detrimental to the society, and therefore from his infancy, throughout his education, we endeavour to increase instead of lessening or destroying this sense of shame; and the only remedy prescribed is a strict observance of certain rules to avoid those things that might bring this troublesome sense of shame upon him. But as to rid or cure him of it, the politician would sooner take away his life.

The rules I speak of consist in a dextrous management of ourselves, a stifling of our appetites, and hiding the real sentiments of our hearts before others. Those who are not instructed in these rules long before they come to years of maturity seldom make any progress in them afterwards. To acquire and bring to perfection the accomplishment I hint at, nothing is more assisting than pride and good sense. The greediness we have after the esteem of others and the raptures we enjoy in the thoughts of being liked and perhaps admired are equivalents that over-pay the conquest of the strongest passions, and consequently keep us at a great distance from all such words or actions that can bring shame upon us. The passions we chiefly ought to hide for the happiness and embellishment of the society are lust, pride, and selfishness; therefore the word modesty has three different acceptations that vary with the passions it conceals.

As to the first, I mean the branch of modesty that has a general pretension to chastity for its object, it consists in a sincere and painful endeavour with all our faculties to stifle and conceal before others that inclination which nature has given us to propagate our species. The lessons of it, like those of grammar, are taught us long before we have occasion for or understand the usefulness of them; for this reason children often are ashamed and blush out of modesty before the impulse of nature I hint at makes any impression upon them. A girl who is modestly educated may, before she is two years old, begin to observe how careful the women she converses with are of covering themselves before men; and the same caution being inculcated to her by precept as well as example, it is very probable that at six she will be ashamed of showing her leg, without knowing any reason why such an act is blameable or what the tendency of it is.

To be modest, we ought, in the first place, to avoid all unfashionable denudations: a woman is not to be found fault with for going with her neck bare, if the custom of the country allows of it; and when the mode orders the stays to be cut very low, a blooming virgin may, without fear of rational censure, show all the world:

> How firm her pouting breasts, that white as snow,
> On th' ample chest at mighty distance grow.

But to suffer her ankle to be seen, where it is the fashion for women to hide their very feet, is a breach of modesty; and she is imprudent who shows half her face in a country where decency bids her to be veiled. In the second, our language must be chaste and not only free, but remote from obscenities, that is, whatever belongs to the multiplication of our species is not to be spoke of, and the least word or expression that, though at a great distance, has any relation to that performance ought never to come from our lips. Thirdly, all postures and motions that can any ways sully the imagination, that is, put us in mind of what I have called obscenities, are to be forbore with great caution.

A young woman, moreover, that would be thought well-bred, ought to be circumspect before men in all her behaviour and never known to receive from, much less to bestow favours upon them, unless the great age of the man, near consanguinity, or a vast superiority on either side plead her excuse. A young lady of refined education keeps a strict guard over her looks, as well as actions, and in her eyes we may read a consciousness that she has a treasure about her, not out of danger of being lost, and which yet she is resolved not to part with at any terms. Thousand satires have been made against prudes, and as many encomiums to extol the careless graces and negligent air of virtuous beauty. But the wiser sort of mankind are well assured that the free and open countenance of the smiling fair is more inviting and yields greater hopes to the seducer than the ever-watchful look of a forbidding eye.

This strict reservedness is to be complied with by all young women, especially virgins, if they value the esteem of the polite and knowing world; men may take greater liberty because in them the appetite is more violent and ungovernable. Had equal harshness of discipline been imposed upon both, neither of them could have made the first advances, and propagation must have stood still among all the fashionable people: which being far from the politician's aim, it was advisable to ease and indulge the sex that suffered most by the severity and make the rules abate of their rigour, where the passion was the strongest and the burden of a strict restraint would have been the most intolerable.

For this reason, the man is allowed openly to profess the veneration and great esteem he has for women and show greater satisfaction, more mirth and gaiety in their company than he is used to do out of it. He may not only be complaisant and serviceable to them on all occasions, but it is reckoned his duty to protect and defend them. He may praise the good qualities they are possessed of and extol their merit with as many exaggerations as his invention will let him and are consistent with good sense. He may talk of love, he may sigh and complain of the rigours of the fair, and what his tongue must not utter he has the privilege to speak with his eyes, and in that language to say what he pleases; so it be done with decency, and short abrupted glances: but too closely to pursue a woman and fasten upon her with one's eyes is counted very unmannerly; the reason is plain, it makes her uneasy, and, if she be not sufficiently fortified by art and dissimulation, often throws her into visible disorders. As the eyes are the windows of the soul, so this staring impudence flings a raw, unexperienced woman into panic fears that she may be seen through, and that the man will discover or has already betrayed what passes within her: it keeps her on a perpetual rack that commands her to reveal her secret wishes and seems designed to extort from her the grand truth, which modesty bids her with all her faculties to deny.

The multitude will hardly believe the excessive force of education and in the difference of modesty between men and women ascribe that to nature which is altogether owing to early instruction: Miss is scarce three years old, but she is spoke to every day to hide her leg and rebuked in good earnest if she shows it; while little Master at the same age is bid to take up his coats and piss like a man. It is shame and education that contains the seeds of all politeness, and he that has neither and offers to speak the truth of his heart and what he feels within is the most contemptible creature upon earth, though he committed no other fault. If a man should tell a woman that he could like nobody so well to propagate his species upon as herself and that he found a violent desire that moment to go about it and accordingly offered to lay hold of her for that purpose, the consequence would be that he would be called a brute, the woman would run away, and himself be never admitted in any civil company. There is no body that has any sense of shame but would conquer the strongest passion rather than be so served. But a man need not conquer his passions, it is sufficient that he conceals them. Virtue bids us subdue, but good breeding only requires we should hide our appetites. A fashionable gentleman may have as violent an inclination to a woman as the brutish fellow; but then he behaves himself quite otherwise; he first addresses the lady's father and demonstrates his ability splendidly to maintain his daughter; upon this he is admitted into her company, where, by flattery, submission, presents, and assiduity, he endeavours to procure her liking to his person, which if he can compass, the lady in a little while resigns herself to him before witnesses in a most solemn manner; at night they go to bed together, where the most reserved virgin very tamely suffers him to do what he pleases, and the upshot is, that he obtains what he wanted without ever having asked for it.

The next day they receive visits, and nobody laughs at them or speaks a word of what they have been doing. As to the young couple themselves, they take no more notice of one another, I speak of well-bred people, than they did the day before; they eat and drink, divert themselves as usually, and having done nothing to be ashamed of, are looked upon as, what in reality they may be, the most modest people upon earth. What I mean by this is to demonstrate that by being well-bred, we suffer no abridgement in our sensual pleasures, but only labour for our mutual happiness and assist each other in the luxurious enjoyment of all worldly comforts. The fine gentleman I spoke of need not practise any greater self-denial than the savage, and the latter acted more according to the laws of nature and sincerity than the first. The man that gratifies his appetites after the manner the custom of the country allows of has no censure to fear. If he is hotter than goats or bulls, as soon as the ceremony is over, let him sate and fatigue himself with joy and ecstacies of pleasure, raise and indulge his appetites by turns, as extravagantly as his strength and manhood will give him leave, he may with safety laugh at the wise men that should reprove him: all the women, and above nine in ten of the men, are of his side; nay, he has the liberty of valuing himself upon the fury of his unbridled passion, and the more he wallows in lust, and strains every faculty to be abandonedly voluptuous, the sooner he shall have the good-will and gain the affection of the women, not the young, vain, and lascivious only, but the prudent, grave, and most sober matrons.

Because impudence is a vice, it does not follow that modesty is a virtue; it is built upon shame, a passion in our nature, and may be either good or bad according to the actions performed from that motive. Shame may hinder a prostitute from yielding to a man before company, and the same shame may cause a bashful good-natured creature, that has been overcome by frailty, to make away with her infant. Passions may do good by chance, but there can be no merit but in the conquest of them.

Was there virtue in modesty, it would be of the same force in the dark as it is in the light, which it is not. This the men of pleasure know every well, who never trouble their heads with a woman's virtue, so they can but conquer her modesty; seducers, therefore, do not make their attacks at noon-day, but cut their trenches at night.

> Illa verecundis lux est praebenda puellis,
> Qua timidus latebras sperat habere pudor.*

People of substance may sin without being exposed for their stolen pleasure; but servants and the poorer sort of women have seldom the opportunity of concealing a big belly or at least the consequences of it. It is possible that an unfortunate girl of good parentage may be left destitute and know no shift for a livelihood than to become a nursery or a chambermaid: she may be diligent, faithful, and obliging, have abundance of modesty, and if you will, be religious: she may resist temptations and preserve her chastity for years together, and yet at last meet with an unhappy moment in which she gives up her honour to a powerful deceiver, who afterwards neglects her. If she proves with child, her sorrows are unspeakable, and she cannot be reconciled with the wretchedness of her condition; the fear of shame attacks her so lively, that every thought distracts her. All the family she lives in have a great opinion of her virtue, and her last mistress took her for a saint. How will her enemies, that envied her character, rejoice! How will her relations detest her! The more modest she is now, and the more violently the dread of coming to shame hurries her away, the more wicked and more cruel her resolutions will be, either against herself or what she bears.

It is commonly imagined, that she who can destroy her child, her own flesh and blood, must have a vast stock of barbarity and be a savage monster, different from other women; but this is likewise a mistake, which we commit for the want of understanding nature and the force of passions. The same woman that murders her bastard in the most execrable manner, if she is married afterwards, may take care of, cherish, and feel all the tenderness for her infant that the fondest mother can be capable of. All mothers naturally love their children: but as this is a passion and all passions centre in self-love, so it may be subdued by any

---

*Ovid, *Amores*, I, 7-8: "It was such a light as shy maidens desire whose timid modesty hopes to hide away."

superior passion, to soothe that same self-love, which if nothing had intervened, would have bid her fondle her offspring. Common whores, whom all the world knows to be such, hardly ever destroy their children; nay, even those who assist in robberies and murders seldom are guilty of this crime; not because they are less cruel or more virtuous, but because they have lost their modesty to a greater degree, and the fear of shame makes hardly any impression upon them.

Our love to what never was within the reach of our senses is but poor and inconsiderable, and therefore women have no natural love to what they bear; their affection begins after the birth: what they feel before is the result of reason, education, and the thoughts of duty. Even when children first are born, the mother's love is but weak, and increases with the sensibility of the child, and grows up to a prodigious height, when by signs it begins to express his sorrows and joys, makes his wants known, and discovers his love to novelty and the multiplicity of his desires. What labours and hazards have not women undergone to maintain and save their children, what force and fortitude beyond their sex have they not shown in their behalf! but the vilest women have exerted themselves on this head as violently as the best. All are prompted to it by a natural drift and inclination, without any consideration of the injury or benefit the society receives from it. There is no merit in pleasing ourselves, and the very offspring is often irreparably ruined by the excessive fondness of parents: for though infants, for two or three years, may be the better for this indulging care of mothers, yet afterwards, if not moderated, it may totally spoil them, and many it has brought to the gallows.

If the reader thinks I have been too tedious on that branch of modesty, by the help of which we endeavour to appear chaste, I shall make him amends in the brevity with which I design to treat of the remaining part, by which we would make others believe that the esteem we have for them exceeds the value we have for ourselves, and that we have no disregard so great to any interest as we have to our own. This laudable quality is commonly known by the name of Manners and Good-breeding, and consists in a fashionable habit, acquired by precept and example, of flattering the pride and selfishness of others and concealing our own with judgment and dexterity. This must be only understood of our commerce with our equals and superiors, and whilst we are in peace and amity with them; for our complaisance must never interfere with the rules of honour nor the homage that is due to us from servants and others that depend upon us.

With this caution, I believe, that the definition will quadrate with everything that can be alleged as a piece or an example of either good-breeding or ill manners; and it will be very difficult throughout the various accidents of human life and conversation to find out an instance of modesty or impudence that is not comprehended in, and illustrated by it, in all countries and in all ages. A man that asks considerable favours of one who is a stranger to him, without consideration, is called impudent, because he shows openly his selfishness without having any regard to the selfishness of the other. We may see in it, likewise, the reason why a man ought to speak of his wife and children and everything that is dear to him as sparing as is possible and hardly ever of himself, especially in commendation of them. A well-bred man may be desirous and even greedy after praise and the esteem of others, but to be praised to his face offends his modesty: the reason is this; all human creatures, before they are yet polished, receive an extraordinary pleasure in hearing themselves praised: this we are all conscious of, and therefore when we see a man openly enjoy and feast on this delight, in which we have no share, it rouses our selfishness, and immediately we begin to envy and hate him. For this reason, the well-bred man conceals his joy, and utterly denies that he feels any, and by this means consulting and soothing our selfishness, he averts that envy and hatred, which otherwise he would have justly to fear. When from our childhood we observe how those are ridiculed who calmly can hear their own praises, it is possible that we may strenuously endeavour to avoid that pleasure, that in tract of time we grow uneasy at the approach of it: but this is not following the dictates of nature, but warping her by education and custom; for if the generality of mankind took no delight in being praised, there could be no modesty in refusing to hear it.

The man of manners picks not the best, but rather takes the worst out of the dish, and gets of everything, unless it be forced upon him, always the most indifferent share. By this civility the best remains for others, which being a compliment to all that are

present, everybody is pleased with it: the more they love themselves, the more they are forced to approve of his behaviour, and
gratitude stepping in, they are obliged almost, whether they will
or not, to think favourably of him. After this manner, it is the
well-bred man insinuates himself in the esteem of all the companies
he comes in, and if he gets nothing else by it, the pleasure he
receives in reflecting on the applause which he knows is secretly
given him, is to a proud man more than an equivalent for his
former self-denial, and overpays to self-love with interest the loss
it sustained in his complaisance to others.

If there are seven or eight apples or peaches among six people
of ceremony, that are pretty near equal, he who is prevailed upon
to choose first, will take that which, if there be any considerable
difference, a child would know to be the worst: this he does to
insinuate that he looks upon those he is with to be of superior
merit, and that there is not one whom he wishes not better to
than he does to himself. It is custom and a general practice that
makes this modish deceit familiar to us, without being shocked at
the absurdity of it; for if people had been used to speak from the
sincerity of their hearts, and act according to the natural sentiments
they felt within until they were three or four and twenty, it would
be impossible for them to assist at this comedy of manners, without either loud laughter or indignation; and yet it is certain that
such behaviour makes us more tolerable to one another than we
could be otherwise.

It is very advantageous to the knowledge of ourselves to be able
well to distinguish between good qualities and virtues. The bond
of society exacts from every member a certain regard for others,
which the highest is not exempt from in the presence of the
meanest even in an empire: but when we are by ourselves, and
so far removed from company as to be beyond the reach of their
senses, the words modesty and impudence lose their meaning; a
person may be wicked, but he cannot be immodest while he is
alone, and no thought can be impudent that never was communicated to another. A man of exalted pride may so hide it that nobody shall be able to discover that he has any; and yet receive
greater satisfaction from that passion than another who indulges
himself in the declaration of it before all the world. Good manners
having nothing to do with virtue or religion; instead of extinguish-

ing, they rather inflame the passions. The man of sense and education never exults more in his pride than when he hides it with the greatest dexterity; and in feasting on the applause, which he is sure all good judges will pay to his behaviour, he enjoys a pleasure altogether unknown to the short-sighted surly alderman, that shows his haughtiness glaringly in his face, pulls off his hat to nobody, and hardly deigns to speak to an inferior.

A man may carefully avoid everything that in the eye of the world is esteemed to be the result of pride without mortifying himself or making the least conquest of his passion. It is possible that he only sacrifices the insipid outward part of his pride, which none but silly ignorant people take delight in, to that part we all feel within, and which the men of the highest spirit and most exalted genius feed on with so much ecstacy in silence. The pride of great and polite men is nowhere more conspicuous than in the debates about ceremony and precedency, where they have an opportunity of giving their vices the appearance of virtues and can make the world believe that it is their care, their tenderness for the dignity of their office or the honour of their masters, what is the result of their own personal pride and vanity. This is most manifest in all negotiations of ambassadors and plenipotentiaries, and must be known by all that observe what is transacted at public treaties; and it will ever be true that men of the best taste have no relish in their pride as long as any mortal can find out that they are proud.

* * * *

Line 163. And virtue, who from politics
　　　　　Has learn'd a thousand cunning tricks,
　　　　　Was, by their happy influence,
　　　　　Made friends with vice—

It may be said that virtue is made friends with vice, when industrious good people, who maintain their families and bring up their children handsomely, pay taxes, and are several ways useful members of the society, get a livelihood by something that chiefly depends on or is very much influenced by the vices of others, without being themselves guilty of, or accessary to them, any otherwise than by way of trade, as a druggist may be to poisoning, or a sword-cutler to blood-shed.

Thus the merchant, that sends corn or cloth into foreign parts to purchase wines and brandies, encourages the growth or manufactory of his own country; he is a benefactor to navigation, increases the customs, and is many ways beneficial to the public; yet it is not to be denied, but that his greatest dependence is lavishness and drunkenness: For, if none were to drink wine but such only as stand in need of it, nor anybody more than his health required, that multitude of wine-merchants, vintners, coopers, &c. that make such a considerable show in this flourishing city would be in a miserable condition. The same may be said not only of card and dice-makers that are the immediate ministers to a legion of vices, but of mercers, upholsterers, tailors, and many others, that would be starved in half a year's time if pride and luxury were at once to be banished the nation.

*　*　*　*

Line 167. The worst of all the multitude
　　　　　Did something for the common good.

This, I know, will seem to be a strange paradox to many; and I shall be asked what benefit the public receives from thieves and house-breakers. They are, I own, very pernicious to human society, and every government ought to take all imaginable care to root out and destroy them; yet if all people were strictly honest, and nobody would meddle with or pry into any thing but his own, half the smiths of the nation would want employment; and abundance of workmanship (which now serves for ornaments as well as defence) is to be seen everywhere both in town and country that would never have been thought of, but to secure us against the attempts of pilferers and robbers.

If what I have said be thought far fetched, and my assertion seems still a paradox, I desire the reader to look upon the consumption of things, and he will find that the laziest and most unactive, the profligate and most mischievous, are all forced to do something for the common good, and whilst their mouths are not sewed up, and they continue to wear and otherwise destroy what the industrious are daily employed about to make, fetch and procure, in spite of their teeth obliged to help, maintain the poor and the public charges. The labour of millions would soon be at an end, if there were not other millions, as I say, in the fable,

.................Employ'd,
To see their handy-works destroy'd.

But men are not to be judged by the consequences that may succeed their actions, but the facts themselves and the motives which it shall appear they acted from. If an ill-natured miser, who is almost a plumb* and spends but fifty pounds a year, though he has no relation to inherit his wealth, should be robbed of five hundred or a thousand guineas, it is certain that as soon as this money should come to circulate, the nation would be the better for the robbery and receive the same and as real a benefit from it as if an archbishop had left the same sum to the public; yet justice and the peace of society require that he or they who robbed the miser should be hanged, though there were half a dozen of them concerned.

Thieves and pick-pockets steal for a livelihood, and either what they can get honestly is not sufficient to keep them, or else they have an aversion to constant working: they want to gratify their senses, have victuals, strong drink, lewd women, and to be idle when they please. The victualler, who entertains them and takes their money, knowing which way they come at it, is very near as great a villain as his guests. But if he fleeces them well, minds his business, and is a prudent man, he may get money, and be punctual with them he deals with. The trusty out-clerk, whose chief aim is his master's profit, sends him in what beer he wants and takes care not to lose his custom; while the man's money is good, he thinks it no business of his to examine whom he gets it by. In the mean time, the wealthy brewer, who leaves all the management to his servants, knows nothing of the matter, but keeps his coach, treats his friends, and enjoys his pleasure with ease and a good conscience; he gets an estate, builds houses, and educates his children in plenty, without ever thinking on the labour which wretches perform, the shifts fools make, and the tricks knaves play to come at the commodity, by the vast sale of which he amasses his great riches.

A highwayman having met with a considerable booty, gives a poor common harlot, he fancies, ten pounds to newrig her from

---

*A *plum*, in the slang of Mandeville's day, meant the sum of £100,000, or a person who had that much money.

top to toe; is there a spruce mercer so conscientious that he will refuse to sell her a thread sattin, though he knew who she was? She must have shoes and stockings, gloves, the stay and mantua-maker, the sempstress, the linen-draper, all must get something by her, and a hundred different tradesmen dependent on those she laid her money out with may touch part of it before a month is at an end. The generous gentleman, in the mean time, his money being near spent, ventured again on the road, but the second day having committed a robbery near Highgate, he was taken with one of his accomplices, and the next sessions both were condemned and suffered the law. The money due on their conviction fell to three country fellows, on whom it was admirably well bestowed. One was an honest farmer, a sober painstaking man, but reduced by misfortunes: The summer before, by the mortality among the cattle, he had lost six cows out of ten, and now his landlord, to whom he owed thirty pounds, had seized on all his stock. The other was a day-labourer, who struggled hard with the world, had a sick wife at home, and several small children to provide for. The third was a gentleman's gardener, who maintained his father in prison, where, being bound for a neighbour, he had lain for twelve pounds almost a year and a half; this act of filial duty was the more meritorious, because he had for some time been engaged to a young woman, whose parents lived in good circumstances, but would not give their consent before our gardener had fifty guineas of his own to show. They received above fourscore pounds each, which extricated every one of them out of the difficulties they laboured under, and made them, in their opinion, the hap-piest people in the world.

Nothing is more destructive, either in regard to the health or the vigilance and industry of the poor, than the infamous liquor, the name of which, derived from Juniper in Dutch, is now by frequent use and the laconic spirit of the nation from a word of meddling length, shrunk into a monosyllable, intoxicating Gin, that charms the unactive, the desperate and crazy of either sex, and makes the starving sot behold his rags and nakedness with stupid indolence, or banter both in senseless laughter and more insipid jests! It is a fiery lake that sets the brain in flame, burns up the entrails, and scorches every part within; and, at the same time, a Lethe of oblivion, in which the wretch immersed drowns his most pinching cares and, with his reason, all anxious reflection on brats that cry for food, hard winter-frosts, and horrid empty home.

In hot and adust* tempers it makes men quarrelsome, renders them brutes and savages, sets them on to fight for nothing, and has often been the cause of murder. It has broke and destroyed the strongest constitutions, thrown them into consumptions, and been the fatal and immediate occasion of apoplexies, phrenzies, and sudden death. But, as these latter mischiefs happen but seldom, they might be overlooked and connived at: but this cannot be said of the many diseases that are familiar to the liquor, and which are daily and hourly produced by it; such as loss of appetite, fevers, black and yellow jaundice, convulsions, stone and gravel, dropsies, and leucophlegmacies.

Among the doting admirers of this liquid poison, many of the meanest rank, from a sincere affection to the commodity itself, become dealers in it, and take delight to help others to what they love themselves, as whores commence bawds to make the profits of one trade subservient to the pleasures of the other. But as these starvelings commonly drink more than their gains, they seldom, by selling, mend the wretchedness of condition they laboured under while they were only buyers. In the fag-end and outskirts of the town and all places of the vilest resort, it is sold in some part or other of almost every house, frequently in cellars, and sometimes in the garret. The petty traders in this Stygian comfort are supplied by others in somewhat higher station, that keep professed brandy shops and are as little to be envied as the former; and among the middling people, I know not a more miserable shift for a livelihood than their calling. Whoever would thrive in it must, in the first place, be of a watchful and suspicious, as well as a bold and resolute temper, that he may not be imposed upon by cheats and sharpers, nor out-bullied by the oaths and imprecations of hackney coachmen and foot soldiers: in the second, he ought to be a dabster at gross jokes and loud laughter, and have all the winning ways to allure customers and draw out their money, and be well versed in the low jests and railleries the mob make use of to banter prudence and frugality. He must be affable and ob-

---

*adust—scorched and dry.

sequious to the most despicable; always ready and officious to help a porter down with his load, shake hands with a basket woman, pull off his hat to an oyster wench, and be familiar with a beggar; with patience and good humour he must be able to endure the filthy actions and viler language of nasty drabs and the lewdest rakehells, and without a frown or the least aversion, bear with all the stench and squalor, noise and impertinence, that the utmost indigence, laziness, and ebriety can produce in the most shameless and abandoned vulgar.

The vast number of the shops I speak of throughout the city and suburbs are an astonishing evidence of the many seducers, that, in a lawful occupation, are accessary to the introduction and increase of all the sloth, sottishness, want, and misery, which the abuse of strong waters is the immediate cause of, to lift above mediocrity perhaps half a score men that deal in the same commodity by wholesale, while, among the retailers, though qualified as I required, a much greater number are broke and ruined for not abstaining from the Circean cup they hold out to others, and the more fortunate are their whole lifetime obliged to take the uncommon pains, endure the hardships, and swallow all the ungrateful and shocking things I named, for little or nothing beyond a bare sustenance and their daily bread.

The short-sighted vulgar in the chain of causes seldom can see further than one link; but those who can enlarge their view and will give themselves the leisure of gazing on the prospect of concatenated events may, in a hundred places, see good spring up and pullulate from evil, as naturally as chickens do from eggs. The money that arises from the duties upon malt is a considerable part of the national revenue, and should no spirits be distilled from it, the public treasure would prodigiously suffer on that head. But if we would set in a true light the many advantages and large catalogue of solid blessings that accrue from, and are owing to the evil I treat of, we are to consider the rents that are received, the ground that is tilled, the tools that are made, the cattle that are employed, and above all, the multitude of poor that are maintained, by the variety of labour, required in husbandry, in malting, in carriage and distillation, before we can have the product of malt, which we call low wines, and is but the beginning from which the various spirits are afterwards to be made.

Besides this, a sharp-sighted good-humoured man might pick up abundance of good from the rubbish, which I have all flung away for evil. He would tell me, that whatever sloth and sottishness might be occasioned by the abuse of malt-spirits, the moderate use of it was of inestimable benefit to the poor, who could purchase no cordials of higher prices, that it was an universal comfort, not only in cold and weariness, but most of the afflictions that are peculiar to the necessitous, and had often to the most destitute supplied the places of meat, drink, clothes, and lodging. That the stupid indolence in the most wretched condition occasioned by those composing draughts, which I complained of, was a blessing to thousands, for that certainly those were the happiest, who felt the least pain. As to diseases, he would say, that, as it caused some, so it cured others, and that if the excess in those liquors had been sudden death to some few, the habit of drinking them daily prolonged the lives of many, whom once it agreed with; that for the loss sustained from the insignificant quarrels it created at home, we were overpaid in the advantage we received from it abroad, by upholding the courage of soldiers, and animating the sailors to the combat; and that in the two last wars no considerable victory had been obtained without.

To the dismal account I have given of the retailers and what they are forced to submit to, he would answer that not many acquired more than middling riches in any trade, and that what I had counted so offensive and intolerable in the calling was trifling to those who were used to it; that what seemed irksome and calamitous to some, was delightful and often ravishing to others; as men differed in circumstances and education. He would put me in mind that the profit of an employment ever made amends for the toil and labour that belong to it, nor forget, *Dulcis odor lucri e re qualibet;** or to tell me that the smell of gain was fragrant even to night-workers.†

If I should ever urge to him that to have here and there one great and eminent distiller was a poor equivalent for the vile means, the certain want, and lasting misery of so many thousand

---

*Juvenal, *Sat*. xiv, 204-5: The smell of gain is sweet whatever its source may be [slightly misquoted by Mandeville].

†*night-workers*—men who carted away garbage and "night-soil", excrements, from the city.

wretches as were necessary to raise them, he would answer that of this I could be no judge, because I do not know what vast benefit they might afterwards be of to the commonwealth. Perhaps, would he say, the man thus raised will exert himself in the commission of the peace or other station with vigilance and zeal against the dissolute and disaffected, and retaining his stirring temper, be as industrious in spreading loyalty and the reformation of manners throughout every cranny of the wide populous town, as once he was in filling it with spirits; till he becomes at last the scourge of whores, of vagabonds and beggars, the terror of rioters and discontented rabbles, and constant plague to sabbath-breaking butchers. Here my good-humoured antagonist would exult and triumph over me, especially if he could instance to me such a bright example, what an uncommon blessing, would he cry out, is this man to his country! how shining and illustrious his virtue!

To justify his exclamation, he would demonstrate to me that it was impossible to give a fuller evidence of self-denial in a grateful mind than to see him at the expence of his quiet and hazard of his life and limbs, be always harassing, and even for trifles persecuting that very class of men to whom he owes his fortune, from no other motive than his aversion to idleness and great concern for religion and the public welfare.

* * * *

Line 173. Parties directly opposite,
         Assist each other, as 'twere for spite.

Nothing was more instrumental in forwarding the Reformation than the sloth and stupidity of the Roman clergy; yet the same Reformation has roused them from the laziness and ignorance they then laboured under; and the followers of Luther, Calvin, and others, may be said to have reformed not only those whom they drew into their sentiment, but likewise those who remained their greatest opposers. The clergy of England, by being severe upon the Schismatics and upbraiding them with want of learning, have raised themselves such formidable enemies as are not easily answered; and again, the Dissenters by prying into the lives, and diligently watching all the actions of their powerful antagonists, render those of the Established Church more cautious of giving offence, than in all probability they would if they had no malicious over-lookers to fear. It is very much owing to the great number of Huguenots that have always been in France, since the late utter extirpation of them, that that kingdom has a less dissolute and more learned clergy to boast of than any other Roman Catholic country. The clergy of that church are nowhere more sovereign than in Italy, and therefore nowhere more debauched; nor any where more ignorant than they are in Spain, because their doctrine is nowhere less opposed.

Who would imagine that virtuous women, unknowingly, should be instrumental in promoting the advantage of prostitutes? Or (what still seems the greater paradox) that incontinence should be made serviceable to the preservation of chastity? and yet nothing is more true. A vicious young fellow, after having been an hour or two at church, a ball, or any other assembly, where there is a great parcel of handsome women dressed to the best advantage, will have his imagination more fired than if he had the same time been polling [voting] at Guildhall or walking in the country among a flock of sheep. The consequence of this is that he will strive to satisfy the appetite that is raised in him; and when he find honest women obstinate and uncomatable,* it is very natural to think that he will hasten to others that are more compliable. Who would so much as surmise that this is the fault of the virtuous women? They have no thoughts of men in dressing themselves, poor souls, and endeavour only to appear clean and decent, every one according to her quality.

I am far from encouraging vice and think it would be an unspeakable felicity to a state if the sin of uncleanness could be utterly banished from it; but I am afraid it is impossible: The passions of some people are too violent to be curbed by any law or precept; and it is wisdom in all governments to bear with lesser inconveniencies to prevent greater. If courtezans and strumpets were to be prosecuted with as much rigour as some silly people would have it, what locks or bars would be sufficient to preserve the honour of our wives and daughters? For it is not only that the women in general would meet with far greater temptations and the attempts to ensnare the innocence of virgins would seem more excuseable even to the sober part of mankind than they do now:

Un-come-at-able, a term probably coined by Mandeville himself.

but some men would grow outrageous, and ravishing would become a common crime. Where six or seven thousand sailors arrive
at once, as it often happens, at Amsterdam, that have seen none
but their own sex for many months together, how is it to be supposed that honest women should walk the streets unmolested if
there were no harlots to be had at reasonable prices? for which
reason, the wise rulers of that well-ordered city always tolerate
an uncertain number of houses, in which women are hired as
publicly as horses at a livery stable; and there being in this toleration a great deal of prudence and economy to be seen, a short
account of it will be no tiresome digression.

In the first place, the houses I speak of are allowed to be nowhere but in the most slovenly and unpolished part of the town,
where seamen and strangers of no repute chiefly lodge and resort.
The street in which most of them stand is counted scandalous, and
the infamy is extended to all the neighbourhood round it. In the
second, they are only places to meet and bargain in, to make
appointments in order to promote interviews of greater secrecy,
and no manner of lewdness is ever suffered to be transacted in them:
which order is so strictly observed, that bar the ill manners and
noise of the company that frequent them, you will meet with no
more indecency and generally less lasciviousness there, than with
us are to be seen at a playhouse.

Thirdly, the female traders that come to these evening exchanges
are always the scum of the people and generally such as in the
day time carry fruit and other eatables about in wheel-barrows.
The habits, indeed, they appear in at night are very different from
their ordinary ones; yet they are commonly so ridiculously gay
that they look more like the Roman dresses of strolling actresses
than gentlewomen's clothes: if to this you add the awkwardness,
the hard hands, and coarse breeding of the damsels that wear them,
there is no great reason to fear that many of the better sort of
people will be tempted by them.

The music in these temples of Venus is performed by organs,
not out of respect to the deity that is worshipped in them, but
the frugality of the owners, whose business it is to procure as much
sound for as little money as they can, and the policy of the government, who endeavour as little as is possible to encourage the breed
of pipers and scrapers. All seafaring men, especially the Dutch,

are like the element they belong to, much given to loudness and roaring, and the noise of half a-dozen of them, when they call themselves merry, is sufficient to drown twice the number of flutes or violins; whereas, with one pair of organs they can make the whole house ring and are at no other charge than the keeping of one scurvy musician, which can cost them but little: yet notwithstanding the good rules and strict discipline that are observed in these markets of love, the schout and his officers are always vexing, mulcting, and, upon the least complaint, removing the miserable keepers of them: which policy is of two great uses; first, it gives an opportunity to a large parcel of officers, the magistrates make use of on many occasions, and which they could not be without, to squeeze a living out of the immoderate gains accruing from the worst of employments, and, at the same time, punish those necessary profligates, the bawds and panders, which, though they abominate, they desire yet not wholly to destroy. Secondly, as on several accounts it might be dangerous to let the multitude into the secret, that those houses and the trade that is drove in them are connived at, so by this means appearing unblameable, the wary magistrates preserve themselves in the good opinion of the weaker sort of people, who imagine that the government is always endeavouring, though unable, to suppress what it actually tolerates: whereas, if they had a mind to root them out, their power in the administration of justice is so sovereign and extensive, and they know so well how to have it executed, that one week, nay, one night might send them all a packing.

In Italy, the toleration of strumpets is yet more barefaced, as is evident from their public stews. At Venice and Naples, impurity is a kind of merchandise and traffic; the courtezans at Rome and the cantoneras in Spain compose a body in the state and are under a legal tax and impost. It is well known that the reason why so many good politicians as these tolerate lewd houses, is not their irreligion, but to prevent a worse evil, an impurity of a more execrable kind, and to provide for the safety of women of honour. "About two hundred and fifty years ago," says Monsieur de St. Didier, "Venice being in want of courtezans, the republic was obliged to procure a great number from foreign parts." Doglioni, who has written the memorable affairs of Venice, highly extols the wisdom of the republic in this point, which secured the chastity of women of honour daily exposed to public violences, the churches and consecrated places not being a sufficient asylum for their chastity.

Our universities in England are much belied, if in some colleges there was not a monthly allowance *ad expurgandos renes:** and time was when monks and priests in Germany were allowed concubines on paying a certain yearly duty to their prelate. "It is generally believed," says Monsieur Bayle, (to whom I owe the last paragraph) "that avarice was the cause of this shameful indulgence; but it is more probable their design was to prevent their tempting modest women, and to quiet the uneasiness of husbands, whose resentments the clergy do well to avoid." From what has been said, it is manifest that there is a necessity of sacrificing one part of womankind to preserve the other and prevent a filthiness of a more heinous nature. From whence I think I may justly conclude (what was the seeming paradox I went about to prove) that chastity may be supported by incontinence, and the best of virtues want the assistance of the worst of vices.

* * * *

Line 180. That noble sin—

The prodigality I call a noble sin is not that which has avarice for its companion and makes men unreasonably profuse to some of what they unjustly extort from others, but that agreeable good-natured vice that makes the chimney smoke and all the tradesmen smile; I mean the unmixed prodigality of heedless and voluptuous men, that being educated in plenty, abhor the vile thoughts of lucre and lavish away only what others took pains to scrape together; such as indulge their inclinations at their own expence, that have the continual satisfaction of bartering old gold for new pleasures, and from the excessive largeness of a diffusive soul are made guilty of despising too much what most people overvalue.

When I speak thus honourably of this vice and treat it with so much tenderness and good manners as I do, I have the same thing at heart that made me give so many ill names to the reverse of it, *viz.*, the interest of the public; for as the avaricious does no good

---

**ad expurgandos renes*—for the relief of the reins, *i.e.*, kidneys, although probably the sexual organs are meant.

to himself and is injurious to all the world besides, except his heir, so the prodigal is a blessing to the whole society and injures no body but himself. It is true that as most of the first are knaves, so the latter are all fools; yet they are delicious morsels for the public to feast on and may with as much justice as the French call the monks the patridges of the women, be styled the wood-cocks of the society. Was it not for prodigality, nothing could make us amends for the rapine and extortion of avarice in power. When a covetous statesman is gone, who spent his whole life in fattening himself with the spoils of the nation and had by pinching and plundering heaped up an immense treasure, it ought to fill every good member of the society with joy to behold the uncommon profuseness of his son. This is refunding to the public what was robbed from it. Resuming of grants is a barbarous way of strip-ping, and it is ignoble to ruin a man faster than he does it himself, when he sets about it in such good earnest. Does he not feed an infinite number of dogs of all sorts and sizes, though he never hunts; keep more horses than any nobleman in the kingdom, though he never rides them; and give as large an allowance to an ill-favoured whore as would keep a duchess, though he never lies with her? Is he not still more extravagant in those things he makes use of? Therefore let him alone, or praise him, call him public-spirited lord, nobly bountiful and magnificently generous, and in a few years he will suffer himself to be stript his own way. As long as the nation has its own back again, we ought not to quarrel with the manner in which the plunder is repaid.

Abundance of moderate men, I know, that are enemies to ex-tremes will tell me that frugality might happily supply the place of the two vices I speak of, that if men had not so many profuse ways of spending wealth, they would not be tempted to so many evil practices to scrape it together, and consequently that the same number of men, by equally avoiding both extremes, might render themselves more happy and be less vicious without than they could with them. Whoever argues thus shows himself a better man than he is a politician. Frugality is like honesty, a mean starving virtue, that is only fit for small societies of good peaceable men, who are contented to be poor, so they may be easy but, in a large stirring nation, you may have soon enough of it. It is an idle dreaming virtue that employs no hands, and therefore very useless in a trading country, where there are vast numbers that one way or other must be all set to work. Prodigality has a thousand inventions to keep people from sitting still that frugality would never think of; and as this must consume a prodigious wealth, so avarice again knows innumerable tricks to raise it together, which frugality would scorn to make use of.

Authors are always allowed to compare small things to great ones, especially if they ask leave first. *Si licit exemplis, etc.* but to compare great things to mean trivial ones is unsufferable, unless it be in burlesque; otherwise I would compare the body politic (I confess the simile is very low) to a bowl of punch. Avarice should be the souring, and prodigality the sweetening of it. The water I would call the ignorance, folly, and credulity of the floating insipid multitude; while wisdom, honour, fortitude, and the rest of the sublime qualities of men, which separated by art from the dregs of nature, the fire of glory has exalted and refined into a spiritual essence, should be an equivalent to brandy. I do not doubt but a Westphalian, Laplander, or any other dull stranger that is unacquainted with the wholesome composition, if he was to sell the several ingredients apart, would think it impossible they should make any tolerable liquor. The lemons would be too sour, the sugar too luscious, the brandy he will say is too strong ever to be drank in any quantity, and the water he will call a tasteless liquor only fit for cows and horses: yet experience teaches us that the ingredients I named, judiciously mixed, will make an excellent liquor, liked of and admired by men of exquisite palates.

As to our vices in particular, I could compare avarice, that causes so much mischief and is complained of by everybody who is not a miser, to a griping acid that sets our teeth on edge and is unpleasant to every palate that is not debauched: I could compare the gaudy trimming and splendid equipage of a profuse beau to the glistening brightness of the finest loaf sugar; for as the one, by correcting the sharpness, prevents the injuries which a gnawing sour might do to the bowels, so the other is a pleasing balsam that heals and makes amends for the smart, which the multitude always suffers from the gripes of the avaricious; while the substances of both melt away alike, and they consume themselves by being beneficial to the several compositions they belong to. I could carry on the simile as to proportions and the exact nicety to be observed in them, which would make it appear how little any of the ingredients could be spared in either of the mixtures; but I will not tire my reader by pursuing too far a ludicrous comparison, when I have other matters to entertain him with of greater importance; and to sum up what I have said in this and the foregoing remark, shall only add that I look upon avarice and prodigality in the society as I do upon two contrary poisons in physic, of which it is certain that the noxious qualities being by mutual mischief corrected in both, they may assist each other and often make a good medicine between them.

* * * *

Line 180. . . . . Whilst luxury
Employ'd a million of the poor, etc.

If everything is to be luxury (as in strictness it ought) that is not immediately necessary to make man subsist as he is a living creature, there is nothing else to be found in the world, no not even among the naked savages; of which it is not probable that there are any but what by this time have made some improvements upon their former manner of living; and either in the preparation of their eatables, the ordering of their huts, or otherwise, added something to what once sufficed them. This definition everybody will say is too rigorous: I am of the same opinion; but if we are to abate one inch of this severity, I am afraid we shall not know where to stop. When people tell us they only desire to keep themselves sweet and clean, there is no understanding what they would be at; if they made use of these words in their genuine proper literal sense, they might soon be satisfied without much cost or trouble, if they did not want water: but these two little adjectives are so comprehensive, especially in the dialect of some ladies, that nobody can guess how far they may be stretched. The comforts of life are likewise so various and extensive, that nobody can tell what people mean by them, except he knows what sort of life they lead. The same obscurity I observe in the words *decency* and *conveniency,* and I never understand them unless I am acquainted with the quality of the persons that make use of them. People may go to church together and be all of one mind as much as they please, I am apt to believe that when they pray for their daily bread, the bishop includes several things in that petition which the sexton does not think on.

By what I have said hitherto I would only show that if once we depart from calling everything luxury that is not absolutely necessary to keep a man alive, that then there is no luxury at all; for if the wants of men are innumerable, then what ought to supply them has no bounds; what is called superfluous to some degree of people will be thought requisite to those of higher quality; and neither the world nor the skill of man can produce anything so curious or extravagant but some most gracious sovereign or other, if it either eases or diverts him, will reckon it among the necessaries of life; not meaning everybody's life, but that of his sacred person.

It is a received notion that luxury is as destructive to the wealth of the whole body politic as it is to that of every individual person who is guilty of it, and that a national frugality enriches a country in the same manner as that which is less general increases the estates of private families. I confess, that though I have found men of much better understanding than myself of this opinion, I cannot help dissenting from them in this point. They argue thus: We send, say they, for example, to Turkey of woollen manufactury and other things of our own growth a million's worth every year; for this we bring back silk, mohair, drugs, etc. to the value of twelve hundred thousand pounds, that are all spent in our own country. By this, say they, we get nothing; but if most of us would be content with our own growth and so consume but half the quantity of those foreign commodities, then those in Turkey who would still want the same quantity of our manufactures would be forced to pay ready money for the rest, and so by the balance of that trade only, the nation should get six hundred thousand pounds *per annum*.

To examine the force of this argument, we will suppose (what they would have) that but half the silk, etc. shall be consumed in England of what there is now; we will suppose likewise that those in Turkey, though we refuse to buy above half as much of their commodities as we used to do, either can or will not be without the same quantity of our manufactures they had before and that they will pay the balance in money; that is to say, that they shall give us as much gold or silver as the value of what they buy from us exceeds the value of what we buy from them. Though what we suppose might perhaps be done for one year, it is impossible it should last: Buying is bartering; and no nation can buy goods of others that has none of her own to purchase them with. Spain and Portugal, that are yearly supplied with new gold and silver from their mines, may for ever buy for ready money, as long as their yearly increase of gold or silver continues; but then money is their growth and the commodity of the country. We know that we could not continue long to purchase the goods of other nations if they would not take our manufactures in payment for them; and why should we judge otherwise of other nations? If those in Turkey, then, had no more money fall from the skies than we, let us see what would be the consequence of what we supposed. The six hundred thousand pounds in silk, mohair, etc. that are left upon their hands the first year, must make those commodities fall considerably: Of this the Dutch and French will reap the benefit as much as ourselves; and if we continue to refuse taking their commodities in payment for our manufactures, they can trade no longer with us, but must content themselves with buying what they want of such nations as are willing to take what we refuse, though their goods are much worse than ours; and thus our commerce with Turkey must in few years be infallibly lost.

But they will say, perhaps, that to prevent the ill consequence I have showed, we shall take the Turkish merchandises as formerly and only be so frugal as to consume but half the quantity of them ourselves and send the rest abroad to be sold to others. Let us see what this will do, and whether it will enrich the nation by the balance of that trade with six hundred thousand pounds. In the first place, I will grant them that our people at home making use of so much more of our own manufactures, those who were employed in silk, mohair, etc. will get a living by the various preparations of woollen goods. But, in the second, I cannot allow that the goods can be sold as formerly; for suppose the half that is wore at home to be sold at the same rate as before, certainly the other half that is sent abroad will want very much of it: For we must send those goods to markets already supplied; and besides that, there must be freight, insurance, provision, and all other charges deducted, and the merchants in general must lose much more by this half that is reshipped than they got by the half that is consumed here. For, though the woollen manufactures are our own product, yet they stand the merchant that ships them off to foreign countries, in as much as they do the shopkeeper here that retails them: so that if the returns for what he sends abroad repay him not what his goods cost him here with all other charges, till he has the money and a good interest for it in cash, the merchant must run out, and the upshot would be that the merchants in general, finding they lost by the Turkish commodities they sent abroad, would ship no more of our manufactures than what would pay for as much silk, mohair, etc. as would be consumed here. Other nations would soon find ways to supply them with as much as we should send short, and somewhere or other to dispose of the goods we should refuse: so that all we should get by this frugality would be that those in Turkey would take but half the quantity of our manufactures of what they do now, while we encourage and wear their merchandises, without which they are not able to purchase ours.

As I have had the mortification for several years to meet with abundance of sensible people against this opinion, and who always thought me wrong in this calculation, so I had the pleasure at last to see the wisdom of the nation fall into the same sentiments, as is so manifest from an act of parliament made in the year 1721, where the legislature disobliges a powerful and valuable company and overlooks very weighty inconveniences at home to promote the interest of the Turkey trade, and not only encourages the consumption of silk and mohair, but forces the subjects, on penalties, to make use of them whether they will or not.

What is laid to the charge of luxury besides is that it increases avarice and rapine: And where they are reigning vices, offices of the greatest trust are bought and sold; the ministers that should serve the public, both great and small, corrupted, and the countries every moment in danger of being betrayed to the highest bidders: And, lastly, that it effeminates and enervates the people, by which the nations become an easy prey to the first invaders. These are indeed terrible things; but what is put to the account of luxury belongs to mal-administration and is the fault of bad politics. Every government ought to be thoroughly acquainted with and stedfastly to pursue the interest of the country. Good politicians, by dexterous management, laying heavy impositions on some goods, or totally prohibiting them, and lowering the duties on others may always turn and divert the course of trade which way they please; and as they will ever prefer, if it be equally considerable, the commerce with such countries as can pay with money as well as goods, to those that can make no returns for what they buy, but in the commodities of their own growth and manufactures, so they will always carefully prevent the traffic with such nations as refuse the goods of others and will take nothing but money for their own. But, above all, they will keep a watchful eye over the balance of trade in general, and never suffer that all the foreign commodities together that are imported in one year shall exceed in value what of their own growth or manufacture is in the same imported to others. Note, that I speak now of the interest of those nations that have no gold or silver of their own growth, otherwise this maxim need not to be so much insisted on.

If what I urged last be but diligently looked after and the imports are never allowed to be superior to the exports, no nation can ever be impoverished by foreign luxury; and they may improve it as much as they please if they can but in proportion raise the fund of their own that is to purchase it.

Trade is the principal, but not the only requisite to aggrandize a nation: there are other things to be taken care of besides. The *meum* and *tuum* must be secured, crimes punished, and all other laws concerning the administration of justice wisely contrived and strictly executed. Foreign affairs must be likewise prudently managed, and the ministry of every nation ought to have a good intelligence abroad and be well acquainted with the public transactions of all those countries that either by their neighbourhood, strength, or interest may be hurtful or beneficial to them, to take the necessary measures accordingly of crossing some and assisting others, as policy and the balance of power direct. The multitude must be awed, no man's conscience forced, and the clergy allowed no greater share in state affairs than our Saviour has bequeathed in his testament. These are the arts that lead to worldly greatness: What sovereign power soever makes a good use of them, that has any considerable nation to govern, whether it be a monarchy, a commonwealth, or a mixture of both, can never fail of making it flourish in spite of all the other powers upon earth, and no luxury or other vice is ever able to shake their constitution.—But here

I expect a full-mouthed cry against me. What! has God never punished and destroyed great nations for their sins? Yes, but not without means, by infatuating their governors and suffering them to depart from either all or some of those general maxims I have mentioned; and of all the famous states and empires the world has had to boast of hitherto, none ever came to ruin, whose destruction was not principally owing to the bad politics, neglects, or mismanagements of the rulers.

There is no doubt, but more health and vigour is expected among the people and their offspring from temperance and sobriety than there is from gluttony and drunkenness; yet I confess that as to luxury's effeminating and enervating a nation, I have not such frightful notions now, as I have had formerly. When we hear or read of things which we are altogether strangers to, they commonly bring to our imagination such ideas of what we have seen, as (according to our apprehension) must come the nearest to them: And I remember that when I have read of the luxury of Persia, Egypt, and other countries where it has been a reigning vice, and that were effeminated and enervated by it, it has sometimes put me in mind of the cramming and swilling of ordinary tradesmen at a city feast, and the beastliness their overgorging themselves is often attended with; at other times, it has made me think on the distraction of dissolute sailors, as I had seen them in company of half a dozen lewd women, roaring along with fiddles before them; and was I to have been carried into any of their great cities, I would have expected to have found one third of the people sick abed with surfeits; another laid up with the gout, or crippled by a more ignominious distemper; and the rest, that could go without leading, walk along the streets in petticoats.

It is happy for us to have fear for a keeper, as long as our reason is not strong enough to govern our appetites, and I believe that the great dread I had more particularly against the word, *to enervate,* and some consequent thoughts on the etymology of it, did me abundance of good when I was a schoolboy. But since I have seen something in the world, the consequences of luxury to a nation seem not so dreadful to me as they did. As long as men have the same appetites, the same vices will remain. In all large societies, some will love whoring and others drinking. The lustful that can get no handsome clean women will content themselves with dirty drabs, and those that cannot purchase true Hermitage or Pontack will be glad of more ordinary French claret. Those that cannot reach wine take up with most liquors, and a foot soldier or a beggar may make himself as drunk with stale beer or malt-spirits as a lord with Burgundy, Champaign, or Tockay. The cheapest and most slovenly way of indulging our passions does as much mischief to a man's constitution as the most elegant and expensive.

The greatest excesses of luxury are shown in buildings, furniture, equipages, and clothes. Clean linen weakens a man no more than flannel; tapestry, fine painting, or good wainscot are no more unwholesome than bare walls; and a rich couch or a gilt chariot are no more enervating than the cold floor or a country cart. The refined pleasures of men of sense are seldom injurious to their constitution, and there are many great epicures that will refuse to eat or drink more than their heads or stomachs can bear. Sensual people may take as great care of themselves as any; and the errors of the most viciously luxurious do not so much consist in the frequent repetitions of their lewdness and their eating and drinking too much (which are the things which would most enervate them), as they do in the operose contrivances, the profuseness and nicety they are served with, and the vast expence they are at in their tables and amours.

But let us once suppose that the ease and pleasures the grandees and the rich people of every nation live in render them unfit to endure hardships and undergo the toils of war. I will allow that most of the common council of the city would make but very indifferent foot soldiers; and I believe heartily, that if your horse was to be composed of aldermen, and such as most of them are, a small artillery of squibs would be sufficient to route them. But what have the aldermen, the common council, or indeed all people of any substance to do with the war, but to pay taxes? The hardships and fatigues of war that are personally suffered fall upon them that bear the brunt of everything, the meanest indigent part of the nation, the working slaving people. For how excessive soever the plenty and luxury of a nation may be, somebody must do the work, houses and ships must be built, merchandises must be removed, and the ground tilled. Such a variety of labours in every great nation require a vast multitude, in which there are always loose, idle, extravagant fellows enough to spare for an army; and those that are robust enough to hedge and ditch, plow and thrash, or else not too much enervated to be smiths, carpenters, sawyers, cloth-workers, porters or carmen will always be strong and hardy enough in a campaign or two to make good soldiers, who, where good orders are kept, have seldom so much plenty and superfluity come to their share as to do them any hurt.

The mischief, then, to be feared from luxury among the people of war cannot extend itself beyond the officers. The greatest of them are either men of a very high birth and princely education, or else extraordinary parts, and no less experience; and whoever is made choice of by a wise government to command an army *en chef* should have a consummate knowledge in martial affairs, intrepidity to keep him calm in the midst of danger, and many other qualifications that must be the work of time and application on men of a quick penetration, a distinguished genius, and a world of honor. Strong sinews and supple joints are trifling advantages, not regarded in persons of their reach and grandeur, that can destroy cities a-bed and ruin whole countries while they are at dinner. As they are most commonly men of great age, it would be ridiculous to expect a hale constitution and agility of limbs from them: so their heads be but active and well furnished, it is no great matter what the rest of their bodies are. If they cannot bear the fatigue of being on horseback, they may ride in coaches or be carried in litters. Men's conduct and sagacity are never the less for their being cripples, and the best general the king of France has now can hardly crawl along. Those that are immediately under the chief commanders must be very nigh of the same abilities and are generally men that have raised themselves to those posts by their merit. The other officers are all of them in their several stations obliged to lay out so large a share of their pay in fine clothes, accoutrements, and other things by the luxury of the times called necessary, that they can spare but little money for debauches; for, as they are advanced and their salaries raised, so they are likewise forced to increase their expenses and their equipages which, as well as everything else, must still be proportionable to their quality: by which means, the greatest part of them are in a manner hindered from those excesses that might be destructive to health; while their luxury thus turned another way, serves, moreover, to heighten their pride and vanity, the greatest motives to make them behave themselves like what they would be thought to be (See Remark on 1. 321 [pp. 125 ff.]).

There is nothing refines mankind more than love and honour. Those two passions are equivalent to many virtues, and therefore the greatest schools of breeding and good manners are courts and armies; the first to accomplish the women, the other to polish the men. What the generality of officers among civilized nations affect is a perfect knowledge of the world and the rules of honour, an air of frankness and humanity peculiar to military men of experience, and such a mixture of modesty and undauntedness as may bespeak them both courteous and valiant. Where good sense is fashionable and a genteel behaviour is in esteem, gluttony and drunkenness can be no reigning vices. What officers of distinction chiefly aim at is not a beastly, but a splendid way of living, and the wishes of the most luxurious, in their several degrees of quality, are to appear handsomely and excel each other in finery of equipage, politeness of entertainments, and the reputation of a judicious fancy in everything about them.

But if there should be more dissolute reprobates among officers than there are among men of other professions, which is not true, yet the most debauched of them may be very serviceable if they have but a great share of honour. It is this that covers and makes up for a multitude of defects in them and it is this that none (how abandoned soever they are to pleasure) dare pretend to be without. But as there is no argument so convincing as matter of fact, let us look back on what so lately happened in our two last wars with France. How many puny young striplings have we had in our armies, tenderly educated, nice in their dress, and curious in their diet, that underwent all manner of duties with gallantry and cheerfulness?

Those that have such dismal apprehensions of luxury's enervating and effeminating people might in Flanders and Spain have seen embroidered beaux with fine laced shirts and powdered wigs stand as much fire and lead up to the mouth of a cannon with as little concern as it was possible for the most stinking slovens to have done in their own hair, though it had not been combed in a month, and met with abundance of wild rakes, who had actually impaired their healths, and broke their constitutions with excesses of wine and women that yet behaved themselves with conduct and bravery against their enemies. Robustness is the least thing required in an officer, and if sometimes strength is of use, a firm resolution of mind, which the hopes of preferment, emulation, and the love of glory inspire them with, will at a push supply the place of bodily force.

Those that understand their business and have a sufficient sense of honour as soon as they are used to danger will always be capable officers; and their luxury, as long as they spend nobody's money but their own, will never be prejudicial to a nation.

By all wh'ch I think I have proved what I designed in this remark on luxury. First, that in one sense everything may be called so, and in another there is no such thing. Secondly, that with a wise administration all people may swim in as much foreign luxury as their product can purchase without being impoverished by it. And lastly, that where military affairs are taken care of as they ought and the soldiers well paid and kept in good discipline, a wealthy nation may live in all the ease and plenty imaginable, and in many parts of it show as much pomp and delicacy as human wit can invent, and at the same time be formidable to their neighbours and come up to the character of the bees in the fable, of which I said that

> Flatter'd in peace, and fear'd in wars,
> They were th' esteem of foreigners;
> And lavish of their wealth and lives,
> The balance of all other hives.

(See what is farther said concerning luxury in the Remarks on line 182 and 307 [below, and pp. 119 ff.]).

* * * *

Line 182. And odious pride a million more.

Pride is that natural faculty by which every mortal that has any understanding over-values and imagines better things of himself than any impartial judge, thoroughly acquainted with all his qualities and circumstances, could allow him. We are possessed of no other quality so beneficial to society and so necessary to render it wealthy and flourishing as this, yet it is that which is most generally detested. What is very peculiar to this faculty of ours is that those who are the fullest of it are the least willing to connive at it in others; whereas the heinousness of other vices is the most extenuated by those who are guilty of them themselves. The chaste man hates fornication, and drunkenness is most abhorred by the temperate, but none are so much offended at their neighbour's pride as the proudest of all; and if any one can pardon it, it is the most humble: from which, I think, we may justly infer that it being odious to all the world is a certain sign that all the world is troubled with it. This all men of sense are ready to confess, and nobody denies but that he has pride in general. But, if you come to particulars, you will meet with few that will own any action you can name of theirs to have proceeded from that principle. There are likewise many who will allow that among the sinful nations of the times pride and luxury are the great promoters of trade, but they refuse to own the necessity there is that in a more virtuous age (such a one as should be free from pride) trade would in a great measure decay.

The Almighty, they say, has endowed us with the dominion over all things which the earth and sea produce or contain; there is nothing to be found in either but what was made for the use of man; and his skill and industry above other animals were given him that he might render both them and everything else within the reach of his senses more serviceable to him. Upon this considera-tion they think it impious to imagine that humility, temperance, and other virtues should debar people from the enjoyment of those comforts of life which are not denied to the most wicked nations; and so conclude that without pride or luxury the same things might be eat, wore, and consumed; the same number of handicrafts and artificers employed, and a nation be every way as flourishing as where those vices are the most predominant.

As to wearing apparel in particular, they will tell you that pride, which sticks much nearer to us than our clothes, is only lodged in the heart, and that rags often conceal a greater portion of it than the most pompous attire; and that as it cannot be denied but that there have always been virtuous princes, who, with humble hearts, have wore their splendid diadems and swayed their envied scep-tres, void of ambition, for the good of others; so it is very probable that silver and gold brocades and the richest embroideries may without a thought of pride be wore by many whose quality and fortune are suitable to them. May not (say they) a good man of extraordinary revenues make every year a greater variety of suits than it is possible he should wear out and yet have no other ends than to set the poor at work, to encourage trade, and by employing many, to promote the welfare of his country? And considering food and raiment to be necessaries and the two chief articles to which all our worldly cares are extended, why may not all mankind set aside a considerable part of their income for the one as well as the other without the least tincture of pride? Nay, is not every member of the society in a manner obliged, according to his ability, to contribute toward the maintenance of that branch of trade on which the whole has so great a dependence? Besides that, to appear decently is a civility and often a duty, which, without any regard to ourselves, we owe to those we converse with.

These are the objections generally made use of by haughty moralists who cannot endure to hear the dignity of their species arraigned; but if we look narrowly into them, they may soon be answered.

If we had no vices, I cannot see why any man should ever make more suits than he has occasion for, though he was never so desirous of promoting the good of the nation: for, though in the wearing of a well-wrought silk rather than a slight stuff and the preferring curious fine cloth to coarse, he had no other view but the setting of more people to work and consequently the public welfare, yet he could consider clothes no otherwise than lovers of their country do taxes now; they may pay them with alacrity, but nobody gives more than his due; especially where all are justly rated according to their abilities, as it could no otherwise be expected in a very virtuous age. Besides, that in such golden times nobody would dress above his condition, nobody pinch his family, cheat or overreach his neighbour to purchase finery, and consequently there would not be half the consumption nor a third part of the people employed as now there are. But to make this more plain and demonstrate that for the support of trade there can be nothing equivalent to pride, I shall examine the several views men have in outward apparel and set forth what daily experience may teach everybody as to dress.

Clothes were originally made for two ends, to hide our nakedness and to fence our bodies against the weather and other outward injuries: to these our boundless pride has added a third, which is ornament; for what else but an excess of stupid vanity could have prevailed upon our reason to fancy that ornamental which must continually put us in mind of our wants and misery beyond all other animals that are ready clothed by nature herself? It is indeed to be admired how so sensible a creature as man, that pretends to so many fine qualities of his own, should condescend to value himself upon what is robbed from so innocent and defenceless an animal as a sheep, or what he is beholden for to the most insignificant thing upon earth, a dying worm; yet while he is proud of such trifling depredations, he has the folly to laugh at the Hottentots on the furthest promontory of Afric, who adorn themselves with the guts of their dead enemies without considering that they are the ensigns of their valour those barbarians are fine with, the true *spolia opima,* and that if their pride be more savage than ours, it is certainly less ridiculous because they wear the spoils of the more noble animal.

But whatever reflections may be made on this head, the world has long since decided the matter; handsome apparel is a main point, fine feathers make fine birds, and people, where they are not known, are generally honoured according to their clothes and other accoutrements they have about them; from the richness of them we judge of their wealth, and by their ordering of them we guess at their understanding. It is this which encourages everybody who is conscious of his little merit if he is any ways able to wear clothes above his rank, especially in large and populous cities, where obscure men may hourly meet with fifty strangers to one acquaintance, and consequently have the pleasure of being esteemed by a vast majority, not as what they are, but what they appear to be: which is a greater temptation than most people want to be vain.

Whoever takes delight in viewing the various scenes of low life, may on Easter, Whitsun, and other great holidays, meet with scores of people, especially women, of almost the lowest rank, that wear good and fashionable clothes: if coming to talk with them, you treat them more courteously and with greater respect than what they are conscious they deserve, they will commonly be ashamed of owning what they are; and often you may, if you are a little inquisitive, discover in them a most anxious care to conceal the business they follow, and the place they live in. The reason is plain; while they receive those civilities that are not usually paid them, and which they think only due to their betters, they have the satisfaction to imagine that they appear what they would be, which to weak minds is a pleasure almost as substantial as they could reap from the very accomplishments of their wishes: this golden dream they are unwilling to be disturbed in, and being sure that the meanness of their condition, if it is known, must sink them very low in your opinion, they hug themselves in their disguise and take all imaginable precaution not to forfeit, by a useless discovery, the esteem which they flatter themselves that their good clothes have drawn from you.

Though everybody allows that as to apparel and manner of living we ought to behave ourselves suitable to our conditions and follow the examples of the most sensible and prudent among our equals in rank and fortune, yet how few that are not either miserably covetous or else proud of singularity have this discretion to boast of? We all look above ourselves and, as fast as we can, strive to imitate those that some way or other are superior to us.

The poorest labourer's wife in the parish who scorns to wear a strong wholesome frize, as she might, will half starve herself and her husband to purchase a second-hand gown and petticoat that cannot do her half the service; because, forsooth, it is more genteel. The weaver, the shoemaker, the tailor, the barber, and every mean working fellow that can set up with little has the impudence with the first money he gets to dress himself like a tradesman of substance; the ordinary retailer in the clothing of his wife takes pattern from his neighbour that deals in the same commodity by wholesale, and the reason he gives for it is that twelve years ago the other had not a bigger shop than himself. The druggist, mercer, draper, and other creditable shopkeepers, can find no difference between themselves and merchants and therefore dress and live like them. The merchant's lady, who cannot bear the assurance of those mechanics, flies for refuge to the other end of the town and scorns to follow any fashion but what she takes from thence; this haughtiness alarms the court, the women of quality are frightened to see merchants' wives and daughters dressed like themselves: this impudence of the city, they cry, is intolerable; mantua-makers are sent for, and the contrivance of fashions becomes all their study, that they may have always new modes ready to take up as soon as those saucy cits shall begin to imitate those in being. The same emulation is continued through the several degrees of quality to an incredible expence, till at last the prince's great favourites and those of the first rank of all, having nothing left to outstrip some of their inferiors, are forced to lay out vast estates in pompous equipages, magnificent furniture, sumptuous gardens, and princely palaces.

To this emulation and continual striving to outdo one another it is owing that after so many various shiftings and changes of modes, in trumping up new ones and renewing of old ones, there is still a *plus ultra* left for the ingenious; it is this, or at least the consequence of it, that sets the poor to work, adds spurs to industry, and encourages the skilful artificer to search after further improvements.

It may be objected that many people of good fashion, who have been used to be well dressed out of custom, wear rich clothes with all the indifferency imaginable, and that the benefit to trade accruing from them cannot be ascribed to emulation or pride. To this I answer that it is impossible that those who trouble their heads so little with their dress could ever have wore those rich clothes if both the stuffs and fashions had not been first invented to gratify the vanity of others who took greater delight in fine apparel than they; besides that everybody is not without pride that appears to be so; all the symptoms of that vice are not easily discovered; they are manifold and vary according to the age, humour, circumstances, and often constitution of the people.

The choleric city captain seems impatient to come to action, and expressing his warlike genius by the firmness of his steps, makes his pike for want of enemies tremble at the valour of his arm; his martial finery, as he marches along, inspires him with an unusual elevation of mind, by which, endeavouring to forget his shop as well as himself, he looks up at the balconies with the fierceness of a Saracen conqueror; while the phlegmatic alderman, now become venerable both for his age and his authority, contents himself with being thought a considerable man; and knowing no easier way to express his vanity, looks big in his coach, where being known by his paltry livery, he receives in sullen state the homage that is paid him by the meaner sort of people.

The beardless ensign counterfeits a gravity above his years and with ridiculous assurance strives to imitate the stern countenance of his colonel, flattering himself all the while that by his daring mien you will judge of his prowess. The youthful fair, in a vast concern of being overlooked, by the continual changing of her posture betrays a violent desire of being observed, and catching, as it were, at everybody's eyes, courts with obliging looks the admiration of her beholders. The conceited coxcomb, on the contrary, displaying an air of sufficiency, is wholly taken up with the contemplation of his own perfections, and in public places discovers such a disregard to others that the ignorant must imagine he thinks himself to be alone.

These and such like are all manifest, though different, tokens of pride that are obvious to all the world; but man's vanity is not always so soon found out. When we perceive an air of humanity, and men seem not to be employed in admiring themselves nor altogether unmindful of others, we are apt to pronounce them void of pride when perhaps they are only fatigued with gratifying their vanity and become languid from a satiety of enjoyments. That outward show of peace within and drowsy composure of careless negligence with which a great man is often seen in his plain chariot to loll at ease are not always so free from art as they may seem to be. Nothing is more ravishing to the proud than to be thought happy.

The well-bred gentleman places his greatest pride in the skill he has of covering it with dexterity, and some are so expert in concealing this frailty, that when they are the most guilty of it, the vulgar think them the most exempt from it. Thus the dissembling courtier, when he appears in state, assumes an air of modesty and good humour; and while he is ready to burst with vanity, seems to be wholly ignorant of his greatness, well knowing that those lovely qualities must heighten him in the esteem of others and be an addition to that grandeur which the coronets about his coach and harnesses, with the rest of his equipage, cannot fail to proclaim without his assistance.

And as in these pride is overlooked because industriously concealed, so in others again it is denied that they have any when they show (or at least seem to show) it in the most public manner. The wealthy parson being as well as the rest of his profession debarred from the gaiety of laymen, makes it his business to look out for an admirable black and the finest cloth that money can purchase and distinguishes himself by the fullness of his noble and spotless garment; his wigs are as fashionable as that form he is forced to comply with will admit of; but as he is only stinted in their shape, so he takes care that for goodness of hair and colour few noblemen shall be able to match him; his body is ever clean, as well as his clothes, his sleek face is kept constantly shaved, and his handsome nails are diligently pared; his smooth white hand and a brilliant of the first water, mutually becoming, honour each other with double graces; what linen he discovers is transparently curious, and he scorns ever to be seen abroad with a worse beaver than what a rich banker would be proud of on his wedding day; to all these niceties in dress he adds a majestic gait and expresses a commanding loftiness in his carriage; yet common civility notwithstanding the evidence of so many concurring symptoms will not allow us to suspect any of his actions to be the result of pride: considering the dignity of his office, it is only decency in him what would be vanity in others; and in good manners to his calling we ought to believe that the worthy gentleman, without any regard to his reverend person, puts himself to all this trouble and expence merely out of a respect which is due to the divine order he belongs to and a religious zeal to preserve his holy function from the contempt of scoffers. With all my heart, nothing of all this shall be called pride; let me only be allowed to say that to our human capacities it looks very like it.

But if at last I should grant that there are men who enjoy all the fineries of equipage and furniture, as well as clothes, and yet have no pride in them; it is certain, that if all should be such, that emulation I spoke of before must cease, and consequently trade, which has so great a dependence upon it, suffer in every branch. For to say that if all men were truly virtuous they might without any regard to themselves consume as much out of zeal to serve their neighbours and promote the public good as they do now out of self-love and emulation is a miserable shift and an unreasonable supposition. As there have been good people in all ages, so without doubt we are not destitute of them in this; but let us inquire of the periwig-makers and tailors in what gentlemen, even of the greatest wealth and highest quality, they ever could discover such public-spirited views. Ask the lacemen, the mercers, and the linen-drapers, whether the richest, and if you will, the most virtuous ladies, if they buy with ready money or intend to pay in any reasonable time, will not drive from shop to shop to try the market, make as many words, and stand as hard with them to save a groat or sixpence in a yard as the most necessitous jilts in town. If it be urged that if there are not, it is possible there might be such people, I answer that it is as possible that cats, instead of killing rats and mice, should feed them and go about the house to suckle and nurse their young ones; or that a kite should call the hens to their meat, as the cock does, and sit brooding over their chickens instead of devouring them; but if they should all do so, they would cease to be cats and kites; it is inconsistent with their natures, and the species of creatures which now we mean when we name cats and kites would be extinct as soon as that could come to pass.

* * * *

Line 183. Envy itself, and vanity,
　　　　　 Were ministers of industry.

Envy is that baseness in our nature which makes us grieve and pine at what we conceive to be a happiness in others. I do not believe there is a human creature in his senses arrived to maturity that at one time or other has not been carried away by this passion in good earnest; and yet I never met with any one that dared own he was guilty of it but in jest. That we are so generally ashamed of this vice is owing to that strong habit of hypocrisy, by the help of which we have learned from our cradle to hide even from ourselves the vast extent of self-love and all its different branches. It is impossible man should wish better for another than he does for himself, unless where he supposes an impossibility that himself should attain to those wishes; and from hence we may easily learn after what manner this passion is raised in us. In order to it, we are to consider first that as well as we think of ourselves, so ill we think of our neighbour with equal injustice; and when we apprehend that others do or will enjoy what we think they do not deserve, it afflicts and makes us angry with the cause of that disturbance. Secondly, that we are employed in wishing well for ourselves, everyone according to his judgment and inclinations, and when we observe something we like and yet are destitute of in the possession of others, it occasions first sorrow in us for not having the thing we like. This sorrow is incurable while we continue our esteem for the thing we want: but as self-defence is restless and never suffers us to leave any means untried how to remove evil from us, as far and as well as we are able, experience teaches us that nothing in nature more alleviates this sorrow than our anger against those who are possessed of what we esteem and want. This latter passion, therefore, we cherish and cultivate to save or relieve ourselves at least in part from the uneasiness we felt from the first.

Envy, then, is a compound of grief and anger; the degrees of this passion depend chiefly on the nearness or remoteness of the objects as to circumstances. If one who is forced to walk on foot envies a great man for keeping a coach and six, it will never be with that violence or give him that disturbance which it may to a man who keeps a coach himself, but can only afford to drive with four horses. The symptoms of envy are as various and as hard to describe as those of the plague; at some time it appears in one shape, at others in another quite different. Among the fair the disease is very common and the signs of it very conspicuous in their opinions and censures of one another. In beautiful young women you may often discover this faculty to a high degree; they frequently will hate one another mortally at first sight from no other principle than envy; and you may read this scorn and unreasonable aversion in their very countenances if they have not a great deal of art and well learned to dissemble.

In the rude and unpolished multitude this passion is very barefaced, especially when they envy others for the goods of fortune. They rail at their betters, rip up their faults, and take pains to misconstrue their most commendable actions. They murmur at Providence and loudly complain that the good things of this world are chiefly enjoyed by those who do not deserve them. The grosser sort of them it often affects so violently that if they were not withheld by the fear of the laws, they would go directly and beat those their envy is levelled at from no other provocation than what that passion suggests to them.

The men of letters, labouring under this distemper, discover quite different symptoms. When they envy a person for his parts and erudition, their chief care is industriously to conceal their frailty, which generally is attempted by denying and depreciating the good qualities they envy. They carefully peruse his works and are displeased with every fine passage they meet with; they look for nothing but his errors and wish for no greater feast than a gross mistake. In their censures they are captious as well as severe, make mountains of mole-hills, and will not pardon the least shadow of a fault, but exaggerate the most trifling omission into a capital blunder.

Envy is visible in brute beasts; horses show it in their endeavours of outstripping one another; and the best spirited will run themselves to death before they will suffer another before them. In dogs this passion is likewise plainly to be seen; those who are used to be caressed will never tamely bear that felicity in others. I have seen a lap-dog that would choke himself with victuals rather than leave any thing for a competitor of his own kind; and we may often observe the same behaviour in those creatures which we daily see in infants that are froward and by being over-fondled made humour-some. If out of caprice they at any time refuse to eat what they have asked for, and we can make them believe that somebody else, nay, even the cat or the dog is going to take it from them, they will make an end of their oughts* with pleasure and feed even against their appetite.

If envy was not rivetted in human nature, it would not be so common in children, and youth would not be so generally spurred on by emulation. Those who would derive every thing that is beneficial to the society from a good principle ascribe the effects of emulation in school-boys to a virtue of the mind; as it requires labour and pains, so it is evident that they commit a self-denial who act from that disposition; but if we look narrowly into it, we shall find that this sacrifice of ease and pleasure is only made to envy and the love of glory. If there was not something very like this passion mixed with that pretended virtue it would be impossible to raise and increase it by the same means that create envy. The boy who receives a reward for the superiority of his performance is conscious of the vexation it would have been to him if he should have fallen short of it. This reflection makes him

---

*probably *orts*, scraps and left-overs.

exert himself, not to be outdone by those whom he looks upon as his inferiors, and the greater his pride is, the more self-denial he will practice to maintain his conquest. The other, who, in spite of the pains he took to do well, has missed of the prize, is sorry and consequently angry with him whom he must look upon as the cause of his grief. But to show this anger would be ridiculous and of no service to him, so that he must either be contented to be less esteemed than the other boy, or, by renewing his endeavors, become a greater proficient; and it is ten to one but the disinterested, good-humoured, and peaceable lad will choose the first, and so become indolent and inactive, while the covetous, peevish, and quarrelsome rascal shall take incredible pains and make himself a conqueror in his turn.

Envy, as it is very common among painters, so it is of great use for their improvement. I do not mean that little daubers envy great masters, but most of them are tainted with this vice against those immediately above them. If the pupil of a famous artist is of a bright genius and uncommon application, he first adores his master; but as his own skill increases, he begins insensibly to envy what he admired before. To learn the nature of this passion and that it consists in what I have named, we are but to observe that if a painter, by exerting himself, comes not only to equal but to exceed the man he envied, his sorrow is gone and all his anger disarmed; and if he hated him before, he is now glad to be friends with him if the other will condescend to it.

Married women who are guilty of this vice, which few are not, are always endeavouring to raise the same passion in their spouses; and where they have prevailed, envy and emulation have kept more men in bounds and reformed more ill husbands from sloth, from drinking, and other evil courses, than all the sermons that have been preached since the time of the Apostles.

As everybody would be happy, enjoy pleasure, and avoid pain if he could, so self-love bids us look on every creature that seems satisfied as a rival in happiness; and the satisfaction we have in feeling that felicity disturbed without any advantage to ourselves but what springs from the pleasure we have in beholding it is called loving mischief for mischief's sake; and the motive of which that frailty is the result, malice, another offspring derived from the same original; for if there was no envy, there could be no malice. When the passions lie dormant, we think they have not such a frailty in their nature because that moment they are not affected with it.

A gentleman well dressed, who happens to be dirtied all over by a coach or a cart, is laughed at, and by his inferiors much more than his equals because they envy him more: they know he is vexed at it, and, imagining him to be happier than themselves, they are glad to see him meet with displeasures in his turn! But a young lady, if she be in a serious mood, instead of laughing at, pities him because a clean man is a sight she takes delight in, and there is no room for envy. At disasters we either laugh or pity those that befall them, according to the stock we are possessed of, either malice or compassion. If a man falls or hurts himself so slightly that it moves not the latter, we laugh, and here our pity and malice shake us alternately: Indeed, Sir, I am very sorry for it, I beg your pardon for laughing, I am the silliest creature in the world, then laugh again; and again, I am indeed very sorry, and so on. Some are so malicious, they would laugh if a man broke his leg, and others are so compassionate that they can heartily pity a man for the least spot in his clothes; but nobody is so savage that no compassion can touch him, nor any man so good-natured as never to be affected with any malicious pleasure. How strangely our passions govern us! We envy a man for being rich, and then perfectly hate him. But if we come to be his equals, we are calm, and the least condescension in him makes us friends; but if we become visibly superior to him, we can pity his misfortunes. The reason why men of true good sense envy less than others is because they admire themselves with less hesitation than fools and silly people; for, though they do not show this to others, yet the solidity of their thinking gives them an assurance of their real worth, which men of weak understanding can never feel within, though they often counterfeit it.

The ostracism of the Greeks was a sacrifice of valuable men made to epidemic envy and often applied as an infallible remedy to cure and prevent the mischiefs of popular spleen and rancour. A victim of state often appeases the murmurs of a whole nation, and after-ages frequently wonder at barbarities of this nature, which, under the same circumstances, they would have committed themselves. They are compliments to the people's malice, which is never better gratified than when they can see a great man humbled.

We believe that we love justice and to see merit rewarded; but if men continue long in the first posts of honour, half of us grow weary of them, look for their faults, and, if we can find none, we suppose they hide them, and it is much if the greatest part of us do not wish them discarded. This foul play the best of men ought ever to apprehend from all who are not their immediate friends or acquaintance because nothing is more tiresome to us than the repetition of praises we have no manner of share in.

The more a passion is a compound of many others, the more difficult it is to define it; and the more it is tormenting to those that labour under it, the greater cruelty it is capable of inspiring them with against others. Therefore nothing is more whimsical or mischievous than jealousy, which is made up of love, hope, fear, and a great deal of envy. The last has been sufficiently treated of already; and what I have to say of fear, the reader will find under Remark on 1. 321 [p. 131]. So that the better to explain and illustrate this odd mixture, the ingredients I shall further speak of in this place are hope and love.

Hoping is wishing with some degree of confidence that the thing wished for will come to pass. The firmness and imbecility of our hope depend entirely on the greater or lesser degree of our confidence, and all hope includes doubt; for when our confidence is arrived to that height as to exclude all doubts, it becomes a certainty, and we take for granted what we only hoped for before. A silver inkhorn may pass in speech because everybody knows what we mean by it, but a certain hope* cannot. For a man who makes use of an epithet that destroys the essence of the substantive he joins it to can have no meaning at all; and the more clearly we understand the force of the epithet and the nature of the substantive, the more palpable is the nonsense of the heterogeneous compound. The reason, therefore, why it is no so shocking to some to hear a man speak of certain hope as if he should talk of hot ice or liquid oak is not because there is less nonsense contained in the first than there is in either of the latter, but because the word hope, I mean the essence of it, is not so clearly understood

*certain hope—Since the words certain hope appear in the Anglican liturgy, Mandeville's criticism in this passage was particularly irritating to the orthodox. See Kaye's ed., I, 141.

by the generality of the people as the words and essence of ice and oak are.

Love, in the first place, signifies affection, such as parents and nurses bear to children and friends to one another; it consists in a liking and well-wishing to the person beloved. We give an easy construction to his words and actions and feel a proneness to excuse and forgive his faults if we see any; his interest we make on all accounts our own, even to our prejudice, and receive an inward satisfaction for sympathising with him in his sorrows as well as joys. What I said last is not impossible, whatever it may seem to be; for, when we are sincere in sharing with another in his misfortunes, self-love makes us believe that the sufferings we feel must alleviate and lessen those of our friend; and while this fond reflection is soothing our pain, a secret pleasure arises from our grieving for the person we love.

Secondly, by love we understand a strong inclination in its nature distinct from all other affections of friendship, gratitude, and consanguinity that persons of different sexes, after liking bear to one another; it is in this signification, that love enters into the compound of jealousy and is the effect as well as happy disguise of that passion that prompts us to labour for the preservation of our species. This latter appetite is innate both in men and women who are not defective in their formation, as much as hunger or thirst, though they are seldom affected with it before the years of puberty. Could we undress nature and pry into her deepest recesses, we should discover the the seeds of this passion before it exerts itself as plainly as we see the teeth in an embryo before the gums are formed. There are few healthy people of either sex whom it has made no impression on before twenty. Yet, as the peace and happiness of the civil society require that this should be kept a secret never to be talked of in public, so among well-bred people it is counted highly criminal to mention before company anything in plain words that is relating to this mystery of succession; by which means, the very name of the appetite, though the most necessary for the continuance of mankind, is become odious, and the proper epithets commonly joined to lust are filthy and abominable.

This impulse of nature in people of strict morals and rigid modesty often disturbs the body for a considerable time before it is understood or known to be what it is, and it is remarkable that the most polished and best instructed are generally the most ignorant as to this affair; and here I can but observe the difference between man in the wild state of nature and the same creature in the civil society. In the first, men and women, if left rude and untaught in the sciences of modes and manners, would quickly find out the cause of that disturbance and be at a loss no more than other animals for a present remedy; besides, that it is not probable they would want either precept or example from the more experienced. But, in the second, where the rules of religion, law, and decency, are to be followed and obeyed before any dictates of nature, the youth of both sexes are to be armed and fortified against this impulse and from their infancy artfully frightened from the most remote approaches of it. The appetite itself and all the symptoms of it, though they are plainly felt and understood, are to be stifled with care and severity and in women flatly disowned, and if there be occasion, with obstinacy denied, even when themselves are affected by them. If it throws them into distempers, they must be cured by physic or else patiently bear them in silence; and it is the interest of the society to preserve decency and politeness; that women should linger, waste, and die rather than relieve themselves in an unlawful manner; and among the fashionable part of mankind, the people of birth and fortune, it is expected that matrimony should never be entered upon without a curious regard to family, estate, and reputation, and, in the making of matches, the call of nature be the very last consideration.

Those, then, who would make love and lust synonymous confound the effect with the cause of it; yet such is the force of education and a habit of thinking, as we are taught that sometimes persons of either sex are actually in love without feeling any carnal desires or penetrating into the intentions of nature, the end proposed by her, without which they could never have been affected with that sort of passion. That there are such is certain, but many more whose pretences to those refined notions are only upheld by art and dissimulation. Those who are really such Platonic lovers are commonly pale-faced weakly people of cold and phlegmatic constitutions in either sex; the hale and robust, of bilious temperament and a sanguine complexion, never entertain any love so spiritual as to exclude all thoughts and wishes that relate to the body; but if the most seraphic lovers would know the original of their inclination, let them but suppose that another should have the corporal enjoyment of the person beloved, and by the tortures they will suffer from that reflection they will soon discover the nature of their passions; whereas, on the contrary, parents and friends receive a satisfaction in reflecting on the joys and comforts of a happy marriage to be tasted by those they wish well to.

The curious, that are skilled in anatomizing the invisible part of man, will observe that the more sublime and exempt this love is from all thoughts of sensuality, the more spurious it is and the more it degenerates from its honest original and primitive simplicity. The power and sagacity as well as labour and care of the politician in civilizing the society has been nowhere more conspicuous than in the happy contrivance of playing our passions against one another. By flattering our pride and still increasing the good opinion we have of ourselves on the one hand and inspiring us on the other with a superlative dread and mortal aversion against shame, the artful moralists have taught us cheerfully to encounter ourselves, and if not subdue, at least so to conceal and disguise our darling passion, lust, that we scarce know it when we meet with it in our breasts. Oh! the mighty prize we have in view for all our self-denial! Can any man be so serious as to abstain from laughter when he considers that for so much deceit and insincerity practiced upon ourselves as well as others, we have no other recompense than the vain satisfaction of making our species appear more exalted and remote from that of other animals than it really is, and we in our consciences know it to be? Yet this is fact, and in it we plainly perceive the reason why it was necessary to render odious every word or action by which we might discover the innate desire we feel to perpetuate our kind; and why tamely to submit to the violence of a furious appetite (which is painful to resist) and innocently to obey the most pressing demand of nature without guile or hypocrisy, like other creatures, should be branded with the ignominious name of brutality.

What we call love, then, is not a genuine, but an adulterated appetite, or rather a compound, a heap of several contradictory passions blended in one. As it is a product of nature warped by custom and education, so the true origin and first motive of it, as I have hinted already, is stifled in well-bred people and concealed from themselves: all which is the reason that, as those affected with it vary in age, strength, resolution, temper, circumstances, and manners, the effects of it are so different, whimsical, surprising, and unaccountable.

It is this passion that makes jealousy so troublesome and the envy of it often so fatal; those who imagine that there may be jealousy without love do not understand that passion. Men may not have the least affection for their wives and yet be angry with them for their conduct, and suspicious of them either with or without cause; but what in such cases affects them is their pride, the concern for their reputation. They feel a hatred against them without remorse; when they are outrageous, they can beat them and go to sleep contentedly: such husbands may watch their dames themselves, and have them observed by others; but their vigilance is not so intense; they are not so inquisitive or industrious in their searches, neither do they feel that anxiety of heart at the fear of a discovery as when love is mixed with the passions.

What confirms me in this opinion is that we never observe this behaviour between a man and his mistress; for when his love is gone and he suspects her to be false, he leaves her and troubles his head no more about her; whereas it is the greatest difficulty imaginable even to a man of sense to part with his mistress as long as he loves her, whatever faults she may be guilty of. If in his anger he strikes her, he is uneasy after it; his love makes him reflect on the hurt he has done her, and he wants to be reconciled to her again. He may talk of hating her, and many times from his heart wish her hanged, but if he cannot get entirely rid of his frailty, he can never disentangle himself from her; though she is represented in the most monstrous guilt to his imagination, and he has resolved and swore a thousand times never to come near her again, there is no trusting him, even when he is fully convinced of her infidelity; if his love continues, his despair is never so lasting, but between the blackest fits of it he relents and finds lucid intervals of hope; he forms excuses for her, thinks of pardoning, and in order to [do] it racks his invention for possibilities that may make her appear less criminal.

* * * *

Line 200. Real pleasures, comforts, ease.

That the highest good consisted in pleasure was the doctrine of

Epicurus, who yet led a life exemplary for continence, sobriety, and other virtues, which made people of the succeeding ages quarrel about the signification of pleasure. Those who argued from the temperance of the philosopher said that the delight Epicurus meant was being virtuous; so Erasmus in his Colloquies tells us that there are no greater Epicures than pious Christians. Others that reflected on the dissolute manners of the greatest part of his followers would have it that by pleasures he could have understood nothing but sensual ones and the gratification of our passions. I shall not decide their quarrel, but am of opinion that, whether men be good or bad, what they take delight in is their pleasure; and not to look out for any further etymology from the learned languages, I believe an Englishman may justly call everything a pleasure that pleases him, and according to this definition, we ought to dispute no more about men's pleasures than their tastes: *Trahit sua quemque voluptas.* *

The worldly-minded, voluptuous, and ambitious man, nothwithstanding he is void of merit, covets precedence everywhere and desires to be dignified above his betters. He aims at spacious palaces and delicious gardens; his chief delight is in excelling others in stately horses, magnificent coaches, a numerous attendance, and dear-bought furniture. To gratify his lust, he wishes for genteel, young, beautiful women of different charms and complexions that shall adore his greatness, and be really in love with his person. His cellars he would have stored with the flower of every country that produces excellent wines; his table he desires may be served with many courses, and each of them contain a choice variety of dainties not easily purchased, and ample evidences of elaborate and judicious cookery; while harmonious music and well-couched flattery entertain his hearing by turns. He employs, even in the meanest trifles, none but the ablest and most ingenious workmen, that his judgment and fancy may as evidently appear in the least things that belong to him as his wealth and quality are manifested in those of greater value. He desires to have several sets of witty, facetious, and polite people to converse with, and among them he would have some famous for learning and universal knowledge; for his serious affairs, he wishes to find men

---

*Virgil, *Eclogues,* II, 65: Each pursues his own desire.

of parts and experience, that should be diligent and faithful. Those that are to wait on him he would have handy, mannerly, and discreet, of comely aspect, and a graceful mien: what he requires in them besides, is a respectful care of everything that is his, nimbleness without hurry, dispatch without noise, and an unlimited obedience to his orders. Nothing he thinks more troublesome than speaking to servants; wherefore he will only be attended by such, as by observing his looks have learned to interpret his will from his slightest motions. He loves to see an elegant nicety in everything that approaches him, and in what is to be employed about his person he desires a superlative cleanliness to be religiously observed. The chief officers of his household he would have to be men of birth, honour and distinction, as well as order, contrivance, and economy; for though he loves to be honoured by everybody, and receives the respects of the common people with joy, yet the homage that is paid him by persons of quality is ravishing to him in a more transcendent manner.

While thus wallowing in a sea of lust and vanity, he is wholly employed in provoking and indulging his appetites, he desires the world should think him altogether free from pride and sensuality, and put a favourable construction upon his most glaring vices: nay, if his authority can purchase it, he covets to be thought wise, brave, generous, good-natured, and endued with the virtues he thinks worth having. He would have us believe that the pomp and luxury he is served with are as many tiresome plagues to him; and all the grandeur he appears in is an ungrateful burden, which, to his sorrow, is inseparable from the high sphere he moves in; that his noble mind, so much exalted above vulgar capacities, aims at higher ends and cannot relish such worthless enjoyments; that the highest of his ambition is to promote the public welfare, and his greatest pleasure to see his country flourish, and everybody in it made happy. These are called real pleasures by the vicious and earthly-minded, and whoever is able, either by his skill or fortune, after this refined manner at once to enjoy the world and the good opinion of it, is counted extremely happy by all the most fashionable part of the people.

But, on the other side, most of the ancient philosophers and grave moralists, especially the Stoics, would not allow anything to be a real good that was liable to be taken from them by others.

They wisely considered the instability of fortune and the favour of princes, the vanity of honour and popular applause, the precariousness of riches and all earthly possessions, and therefore placed true happiness in the calm serenity of a contented mind free from guilt and ambition; a mind that, having subdued every sensual appetite, despises the smiles as well as frowns of fortune, and taking no delight but in contemplation, desires nothing but what everybody is able to give to himself: a mind that, armed with fortitude and resolution, has learned to sustain the greatest losses without concern, to endure pain without affliction, and to bear injuries without resentment. Many have owned themselves arrived to this height of self-denial, and then, if we may believe them, they were raised above common mortals, and their strength extended vastly beyond the pitch of their first nature. They could behold the anger of threatening tyrants and the most imminent dangers without terror, and preserved their tranquillity in the midst of torments; death itself they could meet with intrepidity, and left the world with no greater reluctance than they had showed fondness at their entrance into it.

These among the ancients have always bore the greatest sway; yet others that were no fools neither, have exploded those precepts as impracticable, called their notions romantic, and endeavoured to prove that what these Stoics asserted of themselves exceeded all human force and possibility, and that therefore the virtues they boasted of could be nothing but haughty pretence, full of arrogance and hypocrisy; yet notwithstanding these censures, the serious part of the world, and the generality of wise men that have lived ever since to this day, agree with the Stoics in the most material points; as that there can be no true felicity in what depends on things perishable; that peace within is the greatest blessing, and no conquest like that of our passions; that knowledge, temperance, fortitude, humility, and other embellishments of the mind are the most valuable acquisitions; that no man can be happy but he that is good: and that the virtuous are only capable of enjoying real pleasures.

I expect to be asked why in the fable I have called those pleasures real that are directly opposite to those which I own the wise men of all ages have extolled as the most valuable? My answer is, because I do not call things pleasures which men say are best, but such as they seem to be most pleased with; how can I believe that a man's chief delight is in the embellishment of the mind when I see him ever employed about and daily pursue the pleasures that are contrary to them? John never cuts any pudding, but just enough that you cannot say he took none; this little bit, after much chomping and chewing, you see goes down with him like chopped hay; after that he falls upon the beef with a voracious appetite and crams himself up to his throat. Is it not provoking to hear John cry every day that pudding is all his delight and that he does not value the beef of a farthing?

I could swagger about fortitude and the contempt of riches as much as Seneca himself and would undertake to write twice as much in behalf of poverty as ever he did; for the tenth part of his estate, I could teach the way to his *summum bonum* as exactly as I know my way home. I could tell people to extricate themselves from all worldly engagements, and to purify the mind, they must divest themselves of their passions, as men take out the furniture when they would clean a room thoroughly; and I am clearly of the opinion that the malice and most severe strokes of fortune can do no more injury to a mind thus stripped of all fears, wishes, and inclinations, than a blind horse can do in an empty barn. In the theory of all this I am very perfect, but the practice is very difficult; and if you went about picking my pocket, offered to take the victuals from before me when I am hungry, or made but the least motion of spitting in my face, I dare not promise how philosophically I should behave myself. But that I am forced to submit to every caprice of my unruly nature, you will say, is no argument that others are as little masters of theirs, and therefore I am willing to pay adoration to virtue whenever I can meet with it, with a proviso that I shall not be obliged to admit any as such where I can see no self-denial, or to judge of men's sentiments from their words where I have their lives before me. . . .

. . . if virtue was the chief delight of great men, why should their extravagance be extended to things not understood by the mob and wholly removed from public view, I mean their private diversions, the pomp and luxury of the dining-room and the bedchamber, and the curiosities of the closet? Few of the vulgar know that there is wine of a guinea the bottle, that birds no bigger than larks are often sold for half-a-guinea a-piece, or that a single picture may be worth several thousand pounds; besides, is it to be imagined that unless it was to please their own appetites, men should put themselves to such vast expenses for a political show and be so solicitous to gain the esteem of those whom they so much despise in everything else? If we allow that the splendor and all the elegancy of a court are insipid, and only tiresome to the prince himself, and are altogether made use of to preserve royal majesty from contempt, can we say the same of half a dozen illegitimate children, most of them the offspring of adultery by the same majesty, got, educated, and made princes at the expense of the nation? Therefore, it is evident that this awing of the multitude by a distinguished manner of living is only a cloak and pretense, under which great men would shelter their vanity and indulge every appetite about them without reproach.

A burgomaster of Amsterdam in his plain black suit, followed perhaps by one footman, is fully as much respected and better obeyed than a lord mayor of London with all his splendid equipage and great train of attendance. Where there is a real power, it is ridiculous to think that any temperance or austerity of life should ever render the person in whom that power is lodged contemptible in his office, from an emperor to the beadle of a parish. Cato, in his government of Spain, in which he acquitted himself with so much glory, had only three servants to attend him; do we hear that any of his orders were ever slighted for this, notwithstanding that he loved his bottle? And when that great man marched on foot through the scorching sands of Libya, and parched up with thirst, refused to touch the water that was brought him before all his soldiers had drank, do we ever read that this heroic forbearance weakened his authority or lessened him in the esteem of his army? But what need we go so far off? There has not, for these many ages, been a prince less inclined to pomp and luxury than the present king of Sweden [Charles XII], who, enamoured with the title of hero, has not only sacrificed the lives of his subjects and welfare of his dominions, but (what is more uncommon in sovereigns) his own ease and all the comforts of life, to an implacable spirit of revenge; yet he is obeyed to the ruin of his people, in obstinately maintaining a war that has almost utterly destroyed his kingdom.

Thus I have proved that the real pleasures of all men in nature are worldly and sensual, if we judge from their practice; I say all men in nature because devout Christians, who alone are to be excepted here being regenerated and preternaturally assisted by the Divine grace, cannot be said to be in nature. How strange it is they should all so unanimously deny it! Ask not only the divines and moralists of every nation, but likewise all that are rich and powerful, about real pleasure, and they will tell you, with the Stoics, that there can be no true felicity in things mundane and corruptible: but then look upon their lives, and you will find they take delight in no other.

What must we do in this dilemma? Shall we be so uncharitable, as judging from men's actions, to say that all the world prevaricates and that this is not their opinion, let them talk what they will? Or shall we be so silly, as relying on what they say, to think them sincere in their sentiments and so not believe our own eyes? Or shall we rather endeavour to believe ourselves and them too, and say with Montaigne that they imagine and are fully persuaded that they believe what they do not believe? These are his words: "Some impose on the world and would be thought to believe what they really do not: but much the greater number impose upon themselves, not considering, nor thoroughly apprehending what it is to believe." But this is making all mankind either fools or imposters, which, to avoid, there is nothing left us but to say what Mr. Bayle has endeavoured to prove at large in his Reflections on Comets: "that man is so unaccountable a creature as to act most commonly against his principle"; and this is so far from being injurious that it is a compliment to human nature, for we must say either this or worse.

This contradiction in the frame of man is the reason that the theory of virtue is so well understood and the practice of it so rarely to be met with. If you ask me where to look for those beautiful shining qualities of prime ministers and the great favourites of princes that are so finely painted in dedications, addresses, epitaphs, funeral sermons, and inscriptions, I answer, there, and nowhere else. Where would you look for the excellency of a statue, but in that part which you see of it? It is the polished outside only that has the skill and labour of the sculptor to boast of; what is out of sight is untouched. Would you break the head or cut open the breast to look for the brains or the heart, you would only show your ignorance and destroy the workmanship. This has often made me compare the virtues of great men to your large China jars: they make a fine show, and are ornamental even to a chimney; one would, by the bulk they appear in and the value that is set upon them, think they might be very useful, but look into a thousand of them, and you will find nothing in them but dust and cobwebs.

* * * *

Line 201. . . . . The very poor
Liv'd better than the rich before.

If we trace the most flourishing nations in their origin, we shall find, that in the remote beginnings of every society, the richest and most considerable men among them were a great while destitute of a great many comforts of life that are now enjoyed by the meanest and most humble wretches: so that many things were once looked upon as the invention of luxury, are now allowed, even to those that are so miserably poor as to become the objects of public charity, nay, counted so necessary, that we think no human creature ought to want them.

In the first ages, man, without doubt, fed on the fruits of the earth without any previous preparation, and reposed himself naked like other animals on the lap of their common parent. Whatever has contributed since to make life more comfortable, as it must have been the result of thought, experience, and some labour, so it more or less deserves the name of luxury, the more or less trouble it required, and deviated from the primitive simplicity. Our admiration is extended no farther than to what is new to us and we all overlook the excellency of things we are used to, be they never so curious. A man would be laughed at, that should discover luxury in the plain dress of a poor creature that walks along in a thick parish gown, and a coarse shirt underneath it; and yet what a number of people, how many different trades, and what a variety of skill and tools must be employed to have the most ordinary Yorkshire cloth? What depth of thought and ingenuity, what toil and labour, and what length of time must it have cost before man could learn from a seed, to raise and prepare so useful a product as linen.

Must that society not be vainly curious, among whom this

admirable commodity, after it is made, shall not be thought fit to be used even by the poorest of all before it is brought to a perfect whiteness, which is not to be procured but by the assistance of all the elements, joined to a world of industry and patience? I have not done yet: can we reflect not only on the cost laid out upon this luxurious invention, but likewise on the little time the whiteness of it continues, in which part of its beauty consists, that every six or seven days at farthest it wants cleaning, and while it lasts is a continual charge to the wearer; can we, I say, reflect on all this and not think it an extravagant piece of nicety that even those who receive alms of the parish should not only have whole garments made of this operose manufacture, but likewise that as soon as they are soiled, to restore them to their pristine purity, they should make use of one of the most judicious as well as difficult compositions that chemistry can boast of; with which, dissolved in water by the help of fire, the most detersive and yet innocent lixivium* is prepared that human industry has hitherto been able to invent?

It is certain, time was that the things I speak of would have bore those lofty expressions, and in which everybody would have reasoned after the same manner; but the age we live in would call a man fool who should talk of extravagance and nicety if he saw a poor woman, after having wore her crown cloth smock a whole week, wash it with a bit of stinking soap of a groat a pound.

The arts of brewing and making bread have by slow degrees been brought to the perfection they now are in, but to have invented them at once, and *a priori,* would have required more knowledge and a deeper insight into the nature of fermentation than the greatest philosopher has hitherto been endowed with; yet the fruits of both are now enjoyed by the meanest of our species, and a starving wretch knows not how to make a more humble or a more modest petition than by asking for a bit of bread or a draught of small beer.

Man has learned by experience that nothing was softer than the small plumes and down of birds, and found that heaped together, they would by their elasticity gently resist any incumbent weight and heave up again of themselves as soon as the pressure

---

lixivium—cleanser; literally, lye or a solution containing lye.

is over. To make use of them to sleep upon was, no doubt, first invented to compliment the vanity as well as ease of the wealthy and potent; but they are long since become so common that almost everybody lies upon featherbeds, and to substitute flocks* in the room of them is counted a miserable shift of the most necessitous. What a vast height must luxury have been arrived to before it could be reckoned a hardship to repose upon the soft wool of animals!

From caves, huts, hovels, tents, and barracks, with which mankind took up at first, we are come to warm and well-wrought houses, and the meanest habitations to be seen in cities are regular buildings, contrived by persons skilled in proportions and architecture. If the ancient Britons and Gauls should come out of their graves, with what amazement would they gaze on the mighty structures everywhere raised for the poor! Should they behold the magnificence of a Chelsea-College, a Greenwich-Hospital, or what surpasses all them, a *Des Invalides* at Paris, and see the care, the plenty, the superfluities and pomp, which people that have no possessions at all are treated with in those stately palaces, those who were once the greatest and richest of the land would have reason to envy the most reduced of our species now.

Another piece of luxury the poor enjoy, that is not looked upon as such and which there is no doubt but the wealthiest in a golden age would abstain from, is their making use of the flesh of animals to eat. In what concerns the fashions and manners of the ages men live in, they never examine into the real worth or merit of the cause and generally judge of things not as their reason but custom direct them. Time was when the funeral rites in the disposing of the dead were performed by fire and the cadavers of the greatest emperors were burnt to ashes. Then, burying the corpse in the ground was a funeral for slaves or made a punishment for the worst of malefactors. Now nothing is decent or honourable but interring; and burning the body is reserved for crimes of the blackest dye. At some times we look upon trifles with horror, at other times we can behold enormities without concern. If we see a man walk with his hat on in a church, though out of service

---

flocks—material consisting of coarse tufts and refuse of wool or cotton.

time, it shocks us; but if on a Sunday night we meet half a dozen fellows drunk in the street, the sight makes little or no impression upon us. If a woman at a merry-making dresses in man's clothes, it is reckoned a frolic amongst friends, and he that finds too much fault with it is counted censorious; upon the stage it is done without reproach, and the most virtuous ladies will dispense with it in an actress, though everybody has a full view of her legs and thighs; but if the same woman, as soon as she has petticoats on again, should show her leg to a man as high as her knee, it would be a very immodest action, and everybody will call her impudent for it.

I have often thought, if it was not for this tyranny which custom usurps over us, that men of any tolerable good-nature could never be reconciled to the killing of so many animals for their daily food, as long as the bountiful earth so plentifully provides them with varieties of vegetable dainties. I know that reason excites our compassion but faintly, and therefore I would not wonder how men should so little commiserate such imperfect creatures as crayfish, oysters, cockles, and indeed all fish in general; as they are mute and their inward formation, as well as outward figure [is] vastly different from ours, they express themselves unintelligibly to us, and therefore it is not strange that their grief should not affect our understanding which it cannot reach; for nothing stirs us to pity so effectually as when the symptoms of misery strike immediately upon our senses, and I have seen people moved at the noise a live lobster makes upon the spit, that could have killed half a dozen fowls with pleasure. But in such perfect animals as sheep and oxen, in whom the heart, the brain and nerves differ so little from ours, and in whom the separation of the spirits from the blood, the organs of sense, and consequently feeling itself, are the same as they are in human creatures; I cannot imagine how a man not hardened in blood and massacre is able to see a violent death, and the pangs of it, without concern.

In answer to this, most people will think it sufficient to say that all things being allowed to be made for the service of man, there can be no cruelty in putting creatures to the use they were designed for; but I have heard men make this reply while their nature within them has reproached them with the falsehood of the assertion. There is of all the multitude not one man in ten but what will own (if he was not brought up in a slaughter-house) that of all trades he could never have been a butcher; and I question whether ever anybody so much as killed a chicken without reluctancy the first time. Some people are not to be persuaded to taste of any creatures they have daily seen and been acquainted with while they were alive; others extend their scruple no further than to their own poultry and refuse to eat what they fed and took care of themselves; yet all of them will feed heartily and without remorse on beef, mutton, and fowls when they are bought in the market. In this behaviour, methinks, there appears something like a consciousness of guilt, it looks as if they endeavoured to save themselves from the imputation of a crime (which they know sticks somewhere) by removing the cause of it as far as they can from themselves; and I can discover in it some strong remains of primitive pity and innocence, which all the arbitrary power of custom and the violence of luxury have not yet been able to conquer.

What I build upon I shall be told is a folly that wise men are not guilty of: I own it; but while it proceeds from a real passion inherent in our nature, it is sufficient to demonstrate that we are born with a repugnancy to the killing, and consequently the eating, of animals; for it is impossible that a natural appetite should ever prompt us to act or desire others to do what we have an aversion to, be it as foolish as it will.

Everybody knows that surgeons in the cure of dangerous wounds and fractures, the extirpation of limbs, and other dreadful operations, are often compelled to put their patients to extraordinary torments, and that the more desperate and calamitous cases occur to them, the more the outcries and bodily sufferings of others must become familiar to them; for this reason, our English law, out of a most affectionate regard to the lives of the subject, allows them not to be of any jury upon life and death, as supposing that their practice itself is sufficient to harden and extinguish in them that tenderness without which no man is capable of setting a true value upon the lives of his fellow-creatures. Now, if we ought to have no concern for what we do to brute beasts, and there was not imagined to be any cruelty in killing them, why should of all callings butchers, and only they, jointly with surgeons, be excluded from being jurymen by the same law?

I shall urge nothing of what Pythagoras and many other wise men have said concerning this barbarity of eating flesh; I have gone too much out of my way already and shall therefore beg the reader if he would have any more of this to run over the following fable, or else, if he be tired, to let it alone, with an assurance that in doing of either he shall equally oblige me.

A Roman merchant in one of the Carthaginian wars was cast away upon the coast of Afric; himself and his slave with great difficulty got safe ashore; but going in quest of relief were met by a lion of a mighty size. It happened to be one of the breed that ranged in Aesop's days, and one that could not only speak several languages, but seemed, moreover, very well acquainted with human affairs. The slave got upon a tree, but his master not thinking himself safe there and having heard much of the generosity of lions, fell down prostrate before him with all the signs of fear and submission. The lion who had lately filled his belly, bids him rise and for a while lay by his fears, assuring him withal that he should not be touched if he could give him any tolerable reasons why he should not be devoured. The merchant obeyed; and having now received some glimmering hopes of safety, gave a dismal account of the shipwreck he had suffered, and endeavouring from thence to raise the lion's pity, pleaded his cause with abundance of good rhetoric; but observing by the countenance of the beast that flattery and fine words made very little impression, he betook himself to arguments of greater solidity, and reasoning from the excellency of man's nature and abilities, remonstrated how improbable it was that the gods should not have designed him for a better use than to be eat* by savage beasts. Upon this the lion became more attentive and vouchsafed now and then a reply, till at last the following dialogue ensued between them.

Oh vain and covetous animal (said the lion), whose pride and avarice can make him leave his native soil, where his natural wants might be plentifully supplied, and try rough seas and dangerous mountains to find out superfluities, why should you esteem your

---

*eat—eaten (pronounced et).

species above ours? And if the gods have given you a superiority over all creatures, then why beg you of an inferior? Our superiority (answered the merchant) consists not in bodily force, but strength of understanding; the gods have endued us with a rational soul, which, though invisible, is much the better part of us. I desire to touch nothing of you but what is good to eat; but why do you value yourself so much upon that part which is invisible? Because it is immortal, and shall meet with rewards after death for the actions of this life, and the just shall enjoy eternal bliss and tranquillity with the heroes and demi-gods in the Elysian fields. What life have you led? I have honoured the gods, and studied to be beneficial to man. Then why do you fear death if you think the gods as just as you have been? I have a wife and five small children that must come to want if they lose me. I have two whelps that are not big enough to shift for themselves that are in want now and must actually be starved if I can provide nothing for them. Your children will be provided for one way or other; at least as well when I have eat you, as if you had been drowned.

As to the excellency of either species, the value of things among you has ever increased with the scarcity of them, and to a million of men there is hardly one lion; besides that, in the great veneration man pretends to have for his kind, there is little sincerity farther than it concerns the share which everyone's pride has in it for himself; it is a folly to boast of the tenderness shown and attendance given to your young ones, or the excessive and lasting trouble bestowed in the education of them. Man being born the most necessitous and most helpless animal, this is only an instinct of nature, which, in all creatures, has ever proportioned the care of the parents to the wants and imbecillities of the offspring. But if a man had a real value for his kind, how is it possible that often ten thousand of them, and sometimes ten times as many, should be destroyed in few hours for the caprice of two? All degrees of men despise those that are inferior to them; and if you could enter into the hearts of kings and princes, you would hardly find any but what have less value for the greatest part of the multitudes they rule over than those have for the cattle that belong to them. Why should so many pretend to derive their race, though but spuriously, from the immortal gods; why should all of them suffer others to kneel down before them and more or less take delight in having divine honours paid them, but to insinuate that themselves are of a more exalted nature and a species superior to that of their subjects?

Savage I am, but no creature can be called cruel but what either by malice or insensibility extinguishes his natural pity. The lion was born without compassion; we follow the instinct of our nature; the gods have appointed us to live upon the waste and spoil of other animals, and as long as we can meet with dead ones, we never hunt after the living. It is only man, mischievous man, that can make death a sport. Nature taught your stomach to crave nothing but vegetables; but your violent fondness to change and great eagerness after novelties have prompted you to the destruction of animals without justice or necessity, perverted your nature, and warped your appetites which way soever your pride or luxury have called them. The lion has a ferment within him that consumes the toughest skin and hardest bones, as well as the flesh of all animals without exception; your squeamish stomach, in which the digestive heat is weak and inconsiderable, will not so much as admit of the most tender parts of them, unless above half the concoction has been performed by artificial fire before hand; and yet what animal have you spared to satisfy the caprices of a languid appetite? Languid I say; for what is man's hunger if compared to the lion's? Yours, when it is at the worst, makes you faint; mine makes me mad. Oft have I tried with roots and herbs to allay the violence of it, but in vain; nothing but large quantities of flesh can anywise appease it.

Yet the fierceness of our hunger notwithstanding, lions have often requited benefits received; but ungrateful and perfidious man feeds on the sheep that clothes him and spares not her innocent young ones, whom he has taken into his care and custody. If you tell me the gods made man master over all other creatures, what tyranny was it then to destroy them out of wantonness? No, fickle, timorous animal, the gods have made you for society and designed that millions of you, when well joined together, should compose the strong Leviathan*. A single lion bears some sway in the creation, but what is single man? A small and inconsiderable part,

---

*Leviathan—the national state, especially the state as described by Thomas Hobbes in his Leviathan (1651).

a trifling atom of one great beast. What nature designs, she exe-cutes; and it is not safe to judge of what she purposed but from the effects she shows. If she had intended that man, as man from a superiority of species, should lord it over all other animals, the tiger, nay, the whale and eagle, would have obeyed his voice.

But if your wit and understanding exceeds ours, ought not the lion, in deference to that superiority, to follow the maxims of men, with whom nothing is more sacred than that the reason of the strongest is ever the most prevalent? Whole multitudes of you have conspired and compassed the destruction of one, after they had owned the gods had made him their superior; and one has often ruined and cut off whole multitudes, whom, by the same gods, he had sworn to defend and maintain. Man never acknowl-edged superiority without power, and why should I? The excellence I boast of is visible, all animals tremble at the sight of the lion, not out of panic fear. The gods have given me swiftness to over-take and strength to conquer whatever comes near me. Where is there a creature that has teeth and claws like mine, behold the thickness of these massy jawbones, consider the width of them, and feel the firmness of this brawny neck. The nimblest deer, the wildest boar, the stoutest horse, and strongest bull are my prey wherever I meet them. Thus spoke the lion, and the merchant fainted away.

The lion, in my opinion, has stretched the point too far; yet, when to soften the flesh of male animals we have by castration prevented the firmness of their tendons and every fiber would have come to without it, I confess I think it ought to move a human creature, when he reflects upon the cruel care with which they are fattened for destruction. When a large and gentle bullock, after having resisted a ten times greater force of blows than would have killed his murderer, falls stunned at last and his armed head is fastened to the ground with cords; as soon as the wide wound is made and the jugulars are cut asunder, what mortal can, without compassion, hear the painful bellowings intercepted by his blood, the bitter sighs that speak the sharpness of his anguish, and the deep sounding groans, with loud anxiety, fetched from the bottom of his strong palpitating heart; look on the trembling and violent convulsion of his limbs; see, while his reeking gore streams from him, his eyes become dim and languid, and behold his strugglings, gasps and last efforts for life, the certain signs of his approaching fate? When a creature has given such convincing and undeniable proofs of the terrors upon him and the pains and agonies he feels, is there a follower of Descartes so inured to blood as not to refute by his commiseration the philosophy of the vain reasoner?*

* * * *

Line 307. . . . . For frugally
          They now liv'd on their salary.

When people have small comings in and are honest withal, it is then that the generality of them begin to be frugal, and not before. Frugality in ethics is called that virtue from the principle of which men abstain from superfluities and, despising the operose contrivances of art to procure either case of pleasure, content themselves with the natural simplicity of things and are carefully temperate in the enjoyment of them, without any tincture of covetousness. Frugality thus limited is perhaps scarcer than many may imagine; but what is generally understood by it is a quality more often to be met with, and consists in a medium between profuseness and avarice, rather leaning to the latter. As this prudent economy, which some people call saving, is in private families the most certain method to increase an estate, so some imagine that whether a country be barren or fruitful, the same method, if generally pursued (which they think practicable), will have the same effect upon a whole nation, and that, for example, the English might be much richer than they are if they would be as frugal as some of their neighbors. This, I think, is an error which to prove I shall first refer the reader to what has been said upon this head in Remark on 1. 180 [pp. 77 ff.] and then go on thus.

Experience teaches us first that as people differ in their views and perceptions of things, so they vary in their inclinations; one man is given to covetousness, another to prodigality, and a third is only saving. Secondly, that men are never, or at least, very seldom, reclaimed from their darling passions, either by reason or precept, and that if anything ever draws them from what they are

---

Descartes—Having postulated the complete separation of the material from the immaterial, of body from mind and soul, Descartes argued that animals are mechanical bodies, devoid of consciousness, feeling and reason.

naturally propense to, it must be a change in their circumstances or their fortunes. If we reflect upon these observations, we shall find that to render the generality of a nation lavish, the product of the country must be considerable in proportion to the inhabitants, and what they are profuse of cheap; that, on the contrary, to make a nation generally frugal, the necessaries of life must be scarce, and consequently dear; and that, therefore, let the best politician do what he can, the profuseness or frugality of a people in general must always depend upon and will, in spite of his teeth, be ever proportioned to the fruitfulness and product of the country, the number of inhabitants, and the taxes they are to bear. If anybody would refute what I have said, let them only prove from history that there ever was in any country a national frugality without a national necessity.

Let us examine then what things are requisite to aggrandize and enrich a nation. The first desirable blessings for any society of men are a fertile soil, and a happy climate, a mild government, and more land than people. These things will render man easy, loving, honest, and sincere. In this condition they may be as virtuous as they can, without the least injury to the public, and consequently as happy as they please among themselves. But they shall have no arts or sciences or be quiet longer than their neighbors will let them; they must be poor, ignorant, and almost wholly destitute of what we call the comforts of life, and all the cardinal virtues together would not so much as procure a tolerable coat or a porridge-pot among them; for in this state of slothful ease and stupid innocence, as you need not fear great vices, so you must not expect any considerable virtues. Man never exerts himself but when he is roused by his desires; while they lie dormant, and there is nothing to raise them, his excellence and abilities will be forever undiscovered, and the lumpish machine, without the influence of his passions, may by justly compared to a huge windmill without a breath of air.

Would you render a society of men strong and powerful, you must touch their passions. Divide the land, though there be never so much to spare, and their possessions will make them covetous; rouse them, though but in jest, from their idleness with praises, and pride will set them to work in earnest; teach them trades and handicrafts, and you will bring envy and emulation among them;

to increase their numbers, set up a variety of manufactures and leave no ground uncultivated; let property be inviolably secured and privileges equal to all men; suffer nobody to act but what is lawful and everybody to think what he pleases; for a country where everybody may be maintained that will be employed, and the other maxims are observed, must always be thronged and can never want people, as long as there is any in the world. Would you have them bold and warlike, turn to military discipline, make good use of their fear, and flatter their vanity with art and assiduity; but would you, moreover, render them an opulent, knowing, and polite nation, teach them commerce with foreign countries, and, if possible, get into the sea, which to compass spare no labour nor industry, and let no difficulty deter you from it; then promote navigation, cherish the merchant, and encourage trade in every branch of it; this will bring riches, and where they are, arts and sciences will soon follow; and by the help of what I have named and good management, it is that politicians can make a people potent, renowned, and flourishing.

But would you have a frugal and honest society, the best policy is to preserve men in their native simplicity, strive not to increase their numbers; let them never be acquainted with strangers or superfluities, but remove and keep from them everything that might raise their desires or improve their understanding.

Great wealth and foreign treasure will ever scorn to come among men, unless you will admit their inseparable companions, avarice and luxury; where trade is considerable, fraud will intrude. To be at once well-bred and sincere is no less than a contradiction; and therefore, while man advances in knowledge and his manners are polished, we must expect to see, at the same time, his desires enlarged, his appetites refined, and his vices increased.

The Dutch may ascribe their present grandeur to the virtue and frugality of their ancestors as they please; but what made that contemptible spot of ground so considerable among the principal powers of Europe has been their political wisdom in postponing everything to merchandise and navigation, the unlimited liberty of conscience that is enjoyed among them, and the unwearied application with which they have always made use of the most effectual means to encourage and increase trade in general.

* * * *

To convince the champions for national frugality by another argument that what they urge is impracticable, we will suppose that I am mistaken in everything which in Remark, 1. 180, I have said in behalf of luxury and the necessity of it to maintain trade; after that let us examine what a general frugality, if it was by art and management to be forced upon people, whether they have occasion for it or not, would produce in such nations as ours. We will grant, then, that all the people in Great Britain shall consume but four-fifths of what they do now and so lay by one-fifth part of their income; I shall not speak of what influence this would have upon almost every trade, as well as the farmer, the grazier, and the landlord, but favourably suppose (what is yet impossible) that the same work shall be done, and consequently the same handicrafts be employed as there are now. The consequence would be that unless money should all at once fall prodigiously in value and everything else, contrary to reason, grow very dear, at the five years end all the working people and the poorest of labourers (for I would not meddle with any of the rest) would be worth in ready cash as much as they now spend in a whole year; which, by the bye, would be more money than ever the nation had at once.

Let us now, overjoyed with this increase of wealth, take a view of the condition the working people would be in, and, reasoning from experience and what we daily observe of them, judge what their behaviour would be in such a case. Everybody knows that there is a vast number of journeymen weavers, tailors, cloth-workers, and twenty other handicrafts, who, if by four days labour in a week they can maintain themselves, will hardly be persuaded to work the fifth; and that there are thousands of labouring men of all sorts, who will, though they can hardly subsist, put themselves to fifty inconveniences, disoblige their masters, pinch their bellies, and run in debt to make holidays. When men show such extraordinary proclivity to idleness and pleasure, what reason have we to think that they would ever work unless they were obliged to it by immediate necessity? When we see an artificer that cannot be drove to his work before Tuesday because Monday morning he has two shillings left of his last week's pay, why should we imagine he would go to it at all if he had fifteen or twenty pounds in his pocket?

What would, at this rate, become of our manufactures? If the merchant would send cloth abroad, he must make it himself, for the clothier cannot get one man out of twelve that used to work for him. If what I speak of was only to befall the journeymen shoemakers and nobody else, in less than a twelvemonth half of us would go barefoot. The chief and most pressing use there is for money in a nation is to pay the labour of the poor, and when there is a real scarcity of it, those who have a great many workmen to pay will always feel it first; yet notwithstanding this great necessity of coin, it would be easier, where property was well secured, to live without money than without poor; for who would do the work? For this reason the quantity of circulating coin in a country ought always to be proportioned to the number of hands that are employed, and the wages of labourers to the price of provisions. From whence it is demonstrable that whatever procures plenty makes labourers cheap, where the poor are well managed; who as they ought to be kept from starving, so they should receive nothing worth saving. If here and there one of the lowest class by uncommon industry and pinching his belly lifts himself above the condition he was brought up in, nobody ought to hinder him; nay, it is undeniably the wisest course for every person in the society and for every private family to be frugal; but it is the interest of all rich nations that the greatest part of the poor should almost never be idle and yet continually spend what they get.

All men, as Sir William Temple observes very well, are more prone to ease and pleasure than they are to labour when they are not prompted to it by pride and avarice, and those that get their living by their daily labour are seldom powerfully influenced by either; so that they have nothing to stir them up to be serviceable but their wants, which it is prudence to relieve, but folly to cure. The only thing, then, that can render the labouring man industrious is a moderate quantity of money; for as too little will, according as his temper is, either dispirit or make him desperate, so too much will make him insolent and lazy.

A man would be laughed at by most people who should maintain that too much money could undo a nation, yet this has been the fate of Spain; to this the learned Don Diego Saavedra ascribes the ruin of his country. The fruits of the earth in former ages had made Spain so rich that King Lewis XI of France being come to

the court of Toledo was astonished at its splendour and said that
he had never seen anything to be compared to it, either in Europe
or Asia; he that in his travels to the Holy Land had run through
every province of them. In the kingdom of Castile alone (if we
may believe some writers), there were for the holy war from all
parts of the world got together one hundred thousand foot, ten
thousand horse, and sixty thousand carriages for baggage, which
Alfonso III maintained at his own charge and paid every day, as
well soldiers as officers and princes, every one according to his
rank and dignity; nay, down to the reign of Ferdinand and Isabella
(who equipped Columbus) and some time after, Spain was a fertile country, where trade and manufactures flourished, and had
a knowing industrious people to boast of. But as soon as that
mighty treasure that was obtained with more hazard and cruelty
than the world until then had known and which to come at, by the
Spaniard's own confession, had cost the lives of twenty million
of Indians; as soon, I say, as that ocean of treasure came rolling
in upon them, it took away their senses, and their industry forsook
them. The farmer left his plough, the mechanic his tools, the merchant his counting-house, and everybody scorning to work, took
his pleasure and turned gentleman. They thought they had reason
to value themselves above all their neighbours, and now nothing but
the conquest of the world would serve them.

The consequence of this has been that other nations have supplied what their own sloth and pride denied them; and when
everybody saw that notwithstanding all the prohibitions the government could make against the exportation of bullion, the Spaniard would part with his money and bring it [to] you aboard himself
at the hazard of his neck, all the world endeavoured to work for
Spain. Gold and silver being by this means yearly divided and
shared among all the trading countries have made all things dear
and most nations of Europe industrious, except their owners, who,
ever since their mighty acquisitions, sit with their arms across
and wait every year with impatience and anxiety the arrival of
their revenues from abroad to pay others for what they have spent
already; and thus by too much money, the making of colonies
and other mismanagements, of which it was the occasion, Spain
is from a fruitful and well-peopled country, with all its mighty titles
and possessions, made a barren and empty thoroughfare through

which gold and silver pass from America to the rest of the world; and the nation, from a rich, acute, diligent, and labourious, become a slow, idle, proud, and beggarly people. So much for Spain. The next country where money is called the product is Portugal, and the figure which that kingdom with all its gold makes in Europe, I think is not much to be envied.

The great art then to make a nation happy and what we call flourishing consists in giving everybody an opportunity of being employed; which to compass, let a government's first care be to promote as great a variety of manufactures, arts, and handicrafts, as human wit can invent; and the second, to encourage agriculture and fishery in all their branches, that the whole earth may be forced to exert itself as well as man; for as the one is an infallible maxim to draw vast multitudes of people into a nation, so the other is the only method to maintain them.

It is from this policy, and not the trifling regulations of lavishness and frugality (which will ever take their own course, according to the circumstances of the people), that the greatness and felicity of nations must be expected; for let the value of gold and silver either rise or fall, the enjoyment of all societies will ever depend upon the fruits of the earth and the labour of the people; both which joined together are a more certain, a more inexhaustible, and a more real treasure than the gold of Brazil or the silver of Potosi.

* * * *

Line 321. No honour now, &c.

Honour in its figurative sense is a chimera without truth or being, an invention of moralists and politicians, and signifies a certain principle of virtue not related to religion, found in some men that keeps them close to their duty and engagements whatever they be; as for example, a man of honour enters into a conspiracy with others to murder a king; he is obliged to go thorough stitch* with it; and if overcome by remorse or good nature, he startles at the enormity of his purpose, discovers the plot, and turns a witness against his accomplices; he then forfeits his honour, at least among the party he belonged to. The excellency of this prin-

---

*thorough stitch—wholeheartedly.

ciple is that the vulgar are destitute of it, and it is only to be met with in people of the better sort, as some oranges have kernels and others not, though the outside be the same. In great families it is like the gout, generally counted hereditary, and all lords' children are born with it. In some that never felt anything of it, it is acquired by conversation and reading (especially of romances), in others by preferment; but there is nothing that encourages the growth of it more than a sword, and upon the first wearing of one, some people have felt considerable shoots of it in four and twenty hours.

The chief and most important care a man of honour ought to have is the preservation of this principle, and rather than forfeit it, he must lose his employments and estate, nay, life itself; for which reason, whatever humility he may show by way of good-breeding, he is allowed to put an inestimable value upon himself as a possessor of this invisible ornament. The only method to preserve this principle is to live up to the rules of honour, which are laws he is to walk by; himself is obliged always to be faithful to his trust, to prefer the public interest to his own, not to tell lies, nor defraud or wrong anybody, and from others to suffer no affront, which is a term of art for every action designedly done to undervalue him.

The men of ancient honour, of which I reckon Don Quixote to have been the last upon record, were very nice observers of all these laws, and a great many more than I have named; but the moderns seem to be more remiss; they have a profound veneration for the last of them, but they pay not an equal obedience to any of the other; and whoever will but strictly comply with that I hint at shall have abundance of trespasses against all the rest connived at.

A man of honour is always counted impartial, and a man of sense of course; for nobody ever heard of a man of honour that was a fool; for this reason, he has nothing to do with the law and is always allowed to be a judge in his own case; and if the least injury be done either to himself or his friend, his relation, his servant, his dog, or anything which he is pleased to take under his honourable protection, satisfaction must be forthwith demanded; and if it proves an affront and he that gave it likewise a man of honour, a battle must ensue. From all this it is evident that a man of honour must be possessed of courage and that without it his other principle would be no more than a sword without a point. Let us, therefore, examine what courage consists in and whether it be, as most people will have it, a real something that valiant men have in their nature distinct from all their other qualities or not.

There is nothing so universally sincere upon earth as the love which all creatures that are capable of any bear to themselves; and as there is no love but what implies a care to preserve the thing beloved, so there is nothing more sincere in any creature than his will, wishes, and endeavours to preserve himself. This is the law of nature, by which no creature is endued with any appetite or passion but what either directly or indirectly tends to the preservation either of himself or his species.

The means by which nature obliges every creature continually to stir in this business of self-preservation are grafted in him and (in man) called desires, which either compel him to crave what he thinks will sustain or please him, or command him to avoid what he imagines might displease, hurt, or destroy him. These desires or passions have all their different symptoms by which they manifest themselves to those they disturb, and from that variety of disturbances they make within us, their various denominations have been given them, as has been shown already in pride and shame.

The passion that is raised in us when we apprehend that mischief is approaching us is called fear: the disturbance it makes within us is always more or less violent in proportion, not of the danger, but our apprehension of the mischief dreaded, whether real or imaginary. Our fear then being always proportioned to the apprehension we have of the danger, it follows that while that apprehension lasts, a man can no more shake off his fear than he can a leg or an arm. In a fright, it is true, the apprehension of danger is so sudden and attacks us so lively (as sometimes to take away reason and senses), that when it is over we often do not remember that we had any apprehension at all; but from the event it is plain we had it, for how could we have been frightened if we had not apprehended that some evil or other was coming upon us?

Most people are of opinion that this apprehension is to be conquered by reason, but I confess I am not. Those that have been frightened will tell you that as soon as they could recollect themselves, that is, make use of their reason, their apprehension was conquered. But this is no conquest at all, for in a fright the danger was either altogether imaginary, or else it is past by that time they can make use of their reason; and therefore if they find there is no danger, it is no wonder that they should not apprehend any; but when the danger is permanent, let them then make use of their reason, and they will find that it may serve them to examine the greatness and reality of the danger and that, if they find it less than they imagined, the apprehension will be lessened accordingly; but, if the danger proves real and the same in every circumstance as they took it to be at first, then their reason, instead of diminishing, will rather increase their apprehension. While this fear lasts, no creature can fight offensively; and yet we see brutes daily fight obstinately and worry one another to death; so that some other passion must be able to overcome this fear, and the most contrary to it is anger, which to trace to the bottom I must beg leave to make another digression.

No creature can subsist without food, nor any species of them (I speak of the more perfect animals) continue long unless young ones are continually born as fast as the old ones die. Therefore the first and fiercest appetite that nature has given them is hunger, the next is lust; the one prompting them to procreate, as the other bids them eat. Now, if we observe that anger is that passion which is raised in us when we are crossed or disturbed in our desires, and that, as it sums up all the strength in creatures, so it was given them that by it they might exert themselves more vigorously in endeavouring to remove, overcome, or destroy whatever obstructs them in the pursuit of self-preservation; we shall find that brutes, unless themselves or what they love or the liberty of either are threatened or attacked, have nothing worth notice that can move them to anger but hunger or lust. It is they that make them more fierce, for we must observe that the appetites of creatures are as actually crossed while they want and cannot meet with what they desire (though perhaps with less violence) as when hindered from enjoying what they have in view. What I have said will appear more plainly if we but mind what nobody can be ignorant of, which is this: all creatures upon earth live either upon the fruits and product of it, or else the flesh of other animals, their fellow-creatures. The latter, which we call beasts of prey, nature has armed accordingly and given them weapons and strength to overcome and tear asunder those whom she has designed for their food, and likewise a much keener appetite than to other animals that live upon herbs, &c. For, as to the first, if a cow loved mutton as well as she does grass, being made as she is and having no claws or talons and but one row of teeth before that are all of an equal length, she would be starved even among a flock of sheep. Secondly, as to their voraciousness, if experience did not teach us, our reason might; in the first place, it is highly probable that the hunger which can make a creature fatigue, harass and expose himself to danger for every bit he eats is more piercing than that which only bids him eat what stands before him and which he may have for stooping down. In the second, it is to be considered that as beasts of prey have an instinct by which they learn to crave, trace, and discover those creatures that are good food for them, so the others have likewise an instinct that teaches them to shun, conceal themselves, and run away from those that hunt after them; from hence it must follow that beasts of prey, though they could almost eat forever, go yet more often with empty bellies than other creatures, whose victuals neither fly from nor oppose them. This must perpetuate as well as increase their hunger, which hereby becomes a constant fuel to their anger.

If you ask me what stirs up this anger in bulls and cocks that will fight to death and yet are neither animals of prey nor very voracious, I answer, lust. Those creatures whose rage proceeds from hunger, both male and female, attack everything they can master and fight obstinately against all; but the animals whose fury is provoked by a venereal ferment, being generally males, exert themselves chiefly against other males of the same species. They may do mischief by chance to other creatures; but the main objects of their hatred are their rivals, and it is against them only that their prowess and fortitude are shown. We see likewise in all those creatures, of which the male is able to satisfy a great number of females, a more considerable superiority in the male, expressed by nature in his make and features, as well as fierceness, than is observed in other creatures, where the male is contented with one or two females. Dogs, though become domestic animals, are ravenous to a proverb, and those of them that will fight being carnivorous would soon become beasts of prey if not fed by us;

what we may observe in them is an ample proof of what I have hitherto advanced. Those of a true fighting breed, being voracious creatures, both male and female, will fasten upon anything and suffer themselves to be killed before they give over. As the female is rather more salacious than the male, so there is no difference in their make at all, what distinguishes the sexes excepted, and the female is rather the fiercest of the two. A bull is a terrible creature when he is kept up, but where he has twenty or more cows to range among, in a little time he will become as tame as any of them, and a dozen hens will spoil the best game cock in England. Harts and deers are counted chaste and timorous creatures, and so indeed they are almost all the year long, except in rutting time, and then on a sudden they become bold to admiration and often make at the keepers themselves.

That the influence of those two principal appetites, hunger and lust, upon the temper of animals is not so whimsical as some may imagine may be partly demonstrated from what is observable in ourselves; for, though our hunger is infinitely less violent than that of wolves and other ravenous creatures, yet we see that people who are in health and have a tolerable stomach are more fretful and sooner put out of humour for trifles when they stay for their victuals beyond their usual hours than at any other time. And again, though lust in man is not so raging as it is in bulls, and other salacious creatures, yet nothing provokes men and women both sooner and more violently to anger than what crosses their amours when they are heartily in love; and the most fearful and tenderly educated of either sex have slighted the greatest dangers and set aside all other considerations to compass the destruction of a rival.

Hitherto I have endeavoured to demonstrate, that no creature can fight offensively as long as his fear lasts; that fear cannot be conquered but by another passion; that the most contrary to it and most effectual to overcome it is anger; that the two principal appetites which, disappointed, can stir up this last-named passion are hunger and lust; and that in all brute beasts the proneness to anger and obstinacy in fighting generally depend upon the violence of either or both those appetites together. From whence it must follow that what we call prowess or natural courage in creatures is nothing but the effect of anger, and that all fierce animals must be either very ravenous or very lustful, if not both.

Let us now examine what by this rule we ought to judge of our own species. From the tenderness of man's skin and the great care that is required for years together to rear him; from the make of his jaws, the evenness of his teeth, the breadth of his nails, and the slightness of both, it is not probable that nature should have designed him for rapine; for this reason his hunger is not voracious as it is in beasts of prey; neither is he so salacious as other animals that are called so, and being besides very industrious to supply his wants, he can have no reigning appetite to perpetuate his anger and must consequently be a timorous animal.

What I have said last must only be understood of man in his savage state; for, if we examine him as a member of a society and a taught animal, we shall find him quite another creature. As soon as his pride has room to play, and envy, avarice, and ambition begin to catch hold of him, he is roused from his natural innocence and stupidity. As his knowledge increases, his desires are enlarged, and consequently his wants and appetites are multiplied. Hence it must follow that he will often be crossed in the pursuit of them and meet with abundance more disappointment to stir up his anger in this than his former condition, and man would in a little time become the most hurtful and obnoxious creature in the world, if let alone, whenever he could overpower his adversary, if he had no mischief to fear but from the person that angered him.

The first care, therefore, of all governments is by severe punishments to curb his anger when it does hurt and so, by increasing his fears, prevent the mischief it might produce. When various laws to restrain him from using force are strictly executed, self-preservation must teach him to be peaceable; and, as it is everybody's business to be as little disturbed as is possible, his fears will be continually augmented and enlarged as he advances in experience, understanding, and foresight. The consequence of this must be that as the provocations he will receive to anger will be infinite in the civilized state, so his fears to damp it will be the same, and thus in a little time he will be taught by his fears to destroy his anger and by art to consult, in an opposite method, the same self-preservation for which nature before had furnished him with anger, as well as the rest of his passions.

The only useful passion, then, that man is possessed of toward the peace and quiet of a society is his fear, and the more you work upon it, the more orderly and governable he will be; for how useful soever anger may be to man, as he is a single creature by himself, yet the society has no manner of occasion for it. But nature being always the same in the formation of animals produces all creatures as like to those that beget and bear them as the place she forms them in, and the various influences from without, will give her leave; and consequently all men, whether they are born in courts or forests, are susceptible of anger. When this passion overcomes (as among all degrees of people it sometimes does) the whole set of fears man has, he has true courage and will fight as boldly as a lion or a tiger, and at no other time; and I shall endeavour to prove that whatever is called courage in man, when he is not angry, is spurious and artificial.

It is possible by good government to keep a society always quiet in itself, but nobody can ensure peace from without forever. The society may have occasion to extend their limits further and enlarge their territories, or others may invade theirs, or something else will happen that man must be brought to fight; for how civilized soever men may be, they never forget that force goes beyond reason. The politician now must alter his measures and take off some of man's fears; he must strive to persuade him that all what was told him before of the barbarity of killing men ceases as soon as these men are enemies to the public, and that their adversaries are neither so good nor so strong as themselves. These things well managed will seldom fail of drawing the hardiest, the most quarrelsome, and the most mischievous into combat; but unless they are better qualified, I will not answer for their behaviour there. If once you can make them undervalue their enemies, you may soon stir them up to anger, and while that lasts they will fight with greater obstinacy than any disciplined troops. But if any thing happens that was unforeseen, and a sudden great noise, a tempest, or any strange or uncommon accident that seems to threaten them intervenes, fear seizes them, disarms their anger, and makes them run away to a man.

This natural courage, therefore, as soon as people begin to have more wit, must be soon exploded. In the first place, those that have felt the smart of the enemy's blows will not always believe what is said to undervalue him and are often not easily provoked to anger. Secondly, anger consisting in an ebullition of the spirits is a passion of no long continuance (*ira furor brevis est*), and the enemies, if they withstand the first shock of these angry people, have commonly the better of it. Thirdly, as long as people are angry, all counsel and discipline are lost upon them, and they can never be brought to use art or conduct in their battles. Anger then, without which no creature has natural courage, being altogether useless in a war to be managed by stratagem and brought into a regular art, the government must find out an equivalent for courage that will make men fight.

Whoever would civilize men and establish them into a body politic must be thoroughly acquainted with all the passions and appetites, strength and weaknesses of their frame and understand how to turn their greatest frailties to the advantage of the public. In the Inquiry into the Origin of Moral Virtue, I have shown how easily men were induced to believe anything that is said in their praise. If, therefore, a lawgiver or politician whom they have a great veneration for should tell them that the generality of men had within them a principle of valour distinct from anger, or any other passion that made them to despise danger and face death itself with intrepidity, and that they who had the most of it were the most valuable of their kind, it is very likely, considering what has been said, that most of them, though they felt nothing of this principle, would swallow it for truth, and that the proudest, feeling themselves moved at this piece of flattery and not well versed in distinguishing the passions, might imagine that they felt it heaving in their breasts, by mistaking pride for courage. If but one in ten can be persuaded openly to declare that he is possessed of this principle and maintain it against all gainsayers, there will soon be a half a dozen that shall assert the same. Whoever has once owned it is engaged, the politician has nothing to do but to take all imaginable care to flatter the pride of those that brag of and are willing to stand by it a thousand different ways. The same pride that drew him in first will ever after oblige him to defend the assertion, till at last the fear of discovering the reality of his heart comes to be so great that it outdoes the fear of death itself. Do but increase man's pride and his fear of shame will ever be proportioned to it; for the greater value a man sets upon himself, the more pains he will take and the greater hardships he will undergo to avoid shame.

The great art to make man courageous is first to make him own this principle of valour within and afterwards to inspire him with as much horror against shame as nature has given him against death; and that there are things to which man has, or may have, a stronger aversion than he has to death is evident from suicide. He that makes death his choice must look upon it as less terrible than what he shuns by it; for whether the evil dreaded be present or to come, real or imaginary, nobody would kill himself wilfully but to avoid something. Lucretia held out bravely against all the attacks of the ravisher, even when he threatened her life, which shows that she valued her virtue beyond it; but when he threatened her reputation with eternal infamy, she fairly surrendered and then slew herself, a certain sign that she valued her virtue less than her glory and her life less than either. The fear of death did not make her yield, for she resolved to die before she did it, and her compliance must only be considered as a bribe to make Tarquin forbear sullying her reputation; so that life had neither the first nor second place in the esteem of Lucretia. The courage, then, which is only useful to the body politic, and what is generally called true valour, is artificial and consists in a superlative horror against shame, by flattery infused into men of exalted pride.

As soon as the notions of honour and shame are received among a society, it is not difficult to make men fight. First, take care they are persuaded of the justice of their cause; for no man fights heartily that thinks himself in the wrong; then show them that their altars, their possessions, wives, children, and everything that is near and dear to them is concerned in the present quarrel, or at least may be influenced by it hereafter; then put feathers in their caps, and distinguish them from others, talk of public-spiritedness, the love of their country, facing an enemy with intrepidity, despising death, the bed of honour, and such like high-sounding words, and every proud man will take up arms and fight himself to death before he will turn tail, if it be by daylight. One man in an army is a check upon another, and a hundred of them, that single and without witness would be all cowards, are, for fear of incurring one another's contempt, made valiant by being together. To continue and heighten this artificial courage, all that run away ought to be punished with ignominy; those that fought well, whether they did beat or were beaten, must be flattered and solemnly commended; those that lost their limbs rewarded; and those that were killed ought, above all, to be taken notice of, artfully lamented, and to have extraordinary encomiums bestowed upon them; for to pay honours to the dead will ever be a sure method to make bubbles* of the living.

When I say that the courage made use of in the wars is artificial, I do not imagine that by the same art all men may be made equally valiant; as men have not an equal share of pride and differ from one another in shape and inward structure, it is impossible they should be all equally fit for the same uses. Some men will never be able to learn music, and yet make good mathematicians; others will play excellently well upon the violin, and yet be coxcombs as long as they live, let them converse with whom they please. But to show that there is no evasion, I shall prove that, setting aside what I said of artificial courage already, what the greatest hero differs in from the rankest coward is altogether corporeal and depends upon the inward make of man. What I mean is called constitution, by which is understood the orderly or disorderly mixture of the fluids in our body; that constitution which favours courage consists in the natural strength, elasticity, and due contexture of the finer spirits, and upon them wholly depends what we call stedfastness, resolution, and obstinacy. It is the only ingredient that is common to natural and artificial bravery and is to either what size is to white walls, which hinders them from coming off, and makes them lasting. That some people are very much, others very little frightened at things that are strange and sudden to them, is likewise altogether owing to the firmness or imbecility in the tone of the spirits. Pride is of no use in a fright because while it lasts we cannot think, which, being counted a disgrace, is the reason people are always angry with anything that frightens them as soon as the surprise is over; and when at the turn of a battle the conquerors give no quarter and are very cruel, it is a sign their enemies fought well and had put them first into great fears.

That resolution depends upon this tone of the spirits appears

*bubbles—dupes.

likewise from the effects of strong liquors, the fiery particles whereof crowding into the brain, strengthen the spirits; their operation imitates that of anger, which I said before was an ebullition of the spirits. It is for this reason that most people when they are in drink are sooner touched and more prone to anger than at other times, and some raving mad without any provocation at all. It is likewise observed that brandy makes men more quarrelsome at the same pitch of drunkenness than wine, because the spirits of distilled waters have abundance of fiery particles mixed with them, which the other has not. The contexture of spirits is so weak in some, that though they have pride enough, no art can ever make them fight or overcome their fears; but this is a defect in the principle of the fluids, as other deformities are faults of the solids. These pusillanimous people are never thoroughly provoked to anger, where there is any danger, and drinking makes them bolder, but seldom so resolute as to attack any, unless they be women or children or such who they know dare not resist. This constitution is often influenced by health and sickness and impaired by great losses of blood; sometimes it is corrected by diet; and it is this which the Duke de la Rochefoucault means, when he says: vanity, shame, and above all constitution, make up very often the courage of men and virtue of women.

There is nothing that more improves the useful martial courage I treat of, and at the same time shows it to be artificial, than practice; for when men are disciplined, come to be acquainted with all the tools of death and engines of destruction, when the shouts, the outcries, the fire and smoke, the groans of wounded and ghostly looks of dying men, with all the various scenes of mangled carcases and bloody limbs tore off, begin to be familiar to them, their fears abate apace; not that they are now less afraid to die than before, but being used so often to see the same dangers, they apprehend the reality of them less than they did. As they are deservedly valued for every siege they are at and every battle they are in, it is impossible but the several actions they share in must continually become as many solid steps by which their pride mounts up; and thus their fear of shame, as I said before, will always be proportioned to their pride, increasing as the apprehension of the danger decreases. It is no wonder that most of them learn to discover little or no fear, and some great generals are able to preserve a presence of mind and counterfeit a calm serenity within the midst of all the noise, horror, and confusion that attend a battle.

So silly a creature is man as that, intoxicated with the fumes of vanity, he can feast on the thoughts of the praises that shall be paid his memory in future ages with so much ecstacy as to neglect his present life, nay, court and covet death, if he but imagines that it will add to the glory he had acquired before. There is no pitch of self-denial that a man of pride and constitution cannot reach, nor any passion so violent but he will sacrifice it to another which is superior to it; and here I cannot but admire at the simplicity of some good men, who, when they hear of the joy and alacrity with which holy men in persecutions have suffered for their faith, imagine that such constancy must exceed all human force unless it was supported by some miraculous assistance from Heaven. As most people are willing to acknowledge all the frailties of their species, so they are unacquainted with the strength of our nature and know not that some men of firm constitution may work themselves up into enthusiasm by no other help than the violence of their passions; yet it is certain that there have been men who only assisted with pride and constitution to maintain the worst of causes, have undergone death and torments with as much cheerfulness as the best of men, animated with piety and devotion, ever did for the true religion.

To prove this assertion, I could produce many instances; but one or two will be sufficient. Jordanus Bruno of Nola, who wrote that silly piece of blasphemy called *Spaccio della Bestia triumphante,* and the infamous Vanini* were both executed for openly professing and teaching of atheism: the latter might have been pardoned the moment before the execution if he would have retracted his doctrine; but rather than recant, he chose to be burnt to ashes. As he went to the stake, he was so far from showing any concern that he held his hand out to a physician whom he happened to know, desiring him to judge of the calmness of his mind by the regularity of his pulse, and from thence taking an opportunity of making an impious comparison, uttered a sentence too

---

*Giordano Bruno (1548-1600); the title of the work is *Spaccio de la Bestia Trionfante;* Giulio Cesare Lucilio Vanini (1585-1619).

execrable to be mentioned. To these we may join one Mahomet Effendi, who, as Sir Paul Ricaut tells us, was put to death at Constantinople for having advanced some notions against the existence of a God. He likewise might have saved his life by confessing his error and renouncing it for the future, but chose rather to persist in his blasphemies, saying, "Though he had no reward to expect, the love of truth constrained him to suffer martyrdom in its defence."

I have made this digression chiefly to show the strength of human nature and what mere man may perform by pride and constitution alone. Man may certainly be as violently roused by his vanity as a lion is by his anger; and not only this, avarice, revenge, ambition, and almost every passion, pity not excepted, when they are extraordinary, may, by overcoming fear, serve him instead of valour and be mistaken for it even by himself, as daily experience must teach everybody that will examine and look into the motives from which some men act. But that we may more clearly perceive what this pretended principle is really built upon, let us look into the management of military affairs, and we shall find that pride is nowhere so openly encouraged as there. As for clothes, the very lowest of the commission officers have them richer, or at least more gay and splendid, than are generally wore by other people of four or five times their income. Most of them, and especially those that have families and can hardly subsist, would be very glad all Europe over to be less expensive that way; but it is a force put upon them to uphold their pride, which they do not think on.

But the ways and means to rouse man's pride and catch him by it are nowhere more grossly conspicuous than in the treatment which the common soldiers receive, whose vanity is to be worked upon (because there must be so many) at the cheapest rate imaginable. Things we are accustomed to we do not mind, or else what mortal that never had seen a soldier could look without laughing upon a man accoutred with so much paltry gaudiness and affected finery? The coarsest manufacture that can be made of wool, dyed of a brickdust colour, goes down with him because it is in imitation of scarlet or crimson cloth; and to make him think himself as like his officer as it is possible, with little or no cost, instead of silver or gold lace, his hat trimmed with white or yellow worsted, which in others would deserve bedlam; yet these fine allurements and the noise made upon a calf's skin have drawn in and been the destruction of more men in reality than all the killing eyes and bewitching voices of women ever slew in jest. To-day the swine-herd puts on his red coat and believes everybody in earnest that calls him gentleman; and two days after Serjeant Kite gives him a swinging wrap with his cane for holding his musket an inch higher than he should do. As to the real dignity of the employment, in the two last wars officers, when recruits were wanted, were allowed to list fellows that were convicted of burglary and other capital crimes, which shows that to be made a soldier is deemed to be a preferment next to hanging. A trooper is yet worse than a foot soldier, for when he is most at ease, he has the mortification of being groom to a horse that spends more money than himself. When a man reflects on all this, the usage they generally receive from their officers, their pay, and the care that is taken of them when they are not wanted, must he not wonder how wretches can be so silly as to be proud of being called gentlemen soldiers? Yet if there were not, no art, discipline, or money would be capable of making them so brave as thousands of them are.

If we will mind what effects man's bravery, without any other qualifications to sweeten him, would have out of an army, we shall find that it would be very pernicious to the civil society; for if man could conquer all his fears, you would hear of nothing but rapes, murders, and violences of all sorts, and valiant men would be like giants in romances; politics, therefore, discovered in men a mixed-metal principle, which was a compound of justice, honesty, and all the moral virtues joined to courage, and all that were possessed of it turned to knights-errant, of course. They did abundance of good throughout the world by taming monsters, delivering the distressed, and killing the oppressors; but the wings of all the dragons being clipped, the giants destroyed, and the damsels everywhere set at liberty, except some few in Spain and Italy who remained still captivated by their monsters, the order of chivalry, to whom the standard of ancient honour belonged, has been laid aside some time. It was like their armours, very massy and heavy; the many virtues about it made it very troublesome, and as ages grew wiser and wiser, the principle of honour in the beginning of the last century was melted over again and brought to a new standard; they put in the same weight of courage, half the quantity of honesty, and a very little justice, but not a scrap of any other virtue, which has made it very easy and portable to what it was. However, such as it is, there would be no living without it in a large nation; it is the tie of society, and though we are beholden to our frailties for the chief ingredient of it, there is no virtue, at least that I am acquainted with, that has been half so instrumental to the civilizing of mankind, who in great societies would soon degenerate into cruel villains and treacherous slaves, were honour to be removed from among them.

As to the duelling part which belongs to it, I pity the unfortunate whose lot it is; but to say that those who are guilty of it go by false rules or mistake the notions of honour is ridiculous; for either there is no honour at all, or it teaches men to resent injuries and accept of challenges. You may as well deny that it is the fashion what you see everybody wear as to say that demanding and giving satisfaction is against the laws of true honour. Those that rail at duelling do not consider the benefit the society receives from that fashion; if every ill-bred fellow might use what language he pleased without being called to an account for it, all conversation would be spoiled. Some grave people tell us that the Greeks and Romans were such valiant men, and yet knew nothing of duelling but in their country's quarrel. This is very true, but for that reason the kings and princes in Homer gave one another worse language than our porters and hackney coachmen would be able to bear without resentment.

Would you hinder duelling, pardon nobody that offends that way, and make the laws as severe as you can, but do not take away the thing itself, the custom of it. This will not only prevent the frequency of it, but likewise, by rendering the most resolute and most powerful cautious and circumspect in their behaviour, polish and brighten society in general. Nothing civilizes a man equally as his fear, and if not all (as my lord Rochester said), at least most men would be cowards if they durst. The dread of being called to an account keeps abundance in awe; and there are thousands of mannerly and well-accomplished gentlemen in Europe who would have been insolent and insupportable coxcombs without it; besides, if it was out of fashion to ask satisfaction for injuries which the law cannot take hold of, there would be twenty times the mischief done there is now, or else you must have twenty times the constables and other officers to keep the peace. I confess that though it happens but seldom, it is a calamity to the people and generally the families it falls upon; but there can be no perfect happiness in this world, and all felicity has an allay [alloy]. The act itself is uncharitable, but when above thirty in a nation destroy themselves in one year and not half that number are killed by others, I do not think the people can be said to love their neighbours worse than themselves. It is strange that a nation should grudge to see perhaps half-a-dozen men sacrificed in a twelvemonth to obtain so valuable a blessing as the politeness of manners, the pleasure of conversation, and the happiness of company in general that is often so willing to expose and sometimes loses as many thousands in a few hours without knowing whether it will do any good or not.

I would have nobody that reflects on the mean original of honour complain of being gulled and made a property by cunning politicians, but desire everybody to be satisfied that the governors of societies, and those in high stations, are greater bubbles to pride than any of the rest. If some great men had not a superlative pride and everybody understood the enjoyment of life, who would be a lord chancellor of England, a prime minister of state in France, or what gives more fatigue and not a sixth part of the profit of either, a grand pensionary of Holland? The reciprocal services which all men pay to one another are the foundation of the society. The great ones are not flattered with their high birth for nothing; it is to rouse their pride and excite them to glorious actions that we extol their race, whether it deserves it or not; and some men have been complimented with the greatness of their family and the merit of their ancestors when in the whole generation you could not find two but what were uxorious fools, silly bigots, noted poltroons, or debauched whore-masters. The established pride that is inseparable from those that are possessed of titles already makes them often strive as much not to seem unworthy of them, as the working ambition of others that are yet without, renders them industrious and indefatigable to deserve them. When a gentleman is made a baron or an earl, it is as great a check upon him in many respects as a gown and cassock are to a young student that has been newly taken into orders.

The only thing of weight that can be said against modern honour is that it is directly opposite to religion. The one bids you bear injuries with patience; the other tells you if you do not resent them, you are not fit to live. Religion commands you to leave all revenge to God; honour bids you trust your revenge to nobody but yourself, even where the law would do it for you; religion plainly forbids murder; honour openly justifies it; religion bids you not shed blood upon any account whatever; honour bids you fight for the least trifle; religion is built on humility, and honour upon pride; how to reconcile them must be left to wiser heads than mine.

The reason why there are so few men of real virtue and so many of real honour is because all the recompense a man has of a virtuous action is the pleasure of doing it, which most people reckon but poor pay; but the self-denial a man of honour submits to in one appetite is immediately rewarded by the satisfaction he receives from another, and what he abates of his avarice or any other passion is doubly repaid to his pride; besides, honour gives large grains of allowance and virtue none. A man of honour must not cheat or tell a lie; he must punctually repay what he borrows at play, though the creditor has nothing to show for it; but he may drink, and swear, and owe money to all the tradesmen in town without taking notice of their dunning. A man of honour must be true to his prince and country while he is in their service; but if he thinks himself not well used, he may quit it and do them all the mischief he can. A man of honour must never change his religion for interest; but he may be as debauched as he pleases and never practice any. He must make no attempts upon his friend's wife, daughter, sister, or anybody that is trusted to his care; but he may lie with all the world besides.

* * * *

Line 367. .... To live great,
　　　Had made her husband rob the state.

What our common rogues, when they are going to be hanged, chiefly complain of as the cause of their untimely end is, next to the neglect of the Sabbath, their having kept company with ill women, meaning whores; and I do not question but that among the lesser villains many venture their necks to indulge and satisfy their low amours. But the words that have given occasion to this remark may serve to hint to us that among the great ones men are often put upon such dangerous projects and forced into such pernicious measures by their wives as the most subtle mistress never could have persuaded them to. I have shown already that the worst of women and most profligate of the sex, did contribute to the consumption of superfluities, as well as the necessaries of life, and consequently were beneficial to many peaceable drudges that work hard to maintain their families and have no worse design than an honest livelihood. Let them be banished, notwithstanding, says a good man. When every strumpet is gone and the land wholly freed from lewdness, God Almighty will pour such blessings upon it as will vastly exceed the profits that are now got by harlots. This perhaps would be true; but I can make it evident that, with or without prostitutes, nothing could make amends for the detriment trade would sustain if all those of that sex who enjoy the happy state of matrimony should act and behave themselves as a sober wise man could wish them.

The variety of work that is performed and the number of hands employed to gratify the fickleness and luxury of women is prodigious, and if only the married ones should hearken to reason and just remonstrances, think themselves sufficiently answered with the first refusal, and never ask a second time what had been once denied them: if, I say, married women would do this and then lay out no money but what their husbands knew and freely allowed of, the consumption of a thousand things they now make use of would be lessened by at least a fourth part. Let us go from house to house and observe the way of the world only among the middling people, creditable shopkeepers, that spend two or three hundred a year, and we shall find the women when they have half a score suits of clothes, two or three of them not the worse for wearing, will think it a sufficient plea for new ones, if they can say that they have never a gown or petticoat but what they have been often seen in and are known by, especially at church; I do not speak now of profuse and extravagant women, but such as are counted prudent and moderate in their desires.

If by this pattern we should in proportion judge of the highest ranks, where the richest clothes are but a trifle to their other expences, and not forget the furniture of all sorts, equipages, jewels, and buildings of persons of quality, we should find the fourth part I speak of a vast article in trade, and that the loss of it would be a greater calamity to such a nation as ours than it is possible to conceive any other, a raging pestilence not excepted; for the death of half a million of people could not cause a tenth part of the disturbance to the kingdom than the same number of poor unemployed would certainly create if at once they were to be added to those that already, one way or other, are a burden to the society.

Some few men have a real passion for their wives and are fond of them without reserve; others that do not care and have little occasion for women are yet seemingly uxurious and love out of vanity; they take delight in a handsome wife as a coxcomb does in a fine horse, not for the use he makes of it, but because it is his. The pleasure lies in the consciousness of an uncontrollable possession, and what follows from it, the reflection on the mighty thoughts he imagines others to have of his happiness. The men of either sort may be very lavish to their wives, and often preventing* their wishes, crowd new clothes and other finery upon them faster than they can ask it, but the greatest part are wiser than to indulge the extravagances of their wives so far as to give them immediately everything they are pleased to fancy. It is incredible what vast quantity of trinkets as well as apparel are purchased and used by women, which they could never have come at by any other means than pinching their families, marketing, and other ways of cheating and pilfering from their husbands. Others, by ever teasing their spouses, tire them into compliance and conquer even obstinate churls by perseverance and their assiduity of asking. A third sort are outrageous at a denial, and by downright noise and scolding bully their tame fools out of anything they have a mind to; while thousands, by the force of wheedling, know how to overcome the best weighed reasons and the most positive reiterated refusals; the young and beautiful especially laugh at all remonstrances and denials, and few of them scruple to employ the most tender minutes of wedlock to promote a sordid interest. Here, had I time, I could inveigh with warmth against those base, wicked women, who calmly play their arts and false deluding

---

preventing—anticipating.

charms against our strength and prudence and act the harlots with husbands! Nay, she is worse than whore, who impiously profanes and prostitutes the sacred rites of love to vile ignoble ends; that first excites to passion and invites to joy with seeming ardour, then racks our fondness for no other purpose than to extort a gift, while full of guile in counterfeited transports, she watches for the moment when men can least deny.

I beg pardon for this start out of my way and desire the experienced reader duly to weigh what has been said as to the main purpose, and after that call to mind the temporal blessing which men daily hear not only toasted and wished for when people are merry and doing of nothing; but likewise gravely and solemnly prayed for in churches and other religious assemblies by clergymen of all sorts and sizes. And as soon as he shall have laid these things together and, from what he has observed in the common affairs of life, reasoned upon them consequentially without prejudice, I dare flatter myself that he will be obliged to own that a considerable portion of what the prosperity of London and trade in general, and consequently the honour, strength, safety, and all the worldly interest of the nation consist in, depend entirely on the deceit and vile strategems of women; and that humility, content, meekness, obedience to reasonable husbands, frugality, and all the virtues together, if they were possessed of them in the most eminent degree, could not possibly be a thousandth part so serviceable to make an opulent, powerful, and what we call a flourishing kingdom than their most hateful qualities.

I do not question but many of my readers will be startled at this assertion when they look on the consequences that may be drawn from it; and I shall be asked whether people may not as well be virtuous in a populous, rich, wide, extended kingdom, as in a small, indigent state or principality that is poorly inhabited? And if that be impossible, whether it is not the duty of all sovereigns to reduce their subjects as to wealth and numbers as much as they can? If I allow they may, I own myself in the wrong; and if I affirm the other, my tenets will justly be called impious or at least dangerous to all large societies. As it is not in this place of the book only, but a great many others that such queries might be made even by a well-meaning reader, I shall here explain myself and endeavour to solve those difficulties which several passages might have raised in him, in order to demonstrate the consistency of my opinion to reason and the strictest morality.

I lay down as a first principle that in all societies, great or small, it is the duty of every member of it to be good, that virtue ought to be encouraged, vice discountenanced, the laws obeyed, and the transgressors punished. After this I affirm that if we consult history, both ancient and modern, and take a view of what has passed in the world, we shall find that human nature since the fall of Adam has always been the same and that the strength and frailties of it have ever been conspicuous in one part of the globe or other without any regard to ages, climates, or religion. I never said nor imagined that man could not be virtuous as well in a rich and mighty kingdom as in the most pitiful commonwealth; but I own it is my sense that no society can be raised into such a rich and mighty kingdom, or so raised, subsist in their wealth and power for any considerable time without the vices of man.

This, I imagine, is sufficiently proved throughout the book; and as human nature still continues the same as it has always been for so many thousand years, we have no great reason to suspect a future change in it while the world endures. Now, I cannot see what immorality there is in showing a man the origin and power of those passions which so often, even unknowingly to himself, hurry him away from his reason; or that there is any impiety in putting him upon his guard against himself and the secret stratagems of self-love, and teaching him the difference between such actions as proceed from a victory over the passions and those that are only the result of a conquest which one passion obtains over another; that is, between real and counterfeited virtue. It is an admirable saying of a worthy divine, that though many discoveries have been made in the world of self-love, there is yet abundance of *terra incognita* left behind. What hurt do I do to man if I make him more known to himself than he was before? But we are all so desparately in love with flattery that we can never relish a truth that is mortifying, and I do not believe that the immortality of the soul, a truth broached long before Christianity, would have ever found such a general reception in human capacities as it has, had it not been a pleasing one that extolled and was a compliment to the whole species, the meanest and most miserable not excepted.

Everyone loves to hear the thing well spoke of that he has a share in, even bailiffs, gaol-keepers, and the hangman himself would have you think well of their functions; nay, thieves and housebreakers have a greater regard to those of their fraternity than they have for honest people; and I sincerely believe that it is chiefly self-love that has gained this little treatise (as it was before the last impression) so many enemies; everyone looks upon it as an affront done to himself because it detracts from the dignity and lessens the fine notions he had conceived of mankind, the most worshipful company he belongs to. When I say that societies cannot be raised to wealth and power and the top of earthly glory, without vices, I do not think that by so saying I bid men to be vicious any more than I bid them be quarrelsome or covetous when I affirm that the profession of the law could not be maintained in such numbers and splendor if there was not abundance of too selfish and litigious people.

But as nothing would more clearly demonstrate the falsity of my notions than that the generality of the people should fall in with them, so I do not expect the approbation of the multitude. I write not to many nor seek for any well-wishers, but among the few that can think abstractly and have their minds elevated above the vulgar. If I have shown the way to worldly greatness, I have always without hesitation preferred the road that leads to virtue.

Would you banish fraud and luxury, prevent profaneness and irreligion, and make the generality of the people charitable, good, and virtuous; break down the printing presses, melt the founds,* and burn all the books in the island, except those at the universities, where they remain unmolested, and suffer no volume in private hands but a Bible; knock down foreign trade, prohibit all commerce with strangers, and permit no ships to go to sea that ever will return, beyond fisher-boats. Restore to the clergy, the king, and the barons their ancient privileges, prerogatives, and possessions; build new churches and convert all the coin you can come at into sacred utensils; erect monasteries and alms-houses

---

founds—fonts of type.

in abundance, and let no parish be without a charity-school. Enact sumptuary laws, and let your youth be inured to hardship; inspire them with all the nice and most refined notions of honour and shame, of friendship and heroism, and introduce among them a great variety of imaginary rewards; then let the clergy preach abstinence and self-denial to others and take what liberty they please for themselves; let them bear sway in the management of state affairs and no man be made lord-treasurer but a bishop.

But by such pious endeavours and wholesome regulations, the scene would be soon altered; the greatest part of the covetous, the discontented, the restless and ambitious villains would leave the land; vast swarms of cheating knaves would abandon the city and be dispersed throughout the country: artificers would learn to hold the plough, merchants turn farmers, and the sinful overgrown Jerusalem, without famine, war, pestilence, or compulsion, be emptied in the most easy manner and ever after cease to be dreadful to her sovereigns. This happy reformed kingdom would by this means be crowded in no part of it, and everything necessary for the sustenance of man be cheap and abound; on the contrary, the root of so many thousand evils, money, would be very scarce and as little wanted, where every man should enjoy the fruits of his own labour, and our own dear manufacture unmixed, be promiscuously wore by the lord and the peasant. It is impossible that such a change of circumstances should not influence the manners of a nation and render them temperate, honest, and sincere; and from the next generation we might expect a more healthy and robust offspring than the present; an harmless, innocent, and well-meaning people that would never dispute the doctrine of passive obedience* nor any other orthodox principles, but be submissive to superiors and unanimous in religious worship.

Here I fancy myself interrupted by an Epicure, who, not to want a restorative diet in case of necessity, is never without live ortolans; and I am told that goodness and probity are to be had at a cheaper rate than the ruin of a nation and the destruction of all the comforts of life; that liberty and property may be maintained without wickedness or fraud, and men be good subjects

---

*The doctrine of the subject's duty of absolute unquestioning obedience to the Sovereign.

without being slaves, and religious though they refused to be priest-rid; that to be frugal and saving is a duty incumbent only on those whose circumstances require it, but that a man of a good estate does his country a service by living up to the income of it; that as to himself, he is so much master of his appetites that he can abstain from anything upon occasion; that where true Hermitage was not to be had he could content himself with plain Bordeaux if it had a good body; that many a morning, instead of St. Lawrence, he has made a shift with Frontenac, and after dinner given Cyprus wine and even Madeira when he has had a large company and thought it extravagant to treat with Tockay; but that all voluntary mortifications are superstitious, only belonging to blind zealots and enthusiasts. He will quote my Lord Shaftesbury against me and tell me that people may be virtuous and sociable without self-denial; that it is an affront to virtue to make it inaccessible, that I make a bugbear of it to frighten men from it as a thing impracticable; but that for his part he can praise God and at the same time enjoy his creatures with a good conscience. . . . He will ask me at last whether the legislature, the wisdom of the nation itself, while they endeavour as much as possible to discourage profaneness and immorality and promote the glory of God, do not openly profess at the same time to have nothing more at heart than the ease and welfare of the subject, the wealth, strength, honour, and what else is called the true interest of the country? And, moreover, whether the most devout and most learned of our prelates, in their greatest concern for our conversion, when they beseech the Deity to turn their own as well as our hearts from the world and all carnal desires, do not in the same prayer as loudly solicit him to pour all earthly blessings and temporal felicity on the kingdom they belong to?

These are the apologies, the excuses, and common pleas, not only of those who are notoriously vicious, but the generality of mankind, when you touch the copy-hold of their inclinations; and trying the real value they have for spirituals, should actually strip them of what their minds are wholly bent upon. Ashamed of the many frailties they feel within, all men endeavour to hide themselves, their ugly nakedness, from each other, and wrapping up the true motives of their hearts in the specious cloak of sociableness and their concern for the public good, they are in hopes of

concealing their filthy appetites and the deformity of their desires;
while they are conscious within of the fondness for their darling
lusts and their incapacity, bare-faced, to tread the arduous, rugged
path of virtue. . . .

* * * *

Line 411. T' enjoy the world's conveniences.

That the words decency and conveniency were very ambiguous
and not to be understood unless we were acquainted with the
quality and circumstances of the persons that made use of them
has been hinted already.* The goldsmith, mercer, or any other of
the most creditable shopkeepers that has three or four thousand
pounds to set up with must have two dishes of meat every day
and something extraordinary for Sundays. His wife must have a
damask bed against her lying-in and two or three rooms very well
furnished; the following summer she must have a house, or at least
very good lodgings in the country. A man that has a being out of
town must have a horse; his footman must have another. If he
has a tolerable trade, he expects in eight or ten years time to keep
his coach, which, notwithstanding, he hopes that after he has
slaved (as he calls it) for two or three and twenty years, he shall
be worth at least a thousand a-year for his eldest son to inherit
and two or three thousand pounds for each of his other children
to begin the world with; and when men of such circumstances pray
for their daily bread and mean nothing more extravagant by it, they
are counted pretty modest people. Call this pride, luxury, superfluity, or what you please, it is nothing but what ought to be in
the capital of a flourishing nation; those of inferior condition must
content themselves with less costly conveniences, as others of
higher rank will be sure to make theirs more expensive. Some
people call it but decency to be served in plate and reckon a
coach and six among the necessary comforts of life; and if a peer
has not above three or four thousand a-year, his lordship is counted
poor.

Since the first edition of this book, several have attacked me
with demonstrations of the certain ruin which excessive luxury

---

*In *Remark on Line 177* [on Avarice], not included in this edition.

must bring upon all nations, who yet were soon answered when I showed them the limits within which I had confined it; and therefore, that no reader for the future may misconstrue me on this head, I shall point at the cautions I have given and the provisos I have made in the former, as well as this present impression, and which, if not overlooked, must prevent all rational censure and obviate several objections that otherwise might be made against me. I have laid down as maxims never to be departed from that the poor should be kept strictly to work, and that it was prudence to relieve their wants, but folly to cure them; that agriculture and fishery should be promoted in all their branches in order to render provisions, and consequently labour, cheap. I have named ignorance as a necessary ingredient in the mixture of society; from all which it is manifest that I could never have imagined that luxury was to be made general through every part of a kingdom. I have likewise required that property should be well secured, justice impartially administered, and in everything the interest of the nation taken care of; but what I have insisted on the most and repeated more than once is the great regard that is to be had to the balance of trade and the care the legislature ought to take that the yearly imports never exceed the exports; and where this is observed and the other things I spoke of are not neglected, I still continue to assert that no foreign luxury can undo a country; the height of it is never seen but in nations that are vastly populous, and there only in the upper part of it, and the greater that is, the larger still in proportion must be the lowest, the basis that supports all, the multitude of working poor.

Those who would too nearly imitate others of superior fortune must thank themselves if they are ruined. This is nothing against luxury; for whoever can subsist and lives above his income is a fool. Some persons of quality may keep three or four coaches and six and at the same time lay up money for their children; while a young shopkeeper is undone for keeping one sorry horse. It is impossible there should be a rich nation without prodigals, yet I never knew a city so full of spendthrifts but there were covetous people enough to answer their number. As an old merchant breaks for having been extravagant or careless a great while, so a young beginner falling into the same business gets an estate by being saving or more industrious before he is forty years old; besides that, the frailties of men often work by contraries: some narrow souls can never thrive because they are too stingy, while longer heads amass great wealth by spending their money freely and seeming to despise it. But the vicissitudes of fortune are necessary, and the most lamentable are no more detrimental to society than the death of the individual members of it. Christenings are a proper balance to burials. Those who immediately lose by the misfortunes of others are very sorry, complain, and make a noise; but the others who get by them, as there always are such, hold their tongues because it is odious to be thought the better for the losses and calamities of our neighbour. The various ups and downs compose a wheel, that always turning round, gives motion to the whole machine. Philosophers that dare extend their thoughts beyond the narrow compass of what is immediately before them look on the alternate changes in the civil society no otherwise than they do on the risings and fallings of the lungs, the latter of which are much a part of respiration in the most perfect animals as the first, so that the fickle breath of never-stable fortune is to the body politic the same as floating air is to a living creature.

Avarice then and prodigality are equally necessary to the society. That in some countries men are most generally lavish than in others proceeds from the difference in circumstances that dispose to either vice and arise from the condition of the social body, as well as the temperament of the natural. I beg pardon of the attentive reader if here, in behalf of short memories, I repeat some things, the substance of which they have already seen in Remark on line 307 [pp. 119 ff.]. More money than land, heavy taxes and scarcity of provisions, industry, laboriousness, and active and stirring spirit, ill-nature, and saturnine temper; old age, wisdom, trade, riches acquired by our own labour, and liberty and property well secured are all things that dispose to avarice. On the contrary, indolence, content, good-nature, a jovial temper, youth, folly, arbitrary power, money easily got, plenty of provisions and the uncertainty of possessions are circumstances that render men prone to prodigality; where there is the most of the first, the prevailing vice will be avarice, and prodigality where the other turns the scale; but a national frugality there never was nor never will be without a national necessity.

Sumptuary laws may be of use to an indigent country after

great calamities of war, pestilence, or famine, when work has stood still and the labour of the poor been interrupted; but to introduce them into an opulent kingdom is the wrong way to consult the interest of it. I shall end my remarks on the Grumbling Hive with assuring the champions of national frugality that it would be impossible for the Persians and other eastern people to purchase the vast quantities of fine English cloth they consume, should we load our women with less cargoes of Asiatic silks.

[1723]

A

SEARCH
INTO THE
NATURE OF SOCIETY

THE GENERALITY OF moralists and philosophers have hitherto agreed that there could be no virtue without self-denial; but a late author, who is now much read by men of sense, is of a contrary opinion, and imagines that men, without any trouble or violence upon themselves, may be naturally virtuous. He seems to require and expect goodness in his species, as we do a sweet taste in grapes and China oranges, of which, if any of them are sour, we boldly pronounce that they are not come to that perfection their nature is capable of. This noble writer (for it is the Lord Shaftesbury I mean in his *Characteristicks*) fancies that as a man is made for society, so he ought to be born with a kind of affection to the whole, of which he is a part, and a propensity to seek the welfare of it. In pursuance of this supposition he calls every action performed with regard to the public good Virtuous, and all selfishness wholly excluding such a regard Vice. In respect to our species, he looks upon virtue and vice as permanent realities that must ever be the same in all countries and all ages and imagines that a man of sound understanding, by following the rules of good sense, may not only find out that *pulchrum et honestum* both in morality and the works of art and nature, but likewise govern himself by his reason with as much ease and readiness as a good rider manages a well-taught horse by the bridle.

The attentive reader who perused the foregoing part of this book will soon perceive that two systems cannot be more opposite than his Lordship's and mine. His notions I confess are generous and refined; they are a high compliment to human-kind and capable, by a little enthusiasm, of inspiring us with the most noble sentiments concerning the dignity of our exalted nature. What a pity it is that they are not true. I would not advance thus much if I had not already demonstrated in almost every page of this treatise that the solidity of them is inconsistent with our daily experience. But, to leave not the least shadow of an objection that might be made unanswered, I design to expatiate on some things which hitherto I have but slightly touched upon in order to convince the reader, not only that the good and amiable qualities of men are not those that make him beyond other animals a social creature; but, moreover, that it would be utterly impossible either to raise any multitudes into a populous, rich, and flourishing nation, or, when so raised, to keep and maintain them in that condition without the assistance of what we call Evil, both natural and moral.

The better to perform what I have undertaken, I shall previously examine into the reality of the *pulchrum et honestum,* the *to kalon* that the ancients have talked of so much: the meaning of this is to discuss whether there be a real worth and excellency in things, a pre-eminence of one above another; which everybody will always agree to that well understands them; or, that there are few things, if any, that have the same esteem paid them and which the same judgement is passed upon in all countries and all ages. When we first set out in quest of this intrinsic worth and find one thing better than another, and a third better than that, and so on, we begin to entertain great hopes of success; but when we meet with several things that are all very good or all very bad, we are puzzled and agree not always with ourselves, much less with others. There are different faults as well as beauties that as modes and fashions alter and men vary in their tastes and humours will be differently admired or disapproved of.

Judges of painting will never disagree in opinion when a fine picture is compared to the daubing of a novice; but how strangely have they differed as to the works of eminent masters! There are parties among connoisseurs; and few of them agree in their esteem as to ages and countries; and the best pictures bear not always the best prices: a noted original will ever be worth more than any copy that can be made of it by an unknown hand, though it should be better. The value that is set on paintings depends not only on the name of the master and the time of his age he drew them in, but likewise in a great measure on the scarcity of his works; but, what is still more unreasonable, the quality of the persons in whose possession they are, as well as the length of time they have been in great families; and if the cartoons now at Hampton Court were done by a less famous hand than that of Raphael and had a private person for their owner who would be forced to sell them, they would never yield the tenth part of the money which, with all their gross faults, they are now esteemed to be worth.

Notwithstanding all this, I will readily own that the judgement to be made of painting might become of universal certainty, or at least less alterable and precarious than almost anything else. The reason is plain; there is a standard to go by that always remains the same. Painting is an imitation of nature, a copying of things which men have everywhere before them. My good-humoured reader I hope will forgive me if, thinking on this glorious invention, I make a reflection a little out of season, though very much conducive to my main design; which is, that valuable as the art is I speak of, we are beholden to an imperfection in the chief of our senses for all the pleasures and ravishing delight we receive from this happy deceit. I shall explain myself. Air and space are no objects of sight, but as soon as we can see with the least attention, we observe that the bulk of the things we see is lessened by degrees, as they are further remote from us, and nothing but experience gained from these observations can teach us to make any tolerable guesses at the distance of things. If one born blind should remain so till twenty and then be suddenly blessed with sight, he would be strangely puzzled as to the difference of distances, and hardly able immediately by his eyes alone to determine which was nearest to him, a post almost within the reach of his stick or a steeple that should be half a mile off. Let us look as narrowly as we can upon a hole in a wall that has nothing but the open air behind it, and we shall not be able to see otherwise but that the sky fills up the vacuity and is as near us as the back part of the stones that circumscribe the space where they are wanting. This circumstance, not to call it a defect, in our sense of seeing makes us liable to be imposed upon, and everything but motion may by art be represented to us on a flat in the same manner as we see them in life and nature. If a man had never seen this art put into practice, a looking-glass might soon convince him that such a thing was possible, and I cannot help thinking but that the reflections from very smooth and well-polished bodies made upon our eyes must have given the first handle to the inventions of drawings and painting.

In the works of nature, worth and excellency are as uncertain; and even in human creatures, what is beautiful in one country is not so in another. How whimsical is the florist in his choice! Sometimes the tulip, sometimes the auricula, and at other times the carnation shall engross his esteem, and every year a new flower, in his judgement, beats all the old ones, though it is much inferior to them in colour and shape. Three hundred years ago men were shaved as closely as they are now. Since that they have wore beards and cut them in vast variety of forms that were all as becoming, when fashionable, as now they would be ridiculous. How mean and comically a man looks that is otherwise well dressed, in a narrow-brimmed hat when everybody wears broad ones; and again, how monstrous is a very great hat when the other extreme has been in fashion for a considerable time? Experience has taught us that these modes seldom last above ten or twelve years, and a man of threescore must have observed five or six revolutions of them at least! Yet the beginning of these changes, though we have seen several, seem always uncouth and are offensive afresh whenever they return. What mortal can decide which is the handsomest, abstract from the mode in being, to wear great buttons or small ones? The many ways of laying out a garden judiciously are almost innumerable; and what is called beautiful in them, varies according to the different tastes of nations and ages. In grass plats,* knots and parterres, a great diversity of forms is generally agreeable; but a round may be more pleasing to the eye as a square: an oval cannot be more suitable to one

---

plats—plots.

place than it is possible for a triangle to be to another; and the pre-eminence an octagon has over an hexagon is no greater in figures than at hazard eight has above six among the chances.

Churches, ever since Christians have been able to build them, resemble the form of a cross, with the upper end pointing toward the east; and an architect, where there is room and it can be conveniently done, who should neglect it, would be thought to have committed an unpardonable fault; but it would be foolish to expect this of a Turkish mosque or a Pagan temple. Among the many beneficial laws that have been made these hundred years, it is not easy to name one of greater utility and, at the same time, more exempt from all inconveniences than that which has regulated the dresses of the dead. Those who were old enough to take notice of things when that act was made and are yet alive must remember the general clamour that was made against it. At first, nothing could be more shocking to thousands of people than they were to be buried in woollen, and the only thing that made that law supportable was that there was room left for people of some fashion to indulge their weakness without extravagancy, considering the other expences of funerals where mourning is given to several and rings to a great many. The benefit that accrues to the nation from it is so visible that nothing ever could be said in reason to condemn it, which, in few years, made the horror conceived against it lessen every day. I observed then that young people, who had seen but few in their coffins, did the soonest strike in with the innovation; but that those who, when the act was made, had buried many friends and relations, remained averse to it the longest, and I remember many that never could be reconciled to it to their dying day. By this time, burying in linen being almost forgot, it is the general opinion that nothing could be more decent than woollen and the present manner of dressing a corpse; which shows that our liking and disliking of things chiefly depends on mode and custom, and the precept and example of our betters, and such whom one way or other we think to be superior to us.

In morals there is no greater certainty. Plurality of wives is odious among Christians, and all the wit and learning of a great genius in defence of it has been rejected with contempt.* But

---

*Perhaps Sir Thomas More. See Kaye, I, 330 n.

polygamy is not shocking to a Mahometan. What men have learned from their infancy enslaves them, and the force of custom warps nature and, at the same time, imitates her in such a manner that it is often difficult to know which of the two we are influenced by. In the east, formerly sisters married brothers, and it was meritorious for a man to marry his mother. Such alliances are abominable; but it is certain that, whatever horror we conceive at the thoughts of them, there is nothing in nature repugnant against them but what is built upon mode and custom. A religious Mahometan that has never tasted any spirituous liquor and has often seen people drunk, may receive as great an aversion against wine as another with us of the least morality and education may have against lying with his sister, and both imagine that their antipathy proceeds from nature. Which is the best religion is a question that has caused more mischief than all other questions together. Ask it at Pekin, at Constantinople, and at Rome, and you will receive three distinct answers extremely different from one another, yet all of them equally positive and peremptory. Christians are well assured of the falsity of the Pagan and Mahometan superstitions: as to this point, there is a perfect union and concord among them; but inquire of the several sects they are divided into, Which is the true church of Christ? and all of them will tell you it is theirs and to convince you, go together by the ears.

It is manifest, then, that the hunting after this *pulchrum et honestum* is not much better than a wild-goose chase that is but little to be depended on. But this is not the greatest fault I find with it. The imaginary notions that men may be virtuous without self-denial are a vast inlet to hypocrisy; which being once made habitual, we must not only deceive others, but likewise become altogether unknown to ourselves; and in an instance I am going to give, it will appear how, for want of duly examining himself, this might happen to a person of quality, of parts, and erudition, one every way resembling the author of the *Characteristicks* himself.

A man that has been brought up in ease and affluence, if he is of a quiet indolent nature, learns to shun everything that is troublesome and chooses to curb his passions more because of the inconveniences that arise from the eager pursuit after pleasure, and the yielding to all the demands of our inclinations, than any dislike he has to sensual enjoyments; and it is possible, that a person educated under a great philosopher who was a mild and good-natured as well as able tutor may, in such happy circumstances, have a better opinion of his inward state than it really deserves, and believe himself virtuous because his passions lie dormant. He may form fine notions of the social virtues and the contempt of death, write well of them in his closet, and talk eloquently of them in company, but you shall never catch him fighting for his country or labouring to retrieve any national losses. A man that deals in metaphysics may easily throw himself into an enthusiasm and really believe that he does not fear death while it remains out of sight. But should he be asked why, having this intrepidity either from nature or acquired by philosophy, he did not follow arms when his country was involved in war; or when he saw the nation daily robbed by those at the helm and the affairs of the exchequer perplexed, why he did not go to court and make use of all his friends and interest to be a lord treasurer that by his integrity and wise management he might restore the public credit, it is probable he would answer that he loved retirement, had no other ambition than to be a good man, and never aspired to have any share in the government; or that he hated all flattery and slavish attendance, the insincerity of courts and bustle of the world. I am willing to believe him, but may not a man of an indolent temper and unactive spirit say and be sincere in all this and, at the same time, indulge his appetites without being able to subdue them, though his duty summons him to it. Virtue consists in action, and whoever is possessed of this social love and kind affection to his species and by his birth or quality can claim any post in the public management, ought not to sit still when he can be serviceable, but exert himself to the utmost for the good of his fellow subjects. Had this noble person been of a warlike genius or a boisterous temper, he would have chose another part in the drama of life and preached a quite contrary doctrine. For we are ever pushing our reason which way soever we feel passion to draw it, and self-love pleads to all human creatures for their different views, still furnishing every individual with arguments to justify their inclinations.

That boasted middle way and the calm virtues recommended in the *Characteristicks* are good for nothing but to breed drones, and might qualify a man for the stupid enjoyments of a monastic life or at best a country justice of peace, but they would never fit him for labour and assiduity or stir him up to great achievements and perilous undertakings. Man's natural love of ease and idleness and proneness to indulge his sensual pleasures are not to be cured by precept; his strong habits and inclinations can only be subdued by passions of greater violence. Preach and demonstrate to a coward the unreasonableness of his fears, and you will not make him valiant more than you can make him taller by bidding him to be ten foot high, whereas the secret to raise courage, as I have made it public in Remark on 1. 321, is almost infallible.

The fear of death is the strongest when we are in our greatest vigour and our appetite is keen, when we are sharp-sighted, quick of hearing, and every part performs its office. The reason is plain, because then life is most delicious and ourselves most capable of enjoying it. How comes it, then, that a man of honour should so easily accept of a challenge, though at thirty and in perfect health? It is his pride that conquers his fear; for, when his pride is not concerned, this fear will appear most glaringly. If he is not used to the sea, let him but be in a storm or, if he never was ill before, have but a sore throat or a slight fever, and he will show a thousand anxieties and in them the inestimable value he sets on life. Had man been naturally humble and proof against flattery, the politician could never have had his ends or known what to have made of him. Without vices, the excellency of the species would have ever remained undiscovered, and every worthy that has made himself famous in the world is a strong evidence against this amiable system.

If the courage of the great Macedonian [Alexander] came up to distraction when he fought alone against a whole garrison, his madness was not less when he fancied himself to be a god or at least doubted whether he was or not; and as soon as we make this reflection, we discover both the passion and the extravagancy of it that buoyed up his spirits in the most imminent dangers and carried him through all the difficulties and fatigues he underwent.

There never was in the world a brighter example of an able and complete magistrate than Cicero. When I think on his care and vigilance, the real hazards he slighted, and the pains he took for the safety of Rome, his wisdom and sagacity in detecting and disappointing the stratagems of the boldest and most subtle conspirators, and, at the same time, on his love to literature, arts, and sciences, his capacity in metaphysics, the justness of his reasonings, the force of his eloquence, the politeness of his style, and the genteel spirit that runs through his writings; when I think, I say, on all these things together, I am struck with amazement, and the least I can say of him is that he was a prodigious man. But when I have set the many good qualities he had in the best light, it is as evident to me on the other side that had his vanity been inferior to his greatest excellency, the good sense and knowledge of the world he was so eminently possessed of could never have let him be such a fulsome as well as noisy trumpeter as he was of his own praises, or suffered him rather than not proclaim his own merit to make a verse that a school boy would have been laughed at for. *O! Fortunatam*, &c.

How strict and severe was the morality of rigid Cato, how steady and unaffected the virtue of that grand asserter of Roman liberty! But though the equivalent this stoic enjoyed, for all the self-denial and austerity he practiced, remained long concealed, and his peculiar modesty hid from the world and perhaps himself a vast while the frailty of his heart that forced him into heroism, yet it was brought to light in the last scene of his life, and by his suicide it plainly appeared that he was governed by a tyrannical power, superior to the love of his country, and that the implacable hatred and superlative envy he bore to the glory, the real greatness and personal merit of Caesar had for a long time swayed all his actions under the most noble pretences. Had not this violent motive over-ruled his consummate prudence, he might not only have saved himself, but likewise most of his friends that were ruined by the loss of him and would in all probability, if he could have stooped to it, been the second man in Rome. But he knew the boundless mind and unlimited generosity of the victor; it was his clemency he feared, and therefore chose death because it was less terrible to his pride than the thoughts of giving his mortal foe so tempting an opportunity of showing the magnanimity of his soul, as Caesar would have found in forgiving such an inveterate enemy as Cato and offering him his friendship; and which, it is thought by the judicious, that penetrating as well as ambitious conqueror would not have slipped if the other had dared to live.

Another argument to prove the kind of disposition and real

affection we naturally have for our species is our love of company and the aversion men that are in their senses generally have to solitude, beyond any other creatures. This bears a fine gloss in the *Characteristicks* and is set off in very good language to the best advantage; the next day after I read it first, I heard abundance of people cry *fresh herrings,* which, with the reflexion on the vast shoals of that and other fish that are caught together, made me very merry, though I was alone; but as I was entertaining myself with this contemplation came an impertinent idle fellow whom I had the misfortune to be known by and asked me how I did, though I was and dare say looked as healthy and as well as ever I was or did in my life. What I answered him I forgot, but remember that I could not get rid of him in a good while and felt all the uneasiness my friend Horace complains of from a persecution of the like nature.

I would have no sagacious critic pronounce me a man-hater from this short story; whoever does is very much mistaken. I am a great lover of company and, if the reader is not quite tired with mine, before I show the weakness and ridicule of that piece of flattery made to our species and which I was just now speaking of, I will give him a description of the man I would choose for conversation, with a promise that before he has finished what at first he might only take for a digression foreign to my purpose, he shall find the use of it.

By early and artful instruction he should be thoroughly imbued with the notions of honour and shame and have contracted an habitual aversion to everything that has the least tendency to impudence, rudeness, or inhumanity. He should be well versed in the Latin tongue and not ignorant of the Greek and moreover understand one or two of the modern languages besides his own. He should be acquainted with the fashions and customs of the ancients, but thoroughly skilled in the history of his own country and the manners of the age he lives in. He should besides literature have studied some useful science or other, seen some foreign courts and universities, and made the true use of travelling. He should at times take delight in dancing, fencing, riding the great horse, and knowing something of hunting and other country sports, without being attached to any, and he should treat them all as either exercises for health or diversions that should never interfere with business or the attaining to more valuable qualifications. He should have a smatch of geometry and astronomy, as well as anatomy, and the economy of human bodies; to understand music so as to perform is an accomplishment, but there is abundance to be said against it; and instead of it, I would have him know so much of drawing as is required to take a landscape or explain one's meaning of any form or model we would describe, but never to touch a pencil. He should be very early used to the company of modest women and never be a fortnight without conversing with the ladies.

Gross vices, as irreligion, whoring, gaming, drinking, and quarrelling, I will not mention; even the meanest education guards us against them; I would always recommend to him the practice of virtue, but I am for no voluntary ignorance in a gentleman of anything that is done in court or city. It is impossible a man should be perfect, and therefore there are faults I would connive at if I could not prevent them; and if between the years of nineteen and three-and-twenty, youthful heat should sometimes get the better of his chastity, so it was done with caution; should he on some extraordinary occasion, overcome by the pressing solicitations of jovial friends, drink more than was consistent with strict sobriety, so he did it very seldom, and found it not to interfere with his health or temper; or if by the height of his mettle and great provocation in a just cause, he had been drawn into a quarrel which true wisdom and a less strict adherence to the rules of honour might have declined or prevented, so it never befell him above once; if, I say, he should have happened to be guilty of these things, and he would never speak much less brag of them himself, they might be pardoned, or at least overlooked at the age I named, if he left off then and continued discreet forever after. The very disasters of youth have sometimes frightened gentlemen into a more steady prudence than in all probability they would ever have been masters of without them. To keep him from turpitude and things that are openly scandalous, there is nothing better than to procure him free access in one or two noble families where his frequent attendance is counted a duty; and while by that means you preserve his pride, he is kept in a continual dread of shame.

A man of a tolerable fortune, pretty near accomplished as I have required him to be, that still improves himself and sees the world till he is thirty, cannot be disagreeable to converse with, at least while he continues in health and prosperity and has nothing to spoil his temper. When such a one, either by chance or appointment, meets with three or four of our equals and all agree to pass away a few hours together, the whole is what I call good company. There is nothing said in it that is not either instructive or diverting to a man of sense. It is possible they may not always be of the same opinion, but there can be no contest between any but who shall yield first to the other he differs from. One only speaks at a time and no louder than to be plainly understood by him who sits the farthest off. The greatest pleasure aimed at by every one of them is to have the satisfaction of pleasing others, which they all practically know may as effectually be done by hearkening with attention and an approving countenance, as if we said very good things ourselves.

Most people of any taste would like such a conversation and justly prefer it to being alone when they knew not how to spend their time; but if they could employ themselves in something from which they expected either a more solid or a more lasting satisfaction, they would deny themselves this pleasure and follow what was of greater consequence to them. But would not a man, though he had seen no mortal in a fortnight, remain alone as much longer rather than get into company of noisy fellows that take delight in contradiction and place a glory in picking a quarrel? Would not one that has books read forever or set himself to write upon some subject or other rather than be every night with party-men who count the island to be good for nothing while their adversaries are suffered to live upon it? Would not a man be by himself a month and go to bed before seven a clock rather than mix with fox-hunters, who, having all day long tried in vain to break their necks, join at night in a second attempt upon their lives by drinking, and to express their mirth are louder in senseless sounds within doors than their barking and less troublesome companions are only without? I have no great value for a man who would not rather tire himself with walking, or if he was shut up scatter pins about the room in order to pick them up again, than keep company for six hours with half a score common sailors the day their ship was paid off.

I will grant, nevertheless, that the greatest part of mankind, rather than be alone any considerable time, would submit to the things I named; but I cannot see why this love of company, this strong desire after society, should be construed so much in our favour and alleged as a mark of some intrinsic worth in man not to be found in other animals. For to prove from it the goodness of our nature and a generous love in man, extended beyond himself on the rest of his species, by virtue of which he was a sociable creature, this eagerness after company and aversion of being alone ought to have been the most conspicuous and most violent in the best of their kind, the men of the greatest genius, parts, and accomplishments, and those who are the least subject to vice; the contrary of which is true. The weakest minds, who can the least govern their passions, guilty consciences that abhor reflection, and the worthless who are incapable of producing anything of their own that is useful, are the greatest enemies to solitude and will take up with any company rather than be without; whereas the men of sense and of knowledge that can think and contemplate on things and such as are but little disturbed by their passions can bear to be by themselves the longest without reluctancy; and to avoid noise, folly, and impertinence will run away from twenty companies; and rather than meet with anything disagreeable to their good taste will prefer their closet or a garden, nay, a common or a desert, to the society of some men.

But let us suppose the love of company so inseparable from our species that no man could endure to be alone one moment, what conclusions could be drawn from this? Does not man love company, as he does everything else, for his own sake? No friendships or civilities are lasting that are not reciprocal. In all your weekly and daily meetings for diversion, as well as annual feasts and the most solemn carousals, every member that assists at them has his own ends, and some frequent a club which they would never go to unless they were the top of it. I have known a man who was the oracle of the company, be very constant, and as uneasy at anything that hindered him from coming at the hour, leave his society altogether, as soon as another was added that could match, and disputed superiority with him. There are people who are incapable of holding an argument and yet malicious enough to take delight in hearing others wrangle; and though they never concern themselves in the controversy, would think a company insipid where they could not have that diversion. A good house, rich furniture, a fine garden, horses, dogs, ancestors, relations, beauty, strength, excellency in anything whatever; vices as well as virtue may all be accessary to make men long for society, in hopes that what they value themselves upon will at one time or other become the theme of the discourse and give an inward satisfaction to them. Even the most polite people in the world and such as I spoke of at first give no pleasure to others that is not repaid to their self-love and does not at last centre in themselves, let them wind it and turn it as they will. But the plainest demonstration that in all clubs and societies of conversable people everybody has the greatest consideration for himself, is that the disinterested who rather overpays than wrangles, the good humoured that is never waspish nor soon offended, the easy and indolent that hates disputes and never talks for triumph, is everywhere the darling of the company; whereas the man of sense and knowledge that will not be imposed upon or talked out of his reason, the man of genius and spirit that can say sharp and witty things though he never lashes but what deserves it, the man of honour who neither gives nor takes an affront, may be esteemed, but is seldom so well beloved as a weaker man less accomplished.

As in these instances the friendly qualities arise from our contriving perpetually our own satisfaction, so on other occasions they proceed from the natural timidity of man and the solicitous care he takes of himself. Two Londoners whose business oblige them not to have any commerce together, may know, see, and pass by one another every day upon the Exchange with not much greater civility than bulls would: let them meet at Bristol they will pull off their hats, and on the least opportunity enter into conversation, and be glad of one another's company. When French, English, and Dutch meet in China, or any other pagan country, being all Europeans, they look upon one another as countrymen, and if no passion interferes, will feel a natural propensity to love one another. Nay, two men that are at enmity, if they are forced to travel together, will often lay by their animosities, be affable, and converse in a friendly manner, especially if the road be unsafe and they are both strangers in the place they are to go to. These things by superficial judges are attributed to man's sociableness, his natural propensity to friendship and love of company; but whoever will duly examine things and look into man more narrowly will find that on all these occasions we only endeavour to strengthen our interest and are moved by the causes already alleged.

What I have endeavoured hitherto has been to prove that the *pulchrum et honestum,* excellency and real worth of things are most commonly precarious and alterable as modes and customs vary; that consequently the inferences drawn from their certainty are insignificant, and that the generous notions concerning the natural goodness of man are hurtful, as they tend to mislead, and are merely chimerical: the truth of this latter I have illustrated by the most obvious examples in history. I have spoke of our love of company and aversion to solitude, examined thoroughly the various motives of them, and made it appear that they all centre in self-love. I intend now to investigate into the nature of society, and diving into the very rise of it, make it evident that not the good and amiable, but the bad and hateful qualities of man, his imperfections and the want of excellencies which other creatures are endued with, are the first causes that made man sociable beyond other animals, the moment after he lost Paradise; and that if he had remained in his primitive innocence and continued to enjoy the blessings that attended it, there is no shadow of probability that he ever would have become that sociable creature he is now.

How necessary our appetites and passions are for the welfare of all trades and handicrafts has been sufficiently proved throughout the book, and that they are our bad qualities, or at least produce them, nobody denies. It remains then that I should set forth the variety of obstacles that hinder and perplex man in the labour he is constantly employed in, the procuring of what he wants, and which in other words is called the business of self-preservation; while at the same time I demonstrate that the sociableness of man arises only from these two things, *viz.* the multiplicity of his desires and the continual opposition he meets with in his endeavours to gratify them.

The obstacles I speak of relate either to our own frame or the globe we inhabit, I mean the condition of it, since it has been cursed. I have often endeavoured to contemplate separately on the two things I named last, but could never keep them asunder; they always interfere and mix with one another; and at last make up together a frightful chaos of evil. All the elements are our enemies, water drowns and fire consumes those who unskilfully approach them. The earth in a thousand places produces plants and other vegetables that are hurtful to man, while she feeds and cherishes a variety of creatures that are noxious to him, and suffers a legion of poisons to dwell within her. But the most unkind of all the elements is that which we cannot live one moment without; it is impossible to repeat all the injuries we receive from the wind and weather, and though the greatest part of mankind have ever been employed in defending their species from the inclemency of the air, yet no art or labour have hitherto been able to find a security against the wild rage of some meteors.

Hurricanes, it is true, happen but seldom, and few men are swallowed up by earthquakes or devoured by lions; but while we escape those gigantic mischiefs, we are persecuted by trifles. What a vast variety of insects are tormenting to us; what multitudes of them insult and make game of us with impunity! The most despicable scruple not to trample and graze upon us as cattle do upon a field, which yet is often borne with if moderately they use their fortune; but here again our clemency becomes a vice, and so encroaching are their cruelty and contempt of us on our pity that they make laystalls* of our hands and devour our young ones if we are not daily vigilant in pursuing and destroying them.

There is nothing good in all the universe to the best-designing man, if either through mistake or ignorance he commits the least failing in the use of it; there is no innocence or integrity that can protect a man from a thousand mischiefs that surround him; on the contrary, everything is evil which art and experience have not taught us to turn into a blessing. Therefore how diligent in harvest time is the husbandman in getting in his crop and sheltering it from rain without which he could never have enjoyed it! As seasons differ with the climates, experience has taught us differently to make use of them, and in one part of the globe we may see the farmer sow while he is reaping in the other; from all which we may learn how vastly this earth must have been altered since the fall of our first parents. For should we trace man from his beautiful, his divine original, not proud of wisdom acquired by haughty precept or tedious experience, but endued with consummate knowl-

---

laystall—a dump, or midden.

edge the moment he was formed; I mean the state of innocence, in which no animal nor vegetable upon earth, nor mineral under ground was noxious to him, and himself secured from the injuries of the air as well as all other harms, was contented with the necessaries of life which the globe he inhabited furnished him with without his assistance. When yet not conscious of guilt, he found himself in every place to be the well-obeyed, unrivalled lord of all, and unaffected with his greatness, was wholly wrapped up in sublime meditations on the infinity of his Creator, who daily did vouchsafe intelligibly to speak to him and visit without mischief.

In such a golden age, no reason or probability can be alleged why mankind ever should have raised themselves into such large societies as there have been in the world, as long as we can give any tolerable account of it. Where a man has everything he desires and nothing to vex or disturb him, there is nothing can be added to his happiness; and it is impossible to name a trade, art, science, dignity, or employment that would not be superfluous in such a blessed state. If we pursue this thought, we shall easily perceive that no societies could have sprung from the amiable virtues and loving qualities of man; but, on the contrary, that all of them must have had their origin from his wants, his imperfections, and the variety of his appetites; we shall find likewise that the more their pride and vanity are displayed and all their desires enlarged, the more capable they must be of being raised into large and numerous societies.

Was the air always as inoffensive to our naked bodies and as pleasant as to our thinking it is to the generality of birds in fair weather and man had not been affected with pride, luxury and hypocrisy, as well as lust, I cannot see what could have put us upon the invention of clothes and houses. I shall say nothing of jewels, of plate, painting, sculpture, fine furniture, and all that rigid moralists have called unnecessary and superfluous; but if we were not soon tired with walking a-foot and were as nimble as some other animals; if men were naturally laborious and none unreasonable in seeking and indulging their ease, and likewise free from other vices, and the ground was everywhere even, solid, and clean, who would have thought of coaches or ventured on a horse's back? What occasion has the dolphin for a ship, or what carriage would an eagle ask to travel in?

I hope the reader knows that by society I understand a body politic, in which man either subdued by superior force, or by persuasion drawn from his savage state, is become a disciplined creature that can find his own ends in labouring for others, and where under one head or other form of government each member is rendered subservient to the whole, and all of them by cunning management are made to act as one. For if by society we only mean a number of people that without rule or government should keep together out of a natural affection to their species or love of company, as a herd of cows or a flock of sheep, then there is not in the world a more unfit creature for society than man; an hundred of them that should be all equals under no subjection or fear of any superior upon earth could never live together awake two hours without quarrelling, and the more knowledge, strength, wit, courage and resolution there was among them, the worse it would be.

It is probable that in the wild state of nature, parents would keep a superiority over their children, at least while they were in strength, and that even afterwards, the remembrance of what the others had experienced might produce in them something between love and fear, which we call reverence; it is probable, likewise, that the second generation following the example of the first, a man with a little cunning would always be able, as long as he lived and had his senses, to maintain a superior sway over all his own offspring and descendants, how numerous soever they might grow. But the old stock once dead, the sons would quarrel, and there could be no peace long, before there had been war. Eldership in brothers is of no great force, and the pre-eminence that is given to it only invented as a shift to live in peace. Man, as he is a fearful animal, naturally not rapacious, loves peace and quiet, and he would never fight if nobody offended him and he could have what he fights for without it. To this fearful disposition and the aversion he has to his being disturbed are owing all the various projects and forms of government. Monarchy, without doubt, was the first. Aristocracy and democracy were two different methods of mending the inconveniences of the first, and a mixture of these three an improvement on all the rest.

But be we savages or politicians, it is impossible that man, mere fallen man, should act with any other view but to please

himself while he has the use of his organs, and the greatest extravagancy either of love or despair can have no other centre. There
is no difference between will and pleasure in one sense, and every
motion made in spite of them must be unnatural and convulsive.
Since, then, action is so confined, and we are always forced to do
what we please, and at the same time our thoughts are free and
uncontrolled, it is impossible we could be sociable creatures without hypocrisy. The proof of this is plain. Since we cannot prevent
the ideas that are continually arising within us, all civil commerce
would be lost, if by art and prudent dissimulation we had had not
learned to hide and stifle them; and if all we think was to be laid
open to others in the same manner as it is to ourselves, it is
impossible that, endued with speech, we could be sufferable to
one another. I am persuaded that every reader feels the truth of
what I say; and I tell my antagonist that his conscience flies in
his face, while his tongue is preparing to refute me. In all civil
societies men are taught insensibly to be hypocrites from their
cradle; nobody dares to own that* he gets by public calamities or
even by the loss of private persons. The sexton would be stoned
should he wish openly for the death of the parishoners, though
everybody knew that he had nothing else to live upon.

To me it is a great pleasure, when I look on the affairs of human
life, to behold into what various and often strangely opposite forms
the hopes of gain and thoughts of lucre shape men, according to
the different employments they are of and stations they are in.
How gay and merry does every face appear at a well-ordered ball,
and what a solemn sadness is observed at the masquerade of a
funeral! But the undertaker is as much pleased with his gains as
the dancing master: both are equally tired in the occupations, and
the mirth of one is as much forced as the gravity of the other is
affected. Those who have never minded the conversation of a
spruce mercer and a young lady, his customer, that comes to his
shop, have neglected a scene of life that is very entertaining. I
beg of my serious reader that he would for a while abate a little
of his gravity, and suffer me to examine these people separately,
as to their inside, and the different motives they act from.

His business is to sell as much silk as he can at a price by which

---

*that—that which.

he shall get what he proposes to be reasonable, according to the customary profits of the trade. As to the lady, what she would be at is to please her fancy and buy cheaper by a groat or sixpence per yard than the things she wants are commonly sold at. From the impression the gallantry of our sex has made upon her, she imagines (if she be not very deformed) that she has a fine mien and easy behaviour and a peculiar sweetness of voice; that she is handsome, and, if not beautiful, at least more agreeable than most young women she knows. As she has no pretensions to purchase the same thing with less money than other people but what are built on her good qualities, so she sets herself off to the best advantage her wit and discretion will let her. The thoughts of love are here out of the case; so on the one hand, she has no room for playing the tyrant and giving herself angry and peevish airs and, on the other, more liberty of speaking kindly and being affable than she can have almost on any other occasion. She knows that abundance of well-bred people come to his shop and endeavours to render herself as amiable as virtue and the rules of decency allow of. Coming with such a resolution of behaviour, she cannot meet with anything to ruffle her temper.

Before her coach is yet quite stopped, she is approached by a gentleman-like man, that has everything clean and fashionable about him, who in low obeisance pays her homage, and as soon as her pleasure is known that she has a mind to come in, hands her into the shop, where immediately he slips from her, and through a by-way that remains visible only for half a moment, with great address entrenches himself behind the counter; here facing her, with a profound reverence and modish phrase, he begs the favour of knowing her commands. Let her say and dislike what she pleases, she can never be directly contradicted: she deals with a man in whom consummate patience is one of the mysteries of his trade, and whatever trouble she creates she is sure to hear nothing but the most obliging language and has always before her a cheerful countenance, where joy and respect seem to be blended with good humour and altogether make up an artificial serenity more engaging than untaught nature is able to produce.

When two persons are so well met, the conversation must be very agreeable as well as extremely mannerly, though they talk about trifles. While she remains irresolute what to take, he seems to be the same in advising her and is very cautious how to direct her choice; but when once she has made it and is fixed, he immediately becomes positive that it is the best of the sort, extols her fancy, and the more he looks upon it, the more he wonders he should not before have discovered the pre-eminence of it over anything he has in his shop. By precept, example, and great application, he has learned unobserved to slide into the inmost recesses of the soul, sound the capacity of his customers, and find out their blind side unknown to them: by all which he is instructed in fifty other stratagems to make her over-value her own judgment as well as the commodity she would purchase. The greatest advantage he has over her lies in the most material part of the commerce between them, the debate about the price, which he knows to a farthing and she is wholly ignorant of; therefore he nowhere more egregiously imposes on her understanding; and though here he has the liberty of telling what lies he pleases as to the prime cost and the money he has refused, yet he trusts not to them only, but, attacking her vanity, makes her believe the most incredible things in the world concerning his own weakness and her superior abilities; he had taken a resolution, he says, never to part with that piece under such a price, but she has the power of talking him out of his goods beyond anybody he ever sold to; he protests that he loses by his silk, but seeing that she has a fancy for it and is resolved to give no more, rather than disoblige a lady he has such an uncommon value for, he will let her have it and only begs that another time she will not stand so hard with him. In the meantime, the buyer, who knows that she is no fool, and has a voluble tongue, is easily persuaded that she has a very winning way of talking, and thinking it sufficient for the sake of good breeding to disown her merit and in some witty repartee retort the compliment, he makes her swallow very contentedly the substance of everything he tells her. The upshot is that, with the satisfaction of having saved ninepence per yard, she has bought her silk exactly at the same price as anybody else might have done, and often gives sixpence more than, rather than not have sold it, he would have taken.

It is possible that this lady, for want of being sufficiently flattered, for a fault she is pleased to find in his behaviour, or perhaps the tying of neckcloth, or some other dislike as substantial, may be lost, and her custom bestowed on some other of the fraternity. But where many of them live in a cluster, it is not always easily determined which shop to go to, and the reasons some of the fair sex have for their choice are often very whimsical and kept as great a secret. We never follow our inclinations with more freedom than where they cannot be traced, and it is unreasonable for others to suspect them. A virtuous woman has preferred one house to all the rest because she had seen a handsome fellow in it, and another of no bad character for having received greater civility before it than had been paid her anywhere else, when she had no thoughts of buying and was going to Paul's church; for among the fashionable mercers, the fair dealer must keep before his own door, and to draw in random customers, make use of no other freedom or importunities than an obsequious air, with a submissive posture, and perhaps a bow to every well-dressed female that offers to look towards his shop.

What I have said last makes me think on another way of inviting customers, the most distant in the world from what I have been speaking of, I mean that which is practiced by the waterman, especially on those whom by their mien and garb they know to be peasants. It is not unpleasant to see a half a dozen people surround a man they never saw in their lives before, and two of them that can get the nearest, clapping each an arm over his neck, hug him in as loving and familiar manner as if he was their brother newly come home from an East India voyage; a third lays hold of his hand, another of his sleeve, his coat, the buttons of it, or anything he can come at, while a fifth or a sixth, who has scampered twice around him already without being able to get at him, plants himself directly before the man in hold, and within three inches of his nose, contradicting his rivals with an open-mouthed cry, shows him a dreadful set of large teeth and a small remainder of chewed bread and cheese which the countryman's arrival had hindered from being swallowed.

At all this no offence is taken, and the peasant justly thinks they are making much of him; therefore, far from opposing them, he patiently suffers himself to be pushed or pulled which way the strength that surrounds him shall direct. He has not the delicacy to find fault with a man's breath, who has just blown out his pipe, or a greasy head of hair that is rubbing against his chops. Dirt and sweat he has been used to from his cradle, and it is no disturbance to him to hear half a score people, some of them at his ear, and the furthest not five foot from him, bawl out as if he was a hundred yards off. He is conscious that he makes no less noise when he is merry himself and is secretly pleased with their boisterous usages. The hauling and pulling him about he construes the way it is intended; it is a courtship he can feel and understand. He cannot help wishing them well for the esteem they seem to have for him: he loves to be taken notice of, and admires the Londoners for being so pressing in the offers of their service to him for the value of threepence or less; whereas in the country at the shop he uses, he can have nothing but he must first tell them what he wants and, though he lays out three or four shillings at a time, has hardly a word spoke to him unless it be in answer to a question himself is forced to ask first. This alacrity in his behalf moves his gratitude and, unwilling to disoblige any, from his heart he knows not whom to choose. I have seen a man think all this or something like it as plainly as I could see the nose in his face; and, at the same time, move along very contentedly under a load of watermen, and with a smiling countenance carry seven or eight stone more than his own weight to the water side.

If the little mirth I have shown in the drawing of these two images from low life misbecomes me, I am sorry for it, but I promise not to be guilty of that fault any more, and will now, without loss of time, proceed with my argument in artless dull simplicity, and demonstrate the gross error of those who imagine that the social virtues and the amiable qualities that are praiseworthy in us are equally beneficial to the public as they are to the individual persons that are possessed of them, and that the means of thriving, and whatever conduces to the welfare and real happiness of private families, must have the same effect upon the whole society. This, I confess, I have laboured for all along, and I flatter myself not unsuccessfully. But I hope nobody will like a problem the worse for seeing the truth of it proved more ways than one.

It is certain that the fewer desires a man has, and the less he covets, the more easy he is to himself; the more active he is to supply his own wants and the less he requires to be waited upon, the more he will be beloved and the less trouble he is in a family; the more he loves peace and concord, the more charity he has for his neighbour, and the more he shines in real virtue, there is no doubt but that in proportion he is acceptable to God and man. But let us be just, what benefit can these things be of, or what earthly good can they do to promote the wealth, the glory, and worldly greatness of nations? It is the sensual courtier that sets no limits to his luxury; the fickle strumpet that invents new fashions every week; the haughty duchess that in equipage, entertainments, and all her behaviour would imitate a princess; the profuse rake and lavish heir that scatter about their money without wit or judgment, buy everything they see, and either destroy or give it away the next day; the covetous and perjured villain that squeezed an immense treasure from the tears of widows and orphans and left the prodigals the money to spend: it is these that are the prey and proper food of a full-grown Leviathan; or, in other words, such is the calamitous condition of human affairs, that we stand in need of the plagues and monsters I named to have all the variety of labour performed which the skill of men is capable of inventing in order to procure an honest livelihood to the vast multitudes of working poor, that are required to make a large society. And it is folly to imagine that great and wealthy nations can subsist and be at once powerful and polite without.

I protest against Popery as much as ever Luther and Calvin did, or Queen Elizabeth herself; but I believe from my heart that the Reformation has scarce been more instrumental in rendering the kingdoms and states that have embraced it flourishing beyond other nations than the silly and capricious invention of hooped and quilted petticoats. But if this should be denied me by the enemies of priestly power, at least I am sure that, bar the great men who have fought for and against that layman's blessing, it has, from its beginnings to this day, not employed so many hands, honest, industrious labouring hands, as the abominable improvement on female luxury I named has done in few years. Religion is one thing and trade is another. He that gives most trouble to thousands of his neighbours and invents the most operose manufactures is, right or wrong, the greatest friend to the society.

What a bustle is there to be made in several parts of the world before a fine scarlet or crimson cloth can be produced; what multiplicity of trades and artificers must be employed! Not only such as are obvious, as woolcombers, spinners, the weaver, the cloth worker, the scourer, the dyer, the setter, the drawer, and the packer; but others that are more remote and might seem foreign to it; as the mill-wright, the pewterer, and the chemist, which yet are all necessary, as well as a great number of other implements belonging to the trades already named. But all these things are done at home and may be performed without extraordinary fatigue or danger; the most frightful prospect is left behind, when we reflect on the toil and hazard that are to be undergone abroad, the vast seas we are to go over, the different climates we are to endure, and the several nations we must be obliged to for their assistance. Spain alone, it is true, might furnish us with wool to make the finest cloth; but what skill and pains, what experience and ingenuity, are required to dye it of those beautiful colours! How widely are the drugs and other ingredients dispersed through the universe that are to meet in one kettle! Allum, indeed, we have of our own; argol we might have from the Rhine, and vitriol from Hungary; all this is in Europe; but then for saltpetre in quantity we are forced to go as far as the East Indies. Cochineal, unknown to the ancients, is not much nearer to us, though in quite a different part of the earth: we buy it, it is true, from the Spaniards; but not being their product, they are forced to fetch it for us from the remotest corner of the new world in the East Indies. While so many sailors are broiling in the sun and sweltered with heat in the east and west of us, another set of them are freezing in the north to fetch potashes from Russia.

When we are thoroughly acquainted with all the variety of toil and labour, the hardships and calamities that must be undergone to compass the end I speak of, and we consider the vast risks and perils that are run in those voyages, and that few of them are ever made but at the expence, not only of the health and welfare, but even the lives of many; when we are acquainted with, I say, and duly consider the things I named, it is scarce possible to conceive a tyrant so inhuman and void of shame that, beholding things in the same view, he should exact such terrible services from his innocent slaves; and, at the same time, dare to own that he did it for no other reason than the satisfaction a man receives from having a garment made of scarlet or crimson cloth. But to what height of luxury must a nation be arrived where not only the king's officers, but likewise the guards, even the private soldiers, should have such impudent desires!

But if we turn the prospect and look on all those labours as so many voluntary actions belonging to different callings and occupations that men are brought up to for a livelihood, and in which every one works for himself, how much soever he may seem to labour for others; if we consider that even the sailors who undergo the greatest hardships, as soon as one voyage is ended, even after shipwreck are looking out and soliciting for employment in another; if we consider, I say, and look on these things in another view, we shall find that the labour of the poor is so far from being a burden and an imposition upon them, that to have employment is a blessing, which in their addresses to Heaven they pray for, and to procure it for the generality of them is the greatest care of every legislature.

As children and even infants are the apes of others, so all youths have an ardent desire of being men and women, and become often ridiculous by their impatient endeavours to appear what everybody sees they are not; all large societies are not a little indebted to this folly for the perpetuity or at least long continuance of trades once established. What pains will young people take and what violence will they not commit upon themselves to attain to insignificant and often blameable qualifications, which, for want of judgment and experience, they admire in others that are superior to them in age! This fondness of imitation makes them accustom themselves by degrees to the use of things that were irksome, if not intolerable to them at first, till they know not how to leave them and are often very sorry for having inconsiderately increased the necessaries of life without any necessity. What estates have been got by tea and coffee! What a vast traffic is drove, what a variety of labour is performed in the world to the maintenance of thousands of families that altogether depend on two silly if not odious customs, the taking of snuff and smoking of tobacco; both which, it is certain, do infinitely more hurt than good to those that are addicted to them! I shall go further and demonstrate the usefulness of private losses and misfortunes to the public, and the folly of our wishes when we pretend to be most wise and serious.

The fire of London was a great calamity; but if the carpenters, bricklayers, smiths, and all, not only that are employed in building but likewise those that made and dealt in the same manufactures and other merchandises that were burnt, and other trades again that got by them when they were in full employ, were to vote against those who lost by the fire, the rejoicings would equal if not exceed the complaints. In recruiting what is lost and destroyed by fire, storms, sea-fights, sieges, battles, a considerable part of trade consists; the truth of which and whatever I have said of the nature of society will plainly appear from what follows.

It would be a difficult task to enumerate all the advantages and different benefits that accrue to a nation on account of shipping and navigation; but if we only take into consideration the ships themselves and every vessel great and small that is made use of for water-carriage, from the least wherry to a first-rate man of war; the timber and hands that are employed in the building of them; and consider the pitch, tar, rosin, grease; the masts, yards, sails and riggings; the variety of smith's work; the cables, oars, and everything else belonging to them; we shall find that to furnish only such a nation as ours with all these necessaries makes up a considerable part of the traffic of Europe, without speaking of the stores and ammunition of all sorts that are consumed in them, or the mariners, watermen and others, with their families, that are maintained by them.

But should we, on the other hand, take a view of the manifold mischiefs and variety of evils, moral as well as natural, that befall nations on the score of seafaring and their commerce with strangers, the prospect would be very frightful; and could we suppose a large populous island that should be wholly unacquainted with ships and sea affairs, but otherwise a wise and well-governed people; and that some angel or their genius should lay before them a scheme or draught, where they might see, on the one side, all the riches and real advantages that would be acquired by navigation in a thousand years; and on the other, the wealth and lives that would be lost, and all the other calamities that would be unavoidably sustained on account of it during the same time, I am confident they would look upon ships with horror and detestation, and that their prudent rulers would severely forbid the making and inventing all buildings

or machines to go to sea with, of what shape or denomination soever, and prohibit all such abominable contrivances on great penalties, if not the pain of death.

But to let alone the necessary consequence of foreign trade,
the corruption of manners, as well as plagues, poxes, and other
diseases, that are brought to us by shipping, should we only cast
our eyes on what is either to be imputed to the wind and weather,
the treachery of the seas, the ice of the north, the vermin of the
south, the darkness of nights, and unwholesomeness of climates,
or else occasioned by the want of good provisions, and the faults
of mariners, the unskilfulness of some, and the neglect and drunkenness of others; and should we consider the losses of men and
treasure swallowed up in the deep, the tears and necessities of
widows and orphans made by the sea, the ruin of merchants and
the consequences, the continual anxieties that parents and wives
are in for the safety of their children and husbands, and not forget the many pangs and heart-aches that are felt throughout a
trading nation by owners and insurers at every blast of wind;
should we cast our eyes, I say, on these things, consider with due
attention and give them the weight they deserve, would it not be
amazing how a nation of thinking people should talk of their ships
and navigation as a peculiar blessing to them, and placing an
uncommon felicity in having an infinity of vessels dispersed through
the wide world, and always some going to and others coming from
every part of the universe?

But let us once in our consideration on these things confine
ourselves to what the ships suffer only, the vessels themselves
with their rigging and appurtenances, without thinking on the
freight they carry or the hands that work them, and we shall find
that the damage sustained that way only is very considerable and
must one year with another amount to vast sums; the ships that
are foundered at sea, split against rocks and swallowed up by
sands, some by the fierceness of tempests altogether, others by
that and the want of the pilots' experience and knowledge of the
coasts; the masts that are blown down or forced to be cut and
thrown overboard, the yards, sails, and cordage of different sizes
that are destroyed by storms, and the anchors that are lost; add
to these the necessary repairs of leaks sprung and other hurts
received from the rage of winds and the violence of the waves;

many ships are set on fire by carelessness, and the effects of strong liquors, which none are more addicted to than sailors; sometimes unhealthy climates, at others the badness of provision breed fatal distempers that sweep away the greatest part of the crew, and not a few ships are lost for want of hands.

These are all calamities inseparable from navigation and seem to be great impediments that clog the wheels of foreign commerce. How happy would a merchant think himself if his ship should always have fine weather, and the wind he wished for and every mariner he employed, from the highest to the lowest, be a knowing, experienced sailor and a careful, sober, good man! Was such a felicity to be had for prayers, what owner of ships is there or dealer in Europe, nay, the whole world, who would not be all day long teasing Heaven to obtain such a blessing for himself, without regard to what detriment it would do to others? Such a petition would certainly be a very unconscionable one; yet where is the man who imagines not that he has a right to make it? And therefore, as every one pretends to an equal claim to those favours, let us, without reflecting on the impossibility of its being true, suppose all their prayers effectual and their wishes answered and afterwards examine into the result of such a happiness.

Ships would last as long as timber houses to the full because they are as strongly built, and the latter are liable to suffer by high winds and other storms, which the first, by our supposition, are not to be; so that before there would be any real occasion for new ships, the master builders now in being, and everybody under them that is set to work about them, would all die a natural death if they were not starved or come to some untimely end; for, in the first place, all ships having prosperous gales and never waiting for the wind, they would make very quick voyages both out and home; secondly, no merchandises would be damaged by the sea or by stress of weather thrown overboard, but the entire lading would always come safe ashore; and hence it would follow that three parts in four of the merchantmen already made would be superfluous for the present and the stock of ships that are now in the world serve a vast many years. Masts and yards would last as long as the vessels themselves, and we should not need to trouble Norway on that score a great while yet. The sails and rigging, indeed, of the few ships made use of would wear out, but not a quarter part so fast as now they do, for they often suffer more in one hour's storm than in ten days' fair weather.

Anchors and cables there would be seldom any occasion for, and one of each would last a ship time out of mind; this article alone would yield many a tedious holiday to the anchor-smiths and the rope-yards. This general want of consumption would have such an influence on the timber-merchants and all that import iron, sail-cloth, hemp, pitch, tar, &c. that four parts in five of what, in the beginning of this reflection on sea-affairs I said made a considerable branch of the traffic of Europe, would be entirely lost.

I have only touched hitherto on the consequences of this blessing in relation to shipping, but it would be detrimental to all other branches of trade besides and destructive to the poor of every country that exports anything of their own growth or manufacture. The goods and merchandises that every year go to the deep, that are spoiled at sea by salt water, by heat, by vermin, destroyed by fire, or lost to the merchant by other accidents, all owing to storms or tedious voyages or else the neglect or rapacity of sailors; such goods, I say, and merchandises are a considerable part of what every year is sent abroad throughout the world and must have employed great multitudes of poor, before they could come on board. A hundred bales of cloth that are burnt or sunk in the Mediterranean are as beneficial to the poor in England as if they had safely arrived at Smyrna or Aleppo and every yard of them had been retailed in the grand Signor's dominions.

The merchant may break, and by him the clothier, the dyer, the packer, and other tradesmen, the middling people, may suffer; but the poor that were set to work about them can never lose. Day-labourers commonly receive their earnings once a week, and all the various working people that were employed, either in any of the various branches of the manufacture itself or the several land and water carriages it requires to be brought to perfection, from the sheep's back, to the vessel it was entered in, were paid, at least much the greatest part of them, before the parcel came on board. Should any of my readers draw conclusions *in infinitum* from my assertions that goods sunk or burnt are as beneficial to the poor as if they had been well sold and put to their proper uses, I would count him a caviller and not worth answering: should it always rain and the sun never shine, the fruits of the earth would soon be rotten and destroyed; and yet it is no paradox to affirm that to have grass or corn, rain is as necessary as the sunshine.

In what manner this blessing of fair winds and fine weather would affect the mariners themselves and the breed of sailors may be easily conjectured from what has been said already. As there would hardly one ship in four be made use of, so the vessels themselves being always exempt from storms, fewer hands would be required to work them, and consequently five in six of the seamen we have might be spared, which in this nation, most employments of the poor being overstocked, would be but an untoward article. As soon as those superfluous seamen should be extinct, it would be impossible to man such large fleets as we could at present; but I do not look upon this as a detriment, or the least inconveniency; for the reduction of mariners, as to numbers being general throughout the world, all the consequence would be that in case of war the maritime powers would be obliged to fight with fewer ships, which would be an happiness instead of an evil; and would you carry this felicity to the highest pitch of perfection, it is but to add one desirable blessing more, and no nation shall ever fight at all: the blessing I hint at is what all good Christians are bound to pray for, *viz.* that all princes and states would be true to their oaths and promises and just to one another, as well as their own subjects; that they might have a greater regard for the dictates of conscience and religion than those of state politics and worldly wisdom, and prefer the spiritual welfare of others to their own carnal desires, and the honesty, the safety, the peace and tranquility of the nations they govern to their own love of glory, spirit of revenge, avarice, and ambition.

The last paragraph will to many seem a digression that makes little for my purpose; but what I mean by it is to demonstrate that goodness, integrity, and a peaceful disposition in rulers and governors of nations are not the proper qualifications to aggrandize them and increase their numbers, any more than the uninterrupted series of success[es] that every private person would be blest with, if he could, and which I have shown would be injurious and destructive to a large society that should place a felicity in worldly greatness, and being envied by their neighbours, and value themselves upon their honour and their strength.

No man needs to guard himself against blessings, but calamities require hands to avert them. The amiable qualities of man put none of the species upon stirring: his honesty, his love of company, his goodness, content and frugality, are so many comforts to an indolent society, and the more real and unaffected they are, the more they keep everything at rest and peace, and the more they will everywhere prevent trouble and motion itself. The same almost may be said of the gifts and munificence of Heaven and all the bounties and benefits of nature: this is certain, that the more extensive they are and the greater plenty we have of them, the more we save our labour. But the necessities, the vices, and imperfections of man, together with the various inclemencies of the air and other elements, contain in them the seeds of all arts, industry and labour; it is the extremities of heat and cold, the inconstancy and badness of seasons, the violence and uncertainty of winds, the vast power and treachery of water, the rage and untractableness of fire, and the stubbornness and sterility of the earth that rack our invention, how we shall either avoid the mischiefs they may produce or correct the malignity of them and turn their several forces to our own advantage a thousand different ways; while we are employed in supplying the infinite variety of our wants, which will ever be multiplied as our knowledge is enlarged and our desires increase. Hunger, thirst, and nakedness are the first tyrants that force us to stir; afterwards, our pride, sloth, sensuality, and fickleness are the great patrons that promote all arts and sciences, trades, handicrafts and callings; while the great taskmasters, necessity, avarice, envy, and ambition, each in the class that belongs to him, keep the members of the society to their labour, and make them all submit, most of them cheerfully, to the drudgery of their station, kings and princes not excepted.

The greater the variety of trades and manufactures, the more operose they are, and the more they are divided in many branches, the greater numbers may be contained in a society without being in one another's way, and the more easily they may be rendered a rich, potent, and flourishing people. Few virtues employ any hands, and therefore they may render a small nation good, but they can never make a great one. To be strong and laborious, patient in difficulties, and assiduous in all business are commendable qualities; but as they do their own work, so they are their own reward, and neither art not industry have ever paid their compliments to them; whereas the excellency of human thought and contrivance has been and is yet nowhere more conspicuous than in the variety of tools and instruments of workmen and artificers and the multiplicity of engines, that were all invented either to assist the weakness of man, to correct his many imperfections, to gratify his laziness, or obviate his impatience.

It is in morality as it is in nature, there is nothing so perfectly good in creatures that it cannot be hurtful to anyone of the society, nor anything so entirely evil, but it may prove beneficial to some part or other of the creation; so that things are only good and evil in reference to so something else and according to the light and position they are placed in. What pleases us is good in that regard, and by this rule every man wishes well for himself to the best of his capacity with little respect to his neighbour. There never was any rain yet, though in a very dry season when public prayers had been made for it, but somebody or other who wanted to go abroad wished it might be fair weather only for that day. When the corn stands thick in the spring and the generality of the country rejoice at the pleasing object, the rich farmer who kept his last year's crop for a better market pines at the sight and inwardly grieves at the prospect of a plentiful harvest. Nay, we shall often hear your idle people openly wish for the possessions of others, and not to be injurious forsooth add this wise proviso, that it should be without detriment to the owners; but I am afraid they often do it without any such restriction in their hearts.

It is happiness that the prayers as well as wishes of most people are insignificant and good for nothing; or else the only thing that could keep mankind fit for society and the world from falling into confusion would be the impossibility that all the petitions made to Heaven should be granted. A dutiful pretty young gentleman newly come from his travels lies at the Briel waiting with impatience for an easterly wind to waft him over to England, where a dying father, who wants to embrace and give him his blessing before he yields his breath, lies hoaning* after him, melted with grief and tenderness; in the meanwhile a British minister, who

---

to hone—to grumble, murmur, whine, moan.

is to take care of the Protestant interest in Germany, is riding post to Harwich and in violent haste to be at Ratisbone before the diet* breaks up. At the same time a rich fleet lies ready for the Mediterranean and a fine squadron is bound for the Baltic. All these things may probably happen at once, at least there is no difficulty in supposing they should. If these people are not atheists or very great reprobates, they will all have some good thoughts before they go to sleep, and consequently about bed-time, they must all differently pray for a fair wind and a prosperous voyage. I do not say but it is their duty, and it is possible they may be all heard, but I am sure they cannot be all served at the same time.

After this, I flatter myself to have demonstrated that neither the friendly qualities and kind affections that are natural to man nor the real virtues he is capable of acquiring by reason and self-denial are the foundation of society; but that what we call evil in this world, moral as well as natural, is the grand principle that makes us sociable creatures, the solid basis, the life and support of all trades and employments without exception; that there we must look for the true origin of all arts and sciences, and that the moment evil ceases, the society must be spoiled, if not totally dissolved.

I could add a thousand things to enforce and further illustrate this truth with abundance of pleasure; but for fear of being troublesome, I shall make an end, though I confess that I have not been half so solicitous to gain the approbation of others, as I have studied to please myself in this amusement; yet if ever I hear that by following this diversion I have given any to the intelligent reader, it will always add to the satisfaction I have received in the performance. In the hope my vanity forms of this, I leave him with regret and conclude with repeating the seeming paradox, the substance of which is advanced in the title page, that private vices, by the dexterous management of a skilful politician, may be turned into public benefits.

---

*At this period, the imperial diet of the Holy Roman Empire met regularly at Regensburg (Ratisbon) in Bavaria.

[1728]

THE FABLE OF THE BEES

PART II

Opinionum enim Commenta delet dies; Naturae judicia confirmat.
[Time destroys frivolous superstitions but confirms solid judgments
(freely translated).] Cicero de Nat. Deor. Lib. 2

···━◉━···

FROM THE FOURTH

DIALOGUE

BETWEEN

HORATIO AND CLEOMENES

[Cleomenes defends *The Fable of the Bees* and acts as spokesman
for Mandeville.]

CLEOMENES

. . . IT IS EVIDENT that the necessaries of life stand not
everywhere ready dished up before all creatures; therefore
they have instincts that prompt them to look out for those
necessaries and teach them how to come at them. The zeal and
alacrity to gratify their appetites is always proportioned to the
strength and the degree of force with which those instincts work
upon every creature. But, considering the disposition of things

189

upon earth and the multiplicity of animals that have all their own wants to supply, it must be obvious that these attempts of creatures to obey the different calls of nature will be often opposed and frustrated, and that in many animals they would seldom meet with success if every individual was not endued with a passion that, summoning all his strength, inspired him with a transporting eagerness to overcome the obstacles that hinder him in his great work of self-preservation. The passion I describe is called anger. How a creature possessed of this passion and self-liking, when he sees others enjoy what he wants, should be affected with envy can likewise be no mystery. After labour the most savage and the most industrious creature seeks rest. Hence we learn that all of them are furnished, more or less, with of a love of ease. Exerting their strength tires them; and the loss of spirits, experience teaches us, is best repaired by food and sleep. We see that creatures who in their way of living must meet with the greatest opposition have the greatest share of anger and are born with offensive arms. If this anger was to employ a creature always, without consideration of the danger he exposed himself to, he would soon be destroyed. For this reason they are all endued with fear; and the lion himself turns tail if the hunters are armed and too numerous. From what we observe in the behaviour of brutes we have reason to think that among the more perfect animals those of the same species have a capacity, on many occasions, to make their wants known to one another; and we are sure of several, not only that they understand one another, but likewise that they may be made to understand us. In comparing our species with that of other animals, when we consider the make of man and the qualifications that are obvious in him, his superior capacity in the faculties of thinking and reflecting beyond other creatures, his being capable of learning to speak, and the usefulness of his hands and fingers, there is no room to doubt that he is more fit for society than any other animal we know.

Hor. Since you wholly reject my Lord Shaftesbury's system, I wish you would give me your opinion at large concerning society and the sociableness of man; and I will hearken to you with great attention.

Cleo. The cause of sociableness in man, that is, his fitness for society, is no such abstruse matter. A person of middling capacity that has some experience and a tolerable knowledge of human nature may soon find it out, if his desire of knowing the truth be sincere and he will look for it without prepossession; but most people that have treated on this subject had a turn to serve and a cause in view which they were resolved to maintain. It is very unworthy of a philosopher to say, as Hobbes did, that man is born unfit for society, and allege no better reason for it than the incapacity that infants come into the world with; but some of his adversaries have as far overshot the mark when they asserted that everything which man can attain to ought to be esteemed as a cause of his fitness for society.

Hor. But is there in the mind of man a natural affection that prompts him to love his species beyond what other animals have for theirs; or are we born with hatred and aversion that makes us wolves and bears to one another?

Cleo. I believe neither. From what appears to us in human affairs and the works of nature, we have more reason to imagine that the desire as well as aptness of man to associate do not proceed from his love to others, than we have to believe that a mutual affection of the planets to one another, superior to what they feel to stars more remote, is not the true cause why they keep always moving together in the same solar system.

Hor. You do not believe that the stars have any love for one another, I am sure. Then why more reason?

Cleo. Because there are no phenomena plainly to contradict this love of the planets; and we meet with thousands every day to convince us that man centres everything in himself and neither loves nor hates but for his own sake. Every individual is a little world by itself, and all creatures, as far as their understanding and abilities will let them, endeavour to make that self happy. This in all of them is the continual labour and seems to be the whole design of life. Hence it follows that in the choice of things men must be determined by the perception they have of happiness; and no person can commit or set about an action which at that then present time seems not to be the best to him.

Hor. What will you then say to *video meliora proboque, deteriora sequor?**

---

*Ovid, *Metamorphoses*, VII, 20-21. I see the better and approve it, but I follow the worse.

Cleo. That only shows the turpitude of our inclinations. But men may say what they please. Every motion in a free agent which he does not approve of is either convulsive or it is not his; I speak of those that are subject to the will. When two things are left to a person's choice, it is a demonstration that he thinks that most eligible which he chooses, how contradictory, impertinent, or pernicious soever his reason for choosing it may be. Without this, there could be no voluntary suicide; and it would be injustice to punish men for their crimes.

Hor. I believe everybody endeavours to be pleased; but it is inconceivable that creatures of the same species should differ so much from one another, as men do in their notions of pleasure; and that some of them should take delight in what is the greatest aversion to others. All aim at happiness; but the question is, where is it to be found?

Cleo. It is with complete felicity in this world as it is with the philosopher's stone: both have been sought after many different ways by wise men as well as fools, though neither of them has been obtained hitherto. But in searching after either, diligent inquirers have often stumbled by chance on useful discoveries of things they did not look for and which human sagacity, labouring with design *a priori,* never would have detected. Multitudes of our species may in any habitable part of the globe assist one another in a common defence and be raised into a politic body, in which men shall live comfortably together for many centuries, without being acquainted with a thousand things that if known would every one of them be instrumental to render the happiness of the public more complete, according to the common notions men have of happiness. In one part of the world we have found great and flourishing nations that knew nothing of ships; and in others traffic by sea had been in use above two thousand years, and navigation had received innumerable improvements before they knew how to sail by the help of the lodestone. It would be ridiculous to allege this piece of knowledge either as a reason why man first chose to go to sea or as an argument to prove his natural capacity for maritime affairs. To raise a garden it is necessary that we should have a soil and a climate fit for that purpose. When we have these, we want nothing, besides patience, but the seeds of vegetables and proper culture. Fine walks and canals, statues, summer-houses, fountains, and cascades are great improvements on the delights of nature; but they are not essential to the existence of a garden. All nations must have had mean beginnings; and it is in those, the infancy of them, that the sociableness of man is as conspicuous as it can be ever after. Man is called a sociable creature chiefly for two reasons: first, because it is commonly imagined that he is naturally more fond and desirous of society than any other creature; secondly, because it is manifest that associating in men turns to better account than it possibly could do in other animals if they were to attempt it.

Hor. But why do you say of the first that it is commonly imagined; is it not true, then?

Cleo. I have a very good reason for this caution. All men born in society are certainly more desirous of it than any other animal; but whether man be naturally so, that is a question. But, if he was, it is no excellency, nothing to brag of. The love man has for his ease and security and his perpetual desire of meliorating his condition must be sufficient motives to make him fond of society, concerning the necessitous and helpless condition of his nature.

Hor. Do not you fall into the same error which, you say, Hobbes has been guilty of, when you talk of man's necessitous and helpless condition?

Cleo. Not at all; I speak of men and women full grown; and the more extensive their knowledge is, the higher their quality, and the greater their possessions are, the more necessitous and helpless they are in their nature. A nobleman of twenty-five or thirty thousand pounds a year that has three or four coaches and six and above fifty people to serve him is, in his person considered singly, abstract from what he possesses, more necessitous than an obscure man that has but fifty pounds a year and is used to walk a-foot; so, a lady who never stuck a pin in herself and is dressed and undressed from head to foot like a jointed baby by her woman and the assistance of another maid or two is a more helpless creature than Doll the dairy-maid who all the winter long dresses herself in the dark in less time than the other bestows in placing of her patches.

Hor. But is the desire of meliorating our condition which you named so general that no man is without it?

Cleo. Not one that can be called a sociable creature, and I believe this to be as much a characteristic of our species as any can be named; for there is not a man in the world, educated in society, who if he could compass it by wishing would not have something added to, taken from, or altered in his person, possessions, circumstances, or any part of the society he belongs to. This is what is not to be perceived in any creature but man, whose great industry in supplying what he calls his wants could never have been known so well as it is if it had not been for the unreasonableness as well as multiplicity of his desires. From all which it is manifest that the most civilized people stand most in need of society, and consequently, none less than savages. The second reason for which I said man was called sociable is that associating together turned to better account in our species than it would do in any other if they were to try it. To find out the reason of this we must search into human nature for such qualifications as we excel all other animals in and which the generality of men are endued with, taught or untaught. But in doing this, we should neglect nothing that is observable in them from their most early youth to their extreme old age.

Hor. I cannot see why you use this precaution of taking the whole age of man; would it not be sufficient to mind those qualifications which he is possessed of when he is come to the height of maturity or his greatest perfection?

Cleo. A considerable part of what is called docility in creatures depends upon the pliableness of the parts and their fitness to be moved with facility, which are either entirely lost or very much impaired when they are full grown. There is nothing in which our species so far surpasses all others than in the capacity of acquiring the faculty of thinking and speaking well; that this is a peculiar property belonging to our nature is very certain, yet it is as manifest that this capacity vanishes when we come to maturity, if till then it has been neglected. The term of life likewise that is commonly enjoyed by our species, being longer than it is in most other animals, we have a prerogative above them in point of time; and man has a greater opportunity of advancing in wisdom, though not to be acquired but by his own experience, than a creature that lives but half his age, though it had the same capacity. A man of threescore, *ceteris paribus,* knows better what is to be embraced or avoided in life than a man of thirty. What Mitio, in excusing the follies of youth, said to his brother Demea in the *Adelphi, ad omnia alia ætate sapimus rectius,** holds among savages as well as among philosophers. It is the concurrence of these with other properties that together compose the sociableness of man.

Hor. But why may not the love of our species be named as one of these properties?

Cleo. First, because as I have said already, it does not appear that we have it beyond other animals; secondly, because it is out of the question: for if we examine into the nature of all bodies politic, we shall find that no dependence is ever had or stress laid on any such affection, either for the raising or maintaining of them.

Hor. But the epithet itself, the signification of the word, imports this love to one another, as is manifest from the contrary. One who loves solitude is averse to company, or of a singular, reserved, and sullen temper, is the very reverse of a sociable man.

Cleo. When we compare some men to others, the word, I own, is often used in that sense; but when we speak of a quality peculiar to our species and say that man is a sociable creature, the word implies no more than that in our nature we have a certain fitness, by which great multitudes of us co-operating, may be united and formed into one body; that endued with and able to make use of the strength, skill and prudence of every individual shall govern itself and act on all emergencies as if it was animated by one soul and actuated by one will. I am willing to allow that among the motives that prompt man to enter into society, there is a desire which he has naturally after company; but he has it for his own sake, in hopes of being the better for it; and he would never wish for either company or anything else, but for some advantage or other he proposes to himself from it. What I deny is that man naturally has such a desire out of a fondness of his species, superior to what other animals have for theirs. It is a compliment which we commonly pay to ourselves, but there is no more reality in it than in our being one another's humble servants; and I insist upon it that this pretended love of our species and natural affection we are said to have for one another beyond other animals

---

*Terence, *Adelphoe,* 1. 832: . . . in all other respects we become wiser as we grow older (i.e., only in money matters do we remain the same: we think too much of it).

is neither instrumental to the erecting of societies, nor ever trusted to in our prudent commerce with one another when associated, any more than if it had no existence. The undoubted basis of all societies is government; this truth, well examined into, will furnish us with all the reasons of man's excellency as to sociableness. It is evident from it that creatures to be raised into a community must in the first place be governable. This is a qualification that requires fear and some degree of understanding; for a creature not susceptible of fear is never to be governed; and the more sense and courage it has, the more refractory and untractable it will be without the influence of that useful passion; and again, fear without understanding puts creatures only upon avoiding the danger dreaded without considering what will become of themselves afterwards; so wild birds will beat out their brains against the cage before they will save their lives by eating. There is a great difference between being submissive and being governable; for he who barely submits to another only embraces what he dislikes to shun what he dislikes more; and we may be very submissive and be of no use to the person we submit to; but to be governable implies an endeavour to please and a willingness to exert ourselves in behalf of the person that governs; but love beginning everywhere at home, no creature can labour for others and be easy long, whilst self is wholly out of the question; therefore a creature is then truly governable when, reconciled to submission, it has learned to construe his servitude to his own advantage; and rests satisfied with the account it finds for itself in the labour it performs for others. Several kinds of animals are or may with little trouble be made thus governable; but there is not one creature so tame that it can be made to serve its own species but man; yet without this he could never have been made sociable.

Hor. But was not man by nature designed for society?

Cleo. We know from revelation that man was made for society.

Hor. But if it had not been revealed, or you had been a Chinese or a Mexican, what would you answer me as a philosopher?

Cleo. That nature had designed man for society as she has made grapes for wine.

Hor. To make wine is an invention of man, as it is to press oil from olives and other vegetables and to make ropes of hemp.

Cleo. And so it is to form a society of independent multitudes; and there is nothing that requires greater skill.

Hor. But is not the sociableness of man the work of nature or rather of the author of nature, Divine Providence?

Cleo. Without doubt; but so is the innate virtue and peculiar aptitude of everything; that grapes are fit to make wine, and barley and water to make other liquors is the work of Providence; but it is human sagacity that finds out the uses we make of them; all the other capacities of man likewise, as well as his sociableness, are evidently derived from God who made him; everything therefore that our industry can produce or compass is originally owing to the Author of our being. But when we speak of the works of nature to distinguish them from those of art, we mean such as were brought forth without our concurrence. So nature in due season produces peas; but in England you cannot have them green in January without art and uncommon industry. What nature designs, she executes herself; there are creatures of whom it is visible that nature has designed them for society, as is most obvious in bees, to whom she has given instincts for that purpose, as appears from the effects. We owe our being and everything else to the great Author of the universe; but as societies cannot subsist without his preserving power, so they cannot exist without the concurrence of human wisdom; all of them must have a dependance either on mutual compact or the force of the strong exerting itself upon the patience of the weak. The difference between the works of art and those of nature is so immense that it is impossible not to know them asunder. Knowing, *a priori,* belongs to God only, and Divine Wisdom acts with an original certainty, of which what we call demonstration is but an imperfect borrowed copy. Amongst the works of nature, therefore, we see no trials nor essays; they are all complete and such as she would have them at the first production, and, where she has not been interrupted, highly finished beyond the reach of our understanding as well as senses. Wretched man on the contrary is sure of nothing, his own existence not excepted, but from a reasoning *a posteriori.* The consequence of this is that the works of art and human invention are all very lame and defective, and most of them pitifully mean at first; our knowledge is advanced by slow degrees, and

some arts and sciences require the experience of many ages before they can be brought to any tolerable perfection. Have we any
reason to imagine that the society of bees that sent forth the first
swarm made worse wax or honey than any of their posterity have
produced since? And again the laws of nature are fixed and unalterable; in all her orders and regulations there is a stability
nowhere to be met with in things of human contrivance and approbation; *Quid placet aut odio est, quod non mutabile credas?**
Is it probable that amongst the bees there has ever been any
other form of government than what every swarm submits to
now? What an infinite variety of speculations, what ridiculous
schemes have not been proposed amongst men on the subject of
government; what dissensions in opinion and what fatal quarrels
has it not been the occasion of! and which is the best form of it,
is a question to this day undecided. The projects, good and bad,
that have been stated for the benefit and more happy establishment of society are innumerable; but how shortsighted is our
sagacity, how fallible human judgment! What has seemed highly
advantageous to mankind in one age has often been found to be
evidently detrimental by the succeeding; and even among contemporaries, what is revered in one country is the abomination of
another. What changes have ever bees made in their furniture or
architecture? Have they ever made cells that were not sexangular
or added any tools to those which nature furnished them with at
the beginning? What mighty structures have been raised, what
prodigious works have been performed by the great nations of the
world! Toward all these nature has only found materials; the
quarry yields marble, but it is the sculptor that makes a statue
of it. To have the infinite variety of iron tools that have been
invented, nature has given us nothing but the ore, which she has
hid in the bowels of the earth.

Hor. But the capacity of the workmen, the inventors of arts
and those that improved them, has had a great share in bringing
those labours to perfection; and their genius they had from nature.

Cleo. So far as it depended upon the make of their frame, the
accuracy of the machine they had, and no further; but this I have

---

*Horace, *Epistles,* II, i, 101: Do you think that there are any tastes
that do not change? [free translation].

allowed already; and if you remember what I have said on this head, you will find that the part which nature contributed toward the skill and patience of every single person that had a hand in those works was very inconsiderable.

Hor. If I have not misunderstood you, you would insinuate two things: first, that the fitness of man for society beyond other animals is something real, but that it is hardly perceptible in individuals before great numbers of them are joined together and artfully managed; secondly, that this real something, this sociableness, is a compound that consists in a concurrence of several things and not in any one palpable quality that man is endued with and brutes are destitute of.

Cleo. You are perfectly right; every grape contains a small quantity of juice, and when great heaps of them are squeezed together, they yield a liquor which by skilful management may be made into wine; but if we consider how necessary fermentation is to the vinosity of the liquor, I mean, how essential is it to its being wine, it will be evident to us that without great impropriety of speech it cannot be said that in every grape there is wine.

Hor. Vinosity, so far as it is the effect of fermentation, is adventitious and what none of the grapes could ever have received whilst they remained single; and, therefore, if you would compare the sociableness of man to the vinosity of wine, you must show me that in society there is an equivalent for fermentation; I mean something that individual persons are not actually possessed of whilst they remain single and which likewise is palpably adventitious to multitudes when joined together; in the same manner as fermentation is to the juice of grapes and as necessary and essential to the completing of society as that is, that same fermentation, to procure the vinosity of wine.

Cleo. Such an equivalent is demonstrable in mutual commerce; for if we examine every faculty and qualification from and for which we judge and pronounce man to be a sociable creature beyond other animals, we shall find that a very considerable if not the greatest part of the attribute is acquired and comes upon multitudes from their conversing with one another. *Fabricando fabri fimus.** Men become sociable by living together in society.

---

*We become makers by making.

Natural affection prompts all mothers to take care of the offspring they dare own, so far as to feed and keep them from harm whilst they are helpless; but where people are poor and the women have no leisure to indulge themselves in the various expressions of their fondness for their infants, which fondling of them ever increases, they are often very remiss in tending and playing with them; and the more healthy and quiet such children are, the more they are neglected. This want of prattling to and stirring up the spirits in babes is often the principal cause of an invincible stupidity, as well as ignorance, when they are grown up; and we often ascribe to natural incapacity what is altogether owing to the neglect of this early instruction. We have so few examples of human creatures that never conversed with their own species that it is hard to guess what man would be, entirely untaught; but we have good reason to believe that the faculty of thinking would be very imperfect in such a one if we consider that the greatest docility can be of no use to a creature whilst it has nothing to imitate nor any body to teach it.

Hor. Philosophers therefore are very wisely employed when they discourse about the laws of nature, and pretend to determine what a man in the state of nature would think and which way he would reason concerning himself and the creation, uninstructed.

Cleo. Thinking and reasoning justly, as Mr. Locke has rightly observed, require time and practice. Those that have not used themselves to thinking but just on their present necessities, make poor work of it when they try beyond that. In remote parts and such as are least inhabited, we shall find our species come nearer the state of nature than it does in and near great cities and considerable towns, even in the most civilized nations. Among the most ignorant of such people you may learn the truth of my assertion; talk to them about anything that requires abstract thinking, and there is not one in fifty that will understand you any more than a horse would; and yet many of them are useful labourers and cunning enough to tell lies and deceive. Man is a rational creature, but he is not endued with reason when he comes into the world; nor can he afterwards put it on when he pleases, at once, as he may a garment. Speech likewise is a characteristic of our species, but no man is born with it; and a dozen generations proceeding from two savages would not produce any tolerable language; nor have we reason to believe that a man could be taught to speak after five-and-twenty if he had never heard others before that time.

Hor. The necessity of teaching whilst the organs are supple and easily yield to impression, which you have spoke of before, I believe is of great weight, both in speaking and thinking; but could a dog or a monkey ever be taught to speak?

Cleo. I believe not; but I do not think that creatures of another species had ever the pains bestowed upon them that some children have before they can pronounce one word. Another thing to be considered is that though some animals perhaps live longer than we do, there is no species that remains young so long as ours; and besides what we owe to the superior aptitude to learn, which we have from the great accuracy of our frame and inward structure, we are not a little indebted for our docility to the slowness and long gradation of our increases before we are full grown: the organs in other creatures grow stiff before ours are come to half their perfection.

Hor. So that in the compliment we make to our species of its being endued with speech and sociableness, there is no other reality than that by care and industry men may be taught to speak and be made sociable if the discipline begins when they are very young.

Cleo. Not otherwise. A thousand of our species all grown up, that is, above five-and-twenty, could never be made sociable if they had been brought up wild and were all strangers to one another.

Hor. I believe they would not be civilized if their education began so late.

Cleo. But I mean barely sociable, as it is the epithet peculiar to man; that is, it would be impossible by art to govern them any more than so many wild horses unless you had two or three times that number to watch and keep them in awe. Therefore it is highly probable that most societies and beginnings of nations were formed in the manner Sir William Temple supposes it, but nothing near so fast; and I wonder how a man of his unquestionable good sense could form an idea of justice, prudence, and wisdom in an untaught creature; or think of a civilized man before there was any civil society and even before men had commenced to associate.

Hor. I have read it, I am sure, but I do not remember what it is you mean.

Cleo. He is just behind you; the third shelf from the bottom, the first volume; pray reach it me, it is worth your hearing.—It is in his Essay on Government. Here it is. "For if we consider man multiplying his kind by the birth of many children, and his cares by providing even necessary food for them, until they are able to do it for themselves (which happens much later to the generations of men, and makes a much longer dependence of children upon parents, than we can observe among any other creatures); if we consider not only the cares, but the industry he is forced to, for the necessary sustenance of his helpless brood, either in gathering the natural fruits, or raising those which are purchased with labour and toil: if he be forced for supply of this stock, to catch the tamer creatures, and hunt the wilder, sometimes to exercise his courage in defending his little family, and fighting with the strong and savage beasts (that would prey upon him, as he does upon the weak and mild): if we suppose him disposing with discretion and order, whatever he gets among his children, according to each of their hunger or need; sometimes laying up for tomorrow, what was more than enough for today; at other times pinching himself, rather than suffering any of them should want—"

Hor. This man is no savage or untaught creature; he is fit to be a justice of peace.

Cleo. Pray let me go on, I shall only read this paragraph: "And as each of them grows up, and able to share in the common support, teaching them, both by lesson and example, what he is now to do, as the son of his family, and what hereafter, as the father of another; instructing them all what qualities are good, and what are ill, for their health and life, or common society (which will certainly comprehend whatever is generally esteemed virtue or vice among men) cherishing and encouraging dispositions to the good, disfavouring and punishing those to the ill: And lastly, among the various accidents of life, lifting up his eyes to Heaven, when the earth affords him no relief; and having recourse to a higher and a greater nature, whenever he finds the frailty of his own: we must needs conclude, that the children of this man cannot fail of being bred up with a great opinion of his wisdom, his goodness, his valour, and his piety, And if they see constant plenty in the family, they believe well of his fortune, too."

Hor. Did this man spring out of the earth, I wonder, or did he drop from the sky?

Cleo. There is no manner of absurdity in supposing——.

Hor. The discussion of this would too far engage us; I am sure I have tired you already with my impertinence.

Cleo. You have pleased me extremely; the questions you have asked have all been very pertinent and such as every man of sense would make that had not made it his business to think on these things. I read that passage on purpose to you to make some use of it; but if you are weary of the subject, I will not trespass upon your patience any longer.

Hor. You mistake me; I begin to be fond of the subject; but before we talk of it any further, I have a mind to run over that Essay again; it is a great while since I read it; and after that I shall be glad to resume the discourse; the sooner the better. I know you are a lover of fine fruit; if you will dine with me tomorrow, I will give you an ananas [pineapple].

Cleo. I love your company so well that I can refuse no opportunity of enjoying it.

Hor. Au revoir then.

Cleo. Your servant.

* * * *

FROM THE FIFTH

DIALOGUE

BETWEEN

HORATIO AND CLEOMENES

[They have just eaten the pineapple].

CLEOMENES

IT EXCELS EVERYTHING; it is extremely rich without being luscious, and I know nothing to which I can compare the taste of it; to me it seems to be a collection of different fine flavours that puts me in mind of several delicious fruits which yet are all outdone by it.

Hor. I am glad it pleased you.

Cleo. The scent of it likewise is wonderfully reviving. As you was paring it, a fragrancy, I thought perfumed the room that was perfectly cordial.

Hor. The inside of the rind has an oiliness of no disagreeable smell that upon handling of it sticks to one's fingers for a considerable time; for though now I have washed and wiped my hands, the flavour of it will not be entirely gone from them by tomorrow morning.

Cleo. This was the third I ever tasted of our own growth; the production of them in these northern climates is no small instance of human industry and our improvements in gardening. It is very elegant to enjoy the wholesome air of temperate regions and at the same time be able to raise fruit to its highest maturity that naturally requires the sun of the Torrid Zone.

Hor. It is easy enough to procure heat, but the great art consists in finding out and regulating the degrees of it at pleasure; without which it would be impossible to ripen an ananas here, and to compass this with that exactness as it is done by the help of thermometers was certainly a fine invention.

Cleo. I do not care to drink any more.

Hor. Just as you please; otherwise I was going to name a health, which would not have come *mal à propos.*

Cleo. Whose is that, pray?

Hor. I was thinking on the man to whom we are in a great measure obliged for the production and culture of the exotic we were speaking of in this kingdom, Sir Matthew Decker; the first ananas or pineapple that was brought to perfection in England grew in his garden at Richmond.

Cleo. With all my heart; let us finish with that; he is a beneficent and, I believe, a very honest man.

Hor. It would not be easy to name another who with the same knowledge of the world and capacity of getting money, is equally disinterested and inoffensive.

Cleo. Have you considered the things we discoursed of yesterday?

Hor. I have thought on nothing else since I saw you. This morning I went through the whole Essay and with more attention than I did formerly. I like it very well; only that passage which you read yesterday and some others to the same purpose I cannot reconcile with the account we have of man's origin from the Bible. Since all are descendants from Adam and consequently of Noah and his posterity, how came savages into the world?

Cleo. The history of the world, as to very ancient times, is very imperfect. What devastations have been made by war, by pestilence, and by famine; what distress some men have been drove to, and how strangely our race has been dispersed and scattered over the earth since the flood, we do not know.

Hor. But persons that are well instructed themselves never fail of teaching their children; and we have no reason to think that knowing, civilized men, as the sons of Noah were, should have neglected their offspring; but it is altogether incredible, as all are descendants from them, that succeeding generations instead of increasing in experience and wisdom should learn backward and still more and more abandon their broods in such a manner as to degenerate at last to what you call the state of nature.

Cleo. Whether you intend this as a sarcasm or not, I do not know; but you have raised no difficulty that can render the truth of the sacred history suspected. Holy writ has acquainted us with the miraculous origin of our species and the small remainder of it after the deluge. But it is far from informing us of all the revolutions that have happened among mankind since. The Old Testament hardly touches upon any particulars that had no relation to the Jews; neither does Moses pretend to give a full account of everything that happened to or was transacted by our first parents. He names none of Adam's daughters and takes no notice of several things that must have happened in the beginning of the world, as is evident from Cain's building a city and several other circumstances; from which it is plain, that Moses meddled with nothing but what was material and to his purpose; which in that part of his history was to trace the descent of the Patriarchs from the first man. But that there are savages is certain; most nations of Europe have met with wild men and women in several parts of the world that were ignorant of the use of letters, and among whom they could observe no rule or government.

Hor. That there are savages, I do not question; and from the great number of slaves that are yearly fetched from Africa it is manifest that in some parts there must be vast swarms of people that have not yet made a great hand of their sociableness. But how to derive them from all the sons of Noah, I own, is past my skill.

Cleo. You find it as difficult to account for the loss of the many fine arts and useful inventions of the ancients, which the world has certainly sustained. But the fault I find with Sir William Temple is in the character of his savage. Just reasoning and such an orderly way of proceeding as he makes him act in are unnatural to a wild man. In such a one the passions must be boisterous and continually jostling and succeeding one another; no untaught man could have a regular way of thinking or pursue any one design with steadiness.

Hor. You have strange notions of our species. But has not a man, by the time that he comes to maturity, some notions of right and wrong that are natural?

Cleo. Before I answer your question, I would have you consider that among savages there must be always a great difference as to the wildness or tameness of them. All creatures naturally love their offspring whilst they are helpless, and so does man. But in the savage state men are more liable to accidents and misfortunes than they are in society as to the rearing of their young ones; and therefore the children of savages must very often be put to their shifts so as hardly to remember by the time that they are grown up that they had any parents. If this happens too early and they are dropt or lost before they are four or five years of age, they must perish; either die for want or be devoured by beasts of prey unless some other creature takes care of them. Those orphans that survive, and become their own masters very young, must, when they are come to maturity, be much wilder than others that have lived many years under the tuition of parents.

Hor. But would not the wildest man you can imagine have from nature some thoughts of justice and injustice?

Cleo. Such a one, I believe, would naturally, without much thinking in the case, take everything to be his own that he could lay his hands on.

Hor. Then they would soon be undeceived if two or three of them met together.

Cleo. That they would soon disagree and quarrel, is highly probable; but I do not believe they ever would be undeceived.

Hor. At this rate men could never be formed into an aggregate body. How came society into the world?

Cleo. As I told you, from private families; but not without great difficulty and the concurrence of many favourable accidents; and many generations may pass before there is any likelihood of their being formed into a society.

Hor. That men are formed into societies we see. But if they are all born with that false notion and they can never be undeceived, which way do you account for it?

Cleo. My opinion concerning this matter is this: self-preservation bids all creatures gratify their appetites, and that of propagating his kind never fails to affect a man in health many years before he comes to his full growth. If a wild man and a wild woman should meet very young and live together for fifty years undisturbed in a mild wholesome climate where there is plenty of provisions, they might see a prodigious number of descendants. For in the wild state of nature, man multiplies his kind much faster than can be allowed of in any regular society. No male at fourteen would be long without a female if he could get one; and no female of twelve would be refractory if applied to or remain long uncourted if there were men.

Hor. Considering that consanguinity would be no bar among these people, the progeny of two savages might soon amount to hundreds. All this I can grant you; but as parents, no better qualified, could teach their children but little, it would be impossible for them to govern these sons and daughters when they grew up if none of them had any notions of right or wrong; and society is as far off as ever; the false principle, which you say all men are born with, is an obstacle never to be surmounted.

Cleo. From that false principle, as you call it, the right men naturally claim to everything they can get, it must follow that man will look upon his children as his property and make such use of them as is most consistent with his interest.

Hor. What is the interest of a wild man that pursues nothing with steadiness?

Cleo. The demand of the predominant passion for the time it lasts.

Hor. That may change every moment, and such children would be miserably managed.

Cleo. That is true; but still managed they would be; I mean they would be kept under and forced to do as they were bid, at least till they were strong enough to resist. Natural affection would prompt a wild man to love and cherish his child; it would make him provide food and other necessaries for his son till he was ten or twelve years old, or perhaps longer. But this affection is not the only passion he has to gratify; if his son provokes him by stubbornness or doing otherwise than he would have him, this love is suspended; and if his displeasure be strong enough to raise his anger, which is as natural to him as any other passion, it is ten to one but he will knock him down. If he hurts him very much and the condition he has put his son in moves his pity, his anger will cease; and, natural affection returning, he will fondle him again and be sorry for what he has done. Now if we consider that all creatures hate and endeavour to avoid pain and that benefits beget love in all that receive them, we shall find that the consequence of this management would be that the savage child would learn to love and fear his father. These two passions, together with the esteem which we naturally have for everything that far excels us, will seldom fail of producing that compound which we call reverence.

Hor. I have it now; you have opened my eyes, and I see the origin of society as plain as I do that table.

Cleo. I am afraid the prospect is not so clear yet as you imagine.

Hor. Why so? The grand obstacles are removed. Untaught men, it is true, when they are grown up are never to be governed; and our subjection is never sincere where the superiority of the governor is not very apparent. But both these are obviated; the reverence we have for a person when we are young is easily continued as long as we live; and where authority is once acknowledged and that acknowledgement well established, it cannot be a difficult matter to govern. If thus a man may keep up his authority over his children, he will do it still with greater ease over his grandchildren; for a child that has the least reverence for his parents, will seldom refuse homage to the person to whom he sees his father pay it. Besides, a man's pride would be a sufficient motive for him to maintain the authority once gained; and, if some of his progeny proved refractory, he would leave no stone unturned by the help of the rest to reduce the disobedient. The old man being dead, the authority from him would devolve upon the eldest of his children, and so on.

Cleo. I thought you would go on too fast. If the wild man had understood the nature of things and been endued with general knowledge and a language ready made, as Adam was by miracle, what you say might have been easy; but an ignorant creature that knows nothing but what his own experience has taught him is no more fit to govern than he is fit to teach the mathematics.

Hor. He would not have above one or two children to govern at first; and his experience would increase by degrees, as well as his family. This would require no such consummate knowledge.

Cleo. I do not say it would. An ordinary capacity of a man tolerably well educated would be sufficient to begin with; but a man who never had been taught to curb any of his passions would be very unfit for such a task. He would make his children, as soon as they were able, assist him in getting food and teach them how and where to procure it. Savage children, as they got strength, would endeavour to imitate every action they saw their parents do and every sound they heard them make; but all the instructions they received would be confined to things immediately necessary. Savage parents would often take offence at their children, as they grew up, without a cause; and as these increased in years, so natural affection would decrease in the other. The consequence would be that the children would often suffer for failings that were not their own. Savages would often discover faults in the conduct of what was past; but they would not be able to establish rules for future behaviour which they would approve of themselves for any continuance; and want of foresight would be an inexhaustible fund for changes in their resolutions. The savage's wife as well as himself would be highly pleased to see their daughters impregnated and bring forth; and they would both take great delight in their grandchildren.

Hor. I thought that in all creatures the natural affection of parents had been confined to their own young ones.

Cleo. It is so in all but man; there is no species but ours that are so conceited of themselves as to imagine everything to be theirs. The desire of dominion is a never-failing consequence of the pride that is common to all men; and which the brat of a savage is as much born with as the son of an emperor. This good opinion we have of ourselves makes men not only claim a right to their children, but likewise imagine that they have a great share of jurisdiction over their grandchildren. The young ones of other animals, as soon as they can help themselves, are free; but the authority which parents pretend to have over their children never ceases. How general and unreasonable this eternal claim is naturally in the heart of man we may learn from the laws which, to prevent the usurpation of parents and rescue children from their dominion, every civil society is forced to make, limiting paternal authority to a certain term of years. Our savage pair would have a double title to their grandchildren from their undoubted property in each parent of them; and all the progeny being sprung from their own sons and daughters without intermixture of foreign blood, they would look upon the whole race to be their natural vassals; and I am persuaded that the more knowledge and capacity of reasoning this first couple acquired, the more just and unquestionable their sovereignty over all their descendants would appear to them, though they should love to see the fifth or sixth generation.

Hor. Is it not strange that nature should send us all into the world with a visible desire after government and no capacity for it at all?

Cleo. What seems strange to you, is an undeniable instance of Divine Wisdom. For if all had not been born with this desire, all must have been destitute of it; and multitudes could never have been formed into societies if some of them has not been possessed of this thirst of dominion. Creatures may commit force upon themselves, they may learn to warp their natural appetites and divert them from their proper objects, but peculiar instincts that belong to a whole species are never to be acquired by art or discipline; and those that are born without them must remain destitute of them forever. Ducks run to the water as soon as they are hatched; but you can never make a chicken swim any more than you can teach it to suck.

Hor. I understand you very well. If pride had not been innate to all men, none of them could ever have been ambitious. And as to the capacity of governing, experience shows us that it is to be acquired; but how to bring society into the world, I know no more than the wild man himself. What you have suggested to me of his unskilfulness and want of power to govern himself has quite destroyed all the hopes I had conceived of society from this family. But would religion have no influence upon them? Pray, how came that into the world?

Cleo. From God, by miracle.

Hor. Obscurum per obscurius. I do not understand miracles

---

*Obscurity [explained] by greater obscurity.

that break in upon and subvert the order of nature; and I have no notion of things that come to pass *en dépit de bons sens* and are such, that judging from sound reason and known experience, all wise men would think themselves mathematically sure that they could never happen.

Cleo. It is certain that by the word *miracle* is meant an interposition of the Divine Power when it deviates from the common course of nature.

Hor. As when matters easily combustible remain whole and untouched in the midst of a fire fiercely burning or lions in vigour industriously kept hungry forbear eating what they are most greedy after. These miracles are strange things.

Cleo. They are not pretended to be otherwise; the etymology of the word imports it; but it is almost as unaccountable, that men should disbelieve them and pretend to be of a religion that is altogether built upon miracles.

Hor. But when I asked you that general question, why did you confine yourself to revealed religion?

Cleo. Because nothing, in my opinion, deserves the name of religion that has not been revealed; the Jewish was the first that was national, and the Christian the next.

Hor. But Abraham, Noah, and Adam himself were no Jews, and yet they had religion.

Cleo. No other than what was revealed to them. God appeared to our first parents and gave them commands immediately after he had created them. The same intercourse was continued between the Supreme Being and the Patriarchs; but the father of Abraham was an idolater.

Hor. But the Egyptians, the Greeks, and the Romans had religion as well as the Jews.

Cleo. Their gross idolatry and abominable worship I call superstition.

Hor. You may be as partial as you please, but they all called their worship religion as well as we do ours. You say man brings nothing with him but his passions; and when I asked you how religion came into the world, I meant what is there in man's nature, that is not acquired, from which he has a tendency to religion; what is it that disposes him to it?

Cleo. Fear.

Hor. How! *Primus in orbe Deos fecit timor.** Are you of that opinion?

Cleo. No man upon earth less. But that noted Epicurean axiom which irreligious men are so fond of is a very poor one; and it is silly as well as impious to say that fear made a God; you may as justly say that fear made grass or the sun and the moon; but when I am speaking of savages, it is not clashing either with good sense nor the Christian religion to assert that whilst such men are ignorant of the true Deity and yet very defective in the art of thinking and reasoning, fear is the passion that first gives them an opportunity of entertaining some glimmering notions of an invisible Power; which afterwards, as by practice and experience they grow greater proficients and become more perfect in the labour of the brain and the exercise of their highest faculty, will infallibly lead them to the certain knowledge of an Infinite and Eternal Being; whose power and wisdom will always appear the greater and more stupendous to them the more they themselves advance in knowledge and penetration, though both should be carried on to a much higher pitch than it is possible for our limited nature ever to arrive at.

Hor. I beg your pardon for suspecting you, though I am glad it gave you an opportunity of explaining yourself. The word *fear* without any addition sounded very harsh; and even now I cannot conceive how an invisible cause should become the object of a man's fear, that should be so entirely untaught as you have made the first savage; which way can anything invisible and that affects none of the senses make an impression upon a wild creature?

Cleo. Every mischief and every disaster that happens to him of which the cause is not very plain and obvious; excessive heat and cold; wet and drought that are offensive; thunder and lightning, even when they do no visible hurt; noises in the dark, obscurity itself, and everything that is frightful and unknown, are all administering and contributing to the establishment of this fear. The wildest man that can be conceived, by the time that he came to maturity, would be wise enough to know that fruits and other eatables are not to be had either always or everywhere: this would naturally

---

*Statius, *Thebiad,* III, 661: Fear first made the gods in the world.

put him upon hoarding when he had good store; his provision might be spoiled by the rain; he would see that trees were blasted and yielded not always the same plenty; he might not always be in health, or his young ones might grow sick, and die without any wounds or external force to be seen. Some of these accidents might at first escape his attention or only alarm his weak understanding without occasioning much reflection for some time; but as they come often, he would certainly begin to suspect some invisible cause; and as his experience increased, be confirmed in his suspicion. It is likewise highly probable that a variety of different sufferings would make him apprehend several such causes and at least induce him to believe that there was a great number of them which he had to fear. What would very much contribute to this credulous disposition and naturally lead him into such a belief is a false notion we imbibe very early and which we may observe in infants as soon as by their looks, their gestures, and the signs they make they begin to be intelligible to us.

Hor. What is that, pray?

Cleo. All young children seem to imagine that everything thinks and feels in the same manner as they do themselves; and that they generally have this wrong opinion of things inanimate is evident from a common practice among them whenever they labour under any misfortune which their own wildness and want of care have drawn upon them. In all such cases you see them angry at and strike a table, a chair, the floor, or anything else that can seem to have been accessory to their hurting themselves or the production of any other blunder they have committed. Nurses we see, in compliance to their frailty, seem to entertain the same ridiculous sentiment and actually appease wrathful brats by pretending to take their part. Thus you will often see them very serious in scolding at and beating either the real object of the baby's indignation or something else on which the blame of what has happened may be thrown with any show of probability. It is not to be imagined that this natural folly should be so easily cured in a child that is destitute of all instruction and commerce with his own species as it is in those that are brought up in society and hourly improved by conversing with others that are wiser than themselves; and I am persuaded that a wild man would never get entirely rid of it whilst he lived.

Hor. I cannot think so meanly of human understanding.

Cleo. Whence came the Dryades and Hama-Dryades? How came it ever to be thought impious to cut down or even to wound large venerable oaks or other stately trees; and what root did the Divinity spring from, which the vulgar among the ancient heathens apprehended to be in rivers and fountains?

Hor. From the roguery of designing priests and other impostors that invented those lies and made fables for their own advantage.

Cleo. But still it must have been want of understanding; and a tincture, some remainder of that folly which is discovered in young children, that could induce or would suffer men to believe those fables. Unless fools actually had frailties, knaves could not make use of them.

Hor. There may be something in it; but be that as it will, you have owned that man naturally loves those he receives benefits from; therefore, how comes it that man, finding all the good things he enjoys to proceed from an invisible cause, his gratitude should not sooner prompt him to be religious than his fear?

Cleo. There are several substantial reasons why it does not. Man takes everything to be his own, which he has from nature: sowing and reaping, he thinks, deserve a crop, and whatever he has the least hand in is always reckoned to be his. Every art and every invention, as soon as we know them, are our right and property; and whatever we perform by the assistance of them is by the courtesy of the species to itself deemed to be our own. We make use of fermentation and all the chemistry of nature without thinking ourselves beholden to anything but our own knowledge. She that churns the cream makes the butter, without inquiring into the power by which the thin lymphatic particles are forced to separate themselves and slide away from the more unctuous. In brewing, baking, cooking, and almost everything we have a hand in, nature is the drudge that makes all the alterations and does the principal work; yet all, forsooth, is our own. From all which it is manifest that man, who is naturally for making everything centre in himself, must in his wild state have a great tendency and be very prone to look upon everything he enjoys as his due and everything he meddles with as his own performance. It requires knowledge and reflection; and a man must be pretty far advanced in the art of thinking justly and reasoning consequentially before he can from his own light and without being taught be sensible of his obligations to God. The less a man knows and the more shallow his understanding is, the less he is capable either of enlarging his prospect of things or drawing consequences from the little which he does know. Raw, ignorant, and untaught men, fix their eyes on what is immediately before and seldom look further than, as it is vulgarly expressed, the length of their noses. The wild man, if gratitude moves him, would much sooner pay his respects to the tree he gathers his nuts from than he would think of an acknowledgment to him who had planted it; and there is no property so well established but a civilized man would suspect his title to it sooner than a wild one would question the sovereignty he has over his own breath. Another reason why fear is an elder motive to religion than gratitude is that an untaught man would never suspect that the same cause which he received good from would ever do him hurt; and evil without doubt would always gain his attention first.

Hor. Men, indeed, seem to remember one ill turn that is served them better than ten good ones; one month's sickness better than ten years' health.

Cleo. In all the labours of self-preservation man is intent on avoiding what is hurtful to him; but in the enjoyment of what is pleasant his thoughts are relaxed, and he is void of care; he can swallow a thousand delights, one after another, without asking questions; but the least evil makes him inquisitive whence it came in order to shun it. It is very material, therefore, to know the cause of evil; but to know that of good, which is always welcome, is of little use; that is, such a knowledge seems not to promise any addition to his happiness. When a man once apprehends such an invisible enemy, it is reasonable to think that he would be glad to appease and make him his friend if he could find him out; it is highly probable, likewise, that in order to [do] this, he would search, investigate, and look everywhere about him; and that finding all his inquiries upon earth in vain, he would lift up his eyes to the sky.

Hor. And so a wild man might; and look down and up again long enough before he would be the wiser. I can easily conceive that a creature must labour under great perplexities when it actually fears something of which it knows neither what it is nor where

it is; and that, though a man had all the reason in the world to
think it invisible, he would still be more afraid of it in the dark
than when he could see.

Cleo. Whilst a man is but an imperfect thinker and wholly employed in furthering self-preservation in the most simple manner
and removing the immediate obstacles he meets with in that pursuit, this affair perhaps affects him but little; but when he comes
to be a tolerable reasoner and has leisure to reflect, it must produce strange chimeras and surmises; and a wild couple would not
converse together long before they would endeavour to express
their minds to one another concerning this matter; and as in time
they would invent and agree upon certain sounds of distinction for
several things of which the ideas would often occur, so I believe
that this invisible cause would be one of the first which they would
coin a name for. A wild man and a wild woman would not take
less care of their helpless brood than other animals; and it is not
to be imagined but the children that were brought up by them,
though without instruction or discipline, would before they were
ten years old observe in their parents this fear of an invisible cause.
It is incredible likewise, considering how much men differ from
one another in features, complexion, and temper, that all should
form the same idea of this cause; from whence it would follow
that as soon as any considerable number of men could intelligibly
converse together, it would appear that there were different opinions among them concerning the invisible cause; the fear and
acknowledgment of it being universal and man always attributing
his own passions to everything which he conceives to think, everybody would be solicitous to avoid the hatred and ill-will and, if it
was possible, to gain the friendship of such a power. If we consider these things and what we know of the nature of man, it is
hardly to be conceived that any considerable number of our species
could have any intercourse together long in peace or otherwise
but wilful lies would be raised concerning this power, and some
would pretend to have seen or heard it. How different opinions
about invisible power may by the malice and deceit of imposters be made the occasion of mortal enmity among multitudes
is easily accounted for. If we want rain very much and I can be persuaded that it is your fault we have none, there needs no greater
cause to quarrel; and nothing has happened in the world of priest-

craft or inhumanity, folly or abomination, on religious accounts, that cannot be solved or explained with the least trouble from these data and the principle or fear.

Hor. I think I must yield to you that the first motive of religion among savages was fear; but you must allow me in your turn that from the general thankfulness that nations have always paid to their gods for signal benefits and success; the many hecatombs that have been offered after victories; and the various institutions of games and festivals; it is evident that when men came to be wiser and more civilized, the greatest part of their religion was built upon gratitude.

Cleo. You labour hard, I see, to vindicate the honour of our species; but we have no such cause to boast of it; and I shall demonstrate to you that a well-weighed consideration and a thorough understanding of our nature will give us much less reason to exult in our pride than it will furnish us with, for the exercise of our humility. In the first place, there is no difference between the original nature of a savage and that of a civilized man: they are both born with fear; and neither of them, if they have their senses about them, can live many years, but an invisible Power will at one time or other become the object of that fear; and this will happen to every man, whether he be wild and alone or in society and under the best of discipline. We know by experience that empires, states, and kingdoms may excel in arts and sciences, politeness, and all worldly wisdom and at the same time be slaves to the grossest idolatry and submit to all the inconsistencies of a false religion. The most civilized people have been as foolish and absurd in sacred worship as it is possible for any savages to be; and the first have often been guilty of studied cruelties, which the latter would never have thought of. The Carthaginians were a subtle flourishing people, an opulent and formidable nation, and Hannibal had half conquered the Romans when still to their idols they sacrificed the children of their chief nobility. And, as to private persons, there are innumerable instances in the most polite ages of men of sense and virtue that have entertained the most miserable, unworthy, and extravagant notions of the Supreme Being. What confused and unaccountable apprehensions must not some men have had of Providence to act as they did! Alexander Severus, who succeeded Heliogabalus, was a great reformer of abuses and thought to be as good a prince as his predecessor was a bad one. In his palace he had an oratory, a cabinet set aside for his private devotion, where he had the images of Apollonius Tyanæus, Orpheus, Abraham, Jesus Christ, and such like gods, says his historian. What makes you smile?

Hor. To think how industrious priests are in concealing a man's failings when they would have you think well of him. What you say of Severus I had read before; when looking one day for something in Moreri, I happened to cast my eye on the article of that emperor where no mention is made either of Orpheus or Apollonius! which, remembering the passage in Lampridius, I wondered at; and thinking I might have been mistaken, I again consulted that author, where I found it as you have related it. I do not question but Moreri left this out on purpose to repay the civilities of the emperor to the Christians, whom, he tells us, Severus had been very favourable to.

Cleo. That is not impossible in a Roman Catholic. But what I would speak to in the second place is the festivals you mentioned, the hetacombs after victories, and the general thankfulness of nations to their gods. I desire you would consider that in sacred matters, as well as all human affairs, there are rites and ceremonies and many demonstrations of respect to be seen that to outward appearance seem to proceed from gratitude, which upon due examination will be found to have been originally the result of fear. At what time the floral games were first instituted is not well known; but they never were celebrated every year constantly before a very unseasonable spring put the senate upon the decree that made them annual. To make up the true compound of reverence or veneration, love and esteem are as necessary ingredients as fear; but the latter alone is capable of making men counterfeit both the former, as is evident from the duties that are outwardly paid to tyrants at the same time that inwardly they are execrated and hated. Idolators have always behaved themselves to every invisible cause they adored as men do to a lawless arbitrary power, when they reckon it as captious, haughty, and unreasonable as they allow it to be sovereign, unlimited, and irresistible. What motive could the frequent repetitions of the same solemnities spring from whenever it was suspected that the least holy trifle had been omitted? You know how often the same farce was once acted

over again, because after every performance there was still room
to apprehend that something had been neglected. Do but consult,
I beg of you, and call to mind your own reading; cast your eyes
on the infinite variety of ideas men have formed to themselves and
the vast multitude of divisions they have made of the invisible
cause which everyone imagines to influence human affairs; run
over the history of all ages; look into every considerable nation,
their straits and calamities, as well as victories and successes; the
lives of great generals and other famous men, their adverse fortune
and prosperity; mind at which times their devotion was most fer-
vent; when oracles were most consulted, and on what accounts
the gods were most frequently addressed. Do but calmly consider
everything you can remember relating to superstition, whether
grave, ridiculous, or execrable, and you will find, in the first place,
that the heathens and all that have been ignorant of the true Deity,
though many of them were persons otherwise of great knowledge,
fine understanding, and tried probity, have represented their gods,
not as wise, benign, equitable, and merciful; but, on the contrary,
as passionate, revengeful, capricious, and unrelenting beings; not
to mention the abominable vices and gross immoralities the vulgar
were taught to ascribe to them. In the second, that for every one
instance that men have addressed themselves to an invisible cause
from a principle of gratitude, there are a thousand in every false
religion to convince you that divine worship and men's submission
to Heaven have always proceeded from their fear. The word
religion itself and the fear of God are synonomous; and had man's
acknowledgment been originally founded in love as it is in fear,
the craft of impostors could have made no advantage of the passion; and all their boasted acquaintance with gods and goddesses
would have been useless to them if men had worshipped the
immortal powers, as they called their idols, out of gratitude.

Hor. All lawgivers and leaders of people gained their point and
acquired what they expected from those pretences, which is reverence; and which to produce, you have owned yourself, love and
esteem to be as requisite as fear.

Cleo. But from the laws they imposed on men and the punishments they annexed to the breach and neglect of them, it is easily
seen which of the ingredients they most relied upon.

Hor. It would be difficult to name a king or other great man in very ancient times who attempted to govern an infant nation, that laid no claim to some commerce or other with an invisible power, either held by himself or his ancestors. Between them and Moses there is no other difference than that he alone was a true prophet and really inspired, and all the rest were impostors.

Cleo. What would you infer from this?

Hor. That we can say no more for ourselves than what men of all parties and persuasions have done in all ages, everyone for their cause, *viz.* that they alone were in the right and all that differed from them in the wrong.

Cleo. Is it not sufficient that we can say this of ourselves with truth and justice after the strictest examination, when no other cause can stand any test or bear the least inquiry? A man may relate miracles that never were wrought and give an account of things that never happened, but a thousand years hence all knowing men will agree that nobody could have wrote Sir Isaac Newton's *Principia* unless he had been a great mathematician. When Moses acquainted the Israelites with what had been revealed to him, he told them a truth which nobody then upon earth knew but himself.

Hor. You mean the unity of God and His being the Author of the universe.

Cleo. I do so.

Hor. But is not every man of sense capable of knowing this from his reason?

Cleo. Yes, when the art of reasoning consequentially is come to that perfection which it has been arrived at these several hundred years and himself has been led into the method of thinking justly. Every common sailor could steer a course through the midst of the ocean as soon as the use of the lodestone and the mariner's compass were invented. But before that the most expert navigator would have trembled at the thoughts of such an enterprise. When Moses acquainted and imbued the posterity of Jacob with this sublime and important truth, they were degenerated into slaves, attached to the superstitution of the country they dwelled in; and the Egyptians, their masters, though they were great proficients in many arts and sciences and more deeply skilled in the mysteries of nature than any other nation then was, had the most abject and abominable notions of the Deity which it is possible to conceive; and no savages could have exceeded their ignorance and stupidity as to the Supreme Being, the invisible cause that governs the world. He taught the Israelites *a priori;* and their children, before they were nine or ten years old, knew what the greatest philosophers did not attain to by the light of nature till many ages after.

Hod. The advocates for the ancients will never allow that any modern philosophers have either thought or reasoned better than men did in former ages.

Cleo. Let them believe their eyes. What you say every man of sense may know by his own reason was in the beginning of Christianity contested and denied with zeal and vehemence by the greatest men in Rome. Celsus, Symmachus, Porphyry, Hierocles, and other famous rhetoricians and men of unquestionable good sense wrote in defence of idolatry and strenuously maintained the plurality and multiplicity of their gods. Moses lived above fifteen hundred years before the reign of Augustus. If in a place where I was very well assured that nobody understood anything of colouring or drawing, a man should tell me that he had acquired the art of painting by inspiration, I should be more ready to laugh at him than to believe him; but if I saw him draw several fine portraits before my face, my unbelief would cease and I should think it ridiculous any longer to suspect his veracity. All the accounts that other lawgivers and founders of nations have given of the deities which they or their predecessors conversed with contained ideas that were unworthy of the Divine Being; and by the light of nature only, it is easily proved that they must have been false. But the image which Moses gave the Jews of the Supreme Being, that He was One and had made heaven and earth, will stand all tests and is a truth that will outlast the world. Thus I think I have fully proved, on the one hand, that all true religion must be revealed and could not have come into the world without miracle; and, on the other, that what all men are born with towards religion before they receive any instruction is fear.

Hor. You have convinced me many ways that we are poor creatures by nature; but I cannot help struggling against those mortifying truths when I hear them started first. I long to hear the origin of society, and I continually retard your account of it myself with new questions.

Cleo. Do you remember where we left off?

Hor. I do not think we have made any progress yet; for we have nothing towards it but a wild man and a wild woman with some children and grandchildren, which they are not able either to teach or govern.

Cleo. I thought that the introduction of the reverence which the wildest son must feel, more or less, for the most savage father, if he stays with him, had been a considerable step.

Hor. I thought so too, till you destroyed the hopes I had conceived of it yourself by showing me the incapacity of savage parents to make use of it. And since we are still as far from the origin of society as ever we were or ever can be in my opinion, I desire that before you proceed to that main point, you would answer what you have put off once already, which is my question concerning the notions of right and wrong. I cannot be easy before I have your sentiments on this head.

Cleo. Your demand is very reasonable, and I will satisfy you as well as I can. A man of sense, learning, and experience that has been well educated will always find out the difference between right and wrong in things diametrically opposite; and there are certain facts which he will always condemn and others which he will always approve of. To kill a member of the same society that has not offended us, or to rob him, will always be bad; and to cure the sick and be beneficent to the public, he will always pronounce to be good actions; and for a man to do as he will be done by, he will always say is a good rule in life; and not only men of great accomplishments and such as have learned to think abstractly, but all men of middling capacities that have been brought up in society will agree in this in all countries and in all ages. Nothing likewise seems more true to all that have made any tolerable use of their faculty of thinking than that out of the society before any division was made, either by contract or otherwise, all men would have an equal right to the earth. But do you believe that our wild man, if he had never seen any other human creature but his savage consort and his progeny, would ever have entertained the same notions of right and wrong?

Hor. Hardly; his small capacity in the art of reasoning would hinder him from doing it so justly; and the power he found he had over his children would render him very arbitrary.

Cleo. But without that incapacity, suppose that at three-score he was by a miracle to receive a fine judgment and the faculty of thinking and reasoning consequentially in as great a perfection as the wisest man ever did, do you think he would ever alter his notion of the right he had to everything he could manage or have other sentiments in relation to himself and his progeny than from his behaviour it appeared he entertained when he seemed to act almost altogether by instinct?

Hor. Without doubt. For if judgment and reason were given him, what could hinder him from making use of those faculties as well as others do?

Cleo. You seem not to consider that no man can reason but *a posteriori* from something that he knows or supposes to be true. What I said of the difference between right and wrong, I spoke of persons who remembered their education and lived in society; or at least such as plainly saw others of their own species that were independent of them and either their equals or superiors.

Hor. I begin to believe you are in the right. But at second thoughts, why might not a man with great justice think himself the sovereign of a place where he knew no human creature but his own wife and the descendants of both?

Cleo. With all my heart. But may there not be an hundred such savages in the world with large families that might never meet nor ever hear of one another?

Hor. A thousand, if you will, and then there would be so many natural sovereigns.

Cleo. Very well; what I would have you observe is that there are things which are commonly esteemed to be eternal truths that an hundred or a thousand people of fine sense and judgment could have no notion of. What if it should be true that every man is born with this domineering spirit and that we cannot be cured of it but by our commerce with others and the experience of facts, by which we are convinced that we have no such right? Let us examine a man's whole life from his infancy to his grave and see which of the two seems to be most natural to him: a desire of superiority and grasping everything to himself, or a tendency to act according to the reasonable notions of right and wrong; and we shall find that in his early youth the first is very conspicuous; that nothing appears of the second before he has received some instructions, and that this latter will always have less influence upon his actions the more uncivilized he remains. From whence I infer that the notions of right and wrong are acquired; for if they were as natural, or if they affected us as early as the opinion or rather the instinct we are born with of taking everything to be our own, no child would ever cry for his eldest brother's playthings.

Hor. I think there is no right more natural nor more reasonable than that which men have over their children; and what we owe our parents can never be repaid.

Cleo. The obligations we have to good parents for their care and education is certainly very great.

Hor. That is the least. We are indebted to them for our being; we might be educated by an hundred others but without them we could never have existed.

Cleo. So we could have no malt liquor without the ground that bears the barley: I know no obligations for benefits that never were intended. Should a man see a fine parcel of cherries, be tempted to eat, and devour them accordingly with great satisfaction, it is possible he might swallow some of the stones, which we know by experience do not digest. If twelve or fourteen months after, he should find a little sprig of a cherry-tree growing in a field where nobody would expect it, if he recollected the time he had been there before, it is not improbable that he might guess at the true reason how it came there. It is possible, likewise, that for curiosity's sake this man might take up this plant and take care of it; I am well assured that whatever became of it afterwards, the right he would have to it from the merit of his action would be the same which a savage would have to his child.

Hor. I think there would be a vast difference between the one and the other; the cherry-stone was never part of himself nor mixed with his blood.

Cleo. Pardon me; all the difference, as vast as you take it to be, can only consist in this, that the cherry-stone was not part of the man who swallowed it so long, nor received so great an alteration in its figure whilst it was, as some other things which the savage swallowed were, and received in their figure whilst they stayed with him.

Hor. But he that swallowed the cherry-stone did nothing to it;

it produced a plant as a vegetable, which it might have done as well without his swallowing it.

Cleo. That is true; and I own that as to the cause to which the plant owes its existence, you are in the right; but I plainly spoke as to the merit of the action, which in either case could only proceed from their intentions as free agents; and the savage might and would in all probability act with as little design to get a child as the other had eat cherries in order to plant a tree. It is commonly said that our children are our own flesh and blood; but this way of speaking is strangely figurative. However, allow it to be just, though rhetoricians have no name for it, what does it prove, what benevolence in us, what kindness to others in the intention?

Hor. You shall say what you please, but I think that nothing can endear children to their parents more than the reflection that they are their own flesh and blood.

Cleo. I am of your opinion; and it is a plain demonstration of the superlative value we have for our own selves and everything that comes from us if it be good and counted laudable; whereas other things that are offensive, though equally our own, are in compliment to ourselves industriously concealed; and as soon as it is agreed upon that anything is unseemly and rather a disgrace to us than otherwise, presently it becomes ill manners to name or so much as to hint at it. The contents of the stomach are variously disposed of, but we have no hand in that; and whether they go to the blood or elsewhere, the last thing we did to them voluntarily and with our knowledge was swallowing them; and whatever is afterwards performed by the animal economy, a man contributes no more to than he does to the going of his watch. This is another instance of the unjust claim we lay to every performance we are but in the least concerned in, if good comes of it, though nature does all the work; but whoever places a merit in his prolific faculty ought likewise to expect the blame when he has the stone or a fever. Without this violent principle of innate folly no rational creature would value himself on his free agency and at the same time accept of applause for actions that are visibly independent of his will. Life in all creatures is a compound action, but the share they have in it themselves is only passive. We are forced to breathe before we know it; and our continuance palpably depends upon the guardianship and perpetual tutelage of nature; whilst every part of her works, ourselves not excepted, is an impenetrable secret to us that eludes all inquiries. Nature furnishes us with all the substance of our food herself, nor does she trust to our wisdom for an appetite to crave it; to chew it, she teaches us by instinct and bribes us to it by pleasure. This seeming to be an action of choice and ourselves being conscious of the performance, we perhaps may be said to have a part in it; but the moment after, nature resumes her care and, again withdrawn from our knowledge, preserves us in a mysterious manner without any help or concurrence of ours that we are sensible of. Since, then, the management of what we have eat and drank remains entirely under the direction of nature, what honour or shame ought we to receive from any part of the product, whether it is to serve as a doubtful means toward generation or yields to vegetation a less fallible assistance? It is nature that prompts us to propagate as well as to eat; and a savage man multiplies his kind by instinct as other animals do without more thought or design of preserving his species than a newborn infant has of keeping itself alive in the action of sucking.

Hor. Yet nature gave the different instincts to both for those reasons.

Cleo. Without doubt; but what I mean is that the reason of the thing is as much the motive of action in the one as it is in the other; and I verily believe that a wild woman who had never seen or not minded the production of any young animal, would have several children before she would guess at the real cause of them; any more than if she had the colic she would suspect that it proceeded from some delicious fruit she had eaten, especially if she had feasted upon it for several months without perceiving any inconveniency from it. Children all the world over are brought forth with pain, more or less, which seems to have no affinity with pleasure; and an untaught creature, however docile and attentive, would want several clear experiments before it would believe that the one could produce or be the cause of the other.

Hor. Most people marry in hopes, and with a design, of having children.

Cleo. I doubt, not; and believe that there are as many that would rather not have children, or at least not so fast as often they come, as there are that wish for them even in the state of matrimony; but out of it, in the amours of thousands that revel in enjoyments, children are reckoned to be the greatest calamity that can befall them; and often what criminal love gave birth to without thought, more criminal pride destroys with purposed and considerate cruelty. But all this belongs to people in society that are knowing and well acquainted with the natural consequences of things; what I urged, I spoke of a savage.

Hor. Still, the end of love between the different sexes in all animals is the preservation of their species.

Cleo. I have allowed that already. But once more, the savage is not prompted to love from that consideration; he propagates before he knows the consequence of it; and I much question whether the most civilized pair in the most chaste of their embraces ever acted from the care of their species as a real principle. A rich man may with great impatience wish for a son to inherit his name and his estate; perhaps he may marry from no other motive and for no other purpose; but all the satisfaction he seems to receive from the flattering prospect of an happy posterity can only arise from a pleasing reflection on himself as the cause of those descendants. How much soever this man's posterity might be thought to owe him for their being, it is certain that the motive he acted from was to oblige himself; still here is a wishing for posterity, a thought and design of getting children, which no wild couple could have to boast of; yet they would be vain enough to look upon themselves as the principal cause of all their offspring and descendants, though they should live to see the fifth or sixth generation.

Hor. I can find no vanity in that, and I should think them so myself.

Cleo. Yet, as free agents it would be plain that they had contributed nothing to the existence of their posterity.

Hor. Now surely you have overshot the mark; nothing?

Cleo. No, nothing, even to that of their own children knowingly, if you will allow that men have their appetites from nature. There is but one real cause in the universe, to produce that infinite variety of stupendous effects and all the mighty labours that are performed in nature, either within or far beyond the reach of our senses. Parents are the efficients of their offspring with no more truth or propriety of speech than the tools of an artificer that were made and contrived by himself are the cause of the most elaborate of his works. The senseless engine that raises water into the copper and the passive mash-tub have between them as great a share in the art and action of brewing as the liveliest male and female ever had in the production of an animal.

Hor. You make stocks and stones of us; is it not in our choice to act or not to act?

Cleo. Yes, it is my choice now either to run my head against the wall or to let it alone; but I hope it does not puzzle you to guess which of the two I shall choose.

Hor. But do not we move our bodies as we list; and is not every action determined by the will?

Cleo. What signifies that, where there is a passion that manifestly sways and with a strict hand governs that will?

Hor. Still we act with consciousness and are intelligent creatures.

Cleo. Not in the affair I speak of; where, willing or not willing, we are violently urged from within and in a manner compelled not only to assist in, but likewise to long for, and in spite of our teeth be highly pleased with a performance that infinitely surpasses our understanding. The comparison I made is just in every part of it; for the most loving and, if you will, the most sagacious couple you can conceive are as ignorant in the mystery of generation, nay, must remain, after having had twenty children together, as much uninformed and as little conscious of nature's transactions and what has been wrought within them, as inanimate utensils are of the most mystic and most ingenious operations they have been employed in.

Hor. I do not know any man more expert in tracing human pride or more severe in humbling it than yourself; but when the subject comes in your way, you do not know how to leave it. I wish you would at once go over to the origin of society, which, how to derive or bring about at all from the savage family as we left it, is past my skill. It is impossible but those children, when they grew up, would quarrel on innumerable occasions. If men had but three appetites to gratify, that are the most obvious, they could never live together in peace, without government. For though they all paid a deference to the father, yet if he was a man void of all prudence, that could give them no good rules to walk by, I am persuaded that they would live in a perpetual state of war; and the more numerous his offspring grew, the more the old savage would be puzzled between his desire and incapacity of government. As they increased in numbers, they would be forced to extend their limits, and the spot they were born upon would not hold them long; nobody would be willing to leave his native vale, especially if it was a fruitful one. The more I think upon it and the more I look into such multitudes, the less I can conceive which way they could ever be formed into a society.

Cleo. The first thing that could make man associate would be common danger, which unites the greatest enemies; this danger they would certainly be in from wild beasts, considering that no uninhabited country is without them, and the defenceless condition in which men come into the world. This often must have been a cruel article to prevent the increase of our species.

Hor. The supposition, then, that this wild man with his progeny should for fifty years live undisturbed is not very probable, and I need not trouble myself about our savages being embarrassed with too numerous an offspring.

Cleo. You say right; there is no probability that a man and his progeny, all unarmed, should so long escape the ravenous hunger of beasts of prey that are to live upon what animals they can get, that leave no place unsearched, nor pains untried, to come at food, though with the hazard of their lives. The reason why I made that supposition was to show you, first, the improbability that a wild and altogether untaught man should have the knowledge and discretion which Sir William Temple gives him; secondly, that children who conversed with their own species, though they were brought up by savages, would be governable; and consequently, that all such, when come to maturity, would be fit for society, how ignorant and unskilful soever their parents might have been.

Hor. I thank you for it; for it has shown me that the very first generation of the most brutish savages was sufficient to produce sociable creatures, but that to produce a man fit to govern others, much more was required.

Cleo. I return to my conjecture concerning the first motive that would make savages associate: it is not possible to know any thing with certainty of beginnings, where men were destitute of letters, but I think that the nature of the thing makes it highly probable that it must have been their common danger from beasts of prey, as well such sly ones as lay in wait for their children and the defenceless animals men made use of for themselves, as the more bold that would openly attack grown men and women. What much confirms me in this opinion is the general agreement of all the relations we have from the most ancient times in different countries: for in the infancy of all nations, profane history is stuffed with the accounts of the conflicts men had with wild beasts. It took up the chief labours of the heroes of remotest antiquity, and their greatest prowess was shown in killing of dragons and subduing of other monsters.

Hor. Do you lay any stress upon sphinxes, basilisks, flying dragons, and bulls that spit fire?

Cleo. As much as I do on modern witches. But I believe that all those fictions had their rise from noxious beasts, the mischiefs they did, and other realities that struck terror into man; and I believe that if no man had ever been seen on a horse's back, we should never have heard of centaurs. The prodigious force and rage that are apparent in some savage animals, and the astonishing power which, from the various poisons of venomous creatures, we are sure must be hid in others; the sudden and unexpected assaults of serpents, the variety of them; the vast bulk of crocodiles; the irregular and uncommon shapes of some fishes, and the wings of others, are all things that are capable of alarming man's fear; and it is incredible what chimeras that passion alone may produce in a terrified mind. The dangers of the day often haunt men at night with addition of terror, and from what they remember in their dreams, it is easy to forge realities. If you will consider, likewise, that the natural ignorance of man and his hankering after knowledge will augment the credulity which hope and fear first give birth to; the desire the generality have of applause, and the great esteem that is commonly had for the *merveilleux,* and the witnesses and relaters of it: if, I say, you will consider all these, you will easily discover how many creatures came to be talked of, described, and formally painted, that never had any existence.

Hor. I do not wonder at the origin of monstrous figures or the invention of any fables whatever, but in the reason you gave for the first motive that would make men combine in one interest,

I find something perplexing which I own I never thought of before. When I reflect on the condition of man as you have set it fore me, naked and defenceless, and the multitude of ravenous animals that thirst after his blood and are superior to him in strength and completely armed by nature, it is inconceivable to me how our species should have subsisted.

Ceo. What you observe is well worthy our attention.

Hor. It is astonishing. What filthy, abominable beasts are lions and tigers!

Cleo. I think them to be very fine creatures; there is nothing I admire more than a lion.

Hor. We have strange accounts of his generosity and gratitude, but do you believe them?

Cleo. I do not trouble my head about them. What I admire is his fabric, his structure, and his rage, so justly proportioned to one another. There are order, symmetry, and superlative wisdom to be observed in all the works of nature, but she has not a machine of which every part more visibly answers the end for which the whole was formed.

Hor. The destruction of other animals.

Cleo. That is true; but how conspicuous is that end, without mystery or uncertainty! That grapes were made for wine and man for society are truths not accomplished in every individual: but there is a real majesty stamped on every single lion, at the sight of which the stoutest animals submit and tremble. When we look upon and examine his massy talons, the size of them and the laboured firmness with which they are fixed in and fastened to that prodigious paw, his dreadful teeth, the strength of his jaws, and the width of his mouth equally terrible, the use of them is obvious; but when we consider, moreover, the make of his limbs, the toughness of his flesh and tendons, the solidity of his bones beyond that of other animals, and the whole frame of him, together with his never-ceasing anger, speed, and agility, whilst in the desert he ranges king of beasts! When, I say, we consider all these things, it is stupidity not to see the design of nature and with what amazing skill the beautiful creature is contrived for offensive war and conquest.

Hor. You are a good painter. But after all, why would you judge of a creature's nature from what it was perverted to rather

than from its original, the state it was first produced in? The lion
in Paradise was a gentle, loving creature. Hear what Milton says
of his behaviour before Adam and Eve, "as they sate recline on
the soft downy bank, damask'd with flowers":

> ————About them frisking play'd
> All beasts of the earth, since, wild, and of all chase
> In wood or wilderness, forest or den;
> Sporting the lion ramp'd, and in his paw
> Dandel'd the kid; bears, tigers, ounces, pards,
> Gambol'd before them.————

What was it the lion fed upon; what sustenance had all these beasts
of prey in Paradise?

Cleo. I do not know. Nobody who believes the Bible doubts
but that the whole state of Paradise and the intercourse between
God and the first man were as much preternatural as the creation
out of nothing; and, therefore, it cannot be supposed that they
should be accounted for by human reason; and if they were, Moses
would not be answerable for more than he advanced himself.
The history which he has given us of those times is extremely
succinct and ought not to be charged with anything contained in
the glosses and paraphrases that have been made upon it by
others.

Hor. Milton has said nothing of Paradise but what he could
justify from Moses.

Cleo. It is nowhere to be proved from Moses that the state of
innocence lasted so long that goats or any viviparous animals could
have bred and brought forth young ones.

Hor. You mean that there could have been no kid. I should
never have made that cavil in so fine a poem. It was not in my
thoughts; what I aimed at in repeating those lines was to show
you how superfluous and impertinent a lion must have been in
Paradise; and that those who pretend to find fault with the works
of nature might have censured her with justice for lavishing and
throwing away so many excellencies upon a great beast to no
purpose. What a fine variety of destructive weapons, would they
say, what prodigious strength of limbs and sinews are here given
to a creature! What to do with? to be quiet and dandle a kid. I
own that to me this province, the employment assigned to the

lion, seems to be as proper and well chosen as if you would make a nurse of Alexander the Great.

Cleo. You might make as many flights upon a lion now if you saw him asleep. Nobody would think that a bull had occasion for horns, who had never seen him otherwise than quietly grazing among a parcel of cows; but if one should see him attacked by dogs, by a wolf, or a rival of his own species, he would soon find out that his horns were of great use and service to him. The lion was not made to be always in Paradise.

Hor. There I would have you. If the lion was contrived for purposes to be served and executed out of Paradise, then it is manifest from the very creation that the fall of man was determined and predestinated.

Cleo. Foreknown it was: nothing could be hid from Omniscience; that is certain. But that it was predestinated so as to have prejudiced or anywise influenced the free will of Adam, I utterly deny. But that word *predestinated* has made so much noise in the world, and the thing itself has been the cause of so many fatal quarrels, and is so inexplicable, that I am resolved never to engage in any dispute concerning it.

Hor. I cannot make you; but what you have extolled so much must have cost the lives of thousands of our species; and it is a wonder to me how men, when they were but few, could possibly defend themselves before they had firearms, or at least bows and arrows; for what number of naked men and women would be a match for one couple of lions?

Cleo. Yet here we are; and none of those animals are suffered to be wild in any civilized nation; our superior understanding has got the start of them.

Hor. My reason tells me it must be that; but I cannot help observing that when human understanding serves your purpose to solve anything, it is always ready and full grown; but at other times, knowledge and reasoning are the work of time, and men are not capable of thinking justly until after many generations. Pray, before men had arms, what could their understanding do against lions, and what hindered wild beasts from devouring mankind as soon as they were born?

Cleo. Providence.

Hor. Daniel, indeed, was saved by miracle; but what is that to the rest of mankind? Great numbers, we know, have at different times been torn to pieces by savage beasts; what I want to know is the reason that any of them escaped and the whole species was not destroyed by them, when men had yet no weapons to defend nor strongholds to shelter themselves from the fury of those merciless creatures.

Cleo. I have named it to you already, Providence.

Hor. But which way can you prove this miraculous assistance?

Cleo. You still talk of miracles, and I speak of Providence or the all-governing Wisdom of God.

Hor. If you can, demonstrate to me how that Wisdom interposed between our species and that of lions in the beginning of the world without miracle any more than it does at present, *eris mihi magnus Apollo;** for now, I am sure, a wild lion would prey upon a naked man as soon, at least, as he would upon an ox or an horse.

Cleo. Will not you allow me that all properties, instincts, and what we call the nature of things, animate or inanimate, are the produce, the effects of that Wisdom?

Hor. I never thought otherwise.

Cleo. Then it will not be difficult to prove this to you. Lions are never brought forth wild, but in very hot countries, as bears are the product of the cold. But the generality of our species, which loves moderate warmth, are most delighted with the middle regions. Men may against their wills be inured to intense cold or by use and patience accustom themselves to excessive heat; but a mild air and weather between both extremes being more agreeable to human bodies, the greatest part of mankind would naturally settle in temperate climate and with the same conveniency as to everything else never choose any other. This would very much lessen the danger men would be in from the fiercest and most irresistible wild beasts.

Hor. But would lions and tigers in hot countries keep so close within their bounds, and bears in cold ones, as never to straggle or stray beyond them?

Cleo. I do not suppose they would; and men as well as cattle have often been picked up by lions far from the places where they

---

*Virgil, *Eclogues,* iii, 104: you shall be my great Appollo [*i.e.,* my oracle].

were whelped. No wild beasts are more fatal to our species than often we are to one another; and men pursued by their enemies have fled into climates and countries which they would never have chose. Avarice, likewise, and curiosity have, without force or necessity, often exposed men to dangers which they might have avoided if they had been satisfied with what nature required, and laboured for self-preservation in that simple manner which creatures less vain and fantastical content themselves with. In all these cases I do not question but multitudes of our species have suffered from savage beasts and other noxious animals; and on their account only, I verily believe, it would have been impossible for any number of men to have settled or subsisted in either very hot or very cold countries before the invention of bows and arrows, or better arms. But all this does nothing to overthrow my assertion: what I wanted to prove is that all creatures choosing by instinct that degree of heat or cold which is most natural to them, there would be room enough in the world for man to multiply his species for many ages without running almost any risk of being devoured either by lions or by bears; and that the most savage man would find this out without the help of his reason. This I call the work of Providence; by which I mean the unalterable wisdom of the Supreme Being in the harmonious disposition of the universe; the fountain of that incomprehensible chain of causes on which all events have their undoubted dependance.

Hor. You have made this out better than I had expected; but I am afraid that what you alleged as the first motive towards society is come to nothing by it.

Cleo. Do not fear that; there are other savage beasts against which men could not guard themselves unarmed without joining and mutual assistance; in temperate climates most uncultivated countries abound with wolves.

Hor. I have seen them in Germany; they are of the size of a large mastiff; but I thought their chief prey had been sheep.

Cleo. Anything they can conquer is their prey; they are desperate creatures and will fall upon men, cows, and horses, as well as upon sheep, when they are very hungry; they have teeth like mastiffs; but besides them they have sharp claws to tear with, which dogs have not. The stoutest man is hardly equal to them in strength; but what is worse, they often come in troops, and whole villages have been attacked by them; they have five, six, and more whelps at a litter and would soon over-run a country where they breed, if men did not combine against and make it their business to destroy them. Wild boars likewise are terrible creatures that few large forests and uninhabited places in temperate climates are free from.

Hor. Those tusks of theirs are dreadful weapons.

Cleo. And they are much superior to wolves in bulk and strength. History is full of the mischief they have done in ancient times and of the renown that valiant men have gained by conquering them.

Hor. That is true; but those heroes that fought monsters in former days were well armed, at least the generality of them; but what could a number of naked men, before they had any arms at all, have to oppose to the teeth and claws of ravenous wolves that came in troops; and what impression could the greatest blow a man can strike make upon the thick bristly hide of a wild boar?

Cleo. As on the one hand I have named everything that man has to fear from wild beasts, so on the other, we ought not to forget the things that are in his favour. In the first place, a wild man inured to hardship would far exceed a tame one in all feats of strength, nimbleness and activity; in the second, his anger would sooner and more usefully transport and assist him in his savage state than it can do in society, where from his infancy, he is so many ways taught and forced in his own defence to cramp and stifle with his fears the noble gift of nature. In wild creatures we see that most of them, when their own life or that of their young ones is at stake, fight with great obstinacy and continue fighting to the last and do what mischief they can whilst they have breath, without regard to their being overmatched or the disadvantages they labour under. It is observed, likewise, that the more untaught and inconsiderate creatures are, the more entirely they are swayed by the passion that is uppermost; natural affection would make wild men and women, too, sacrifice their lives and die for their children; but they would die fighting; and one wolf would not find it an easy matter to carry off a child from his watchful parents if they were both resolute, though they were naked. As to man's being born defenceless, it is not to be conceived that he should long know the strength of his arms without being acquainted with the articulation of his fingers or, at least, what is owing to it, his faculty of grasping and holding fast; and the most untaught savage would make use of clubs and staves before he came to maturity. As the danger men are in from wild beasts would be of the highest consequence, so it would employ their utmost care and industry; they would dig holes and invent other stratagems to distress their enemies and destroy their young ones; as soon as they found out fire, they would make use of that element to guard themselves and annoy their foes; by the help of it they would soon learn to sharpen wood, which presently would put them upon making spears and other weapons that would cut. When men are angry enough with creatures to strike them, and these are running away or flying from them, they are apt to throw at what they cannot reach; this, as soon as they had spears, would naturally lead them to the invention of darts and javelins. Here, perhaps, they may stop a while; but the same chain of thinking would, in time, produce bows and arrows: the elasticity of sticks and boughs of trees is very obvious; and to make strings of the guts of animals, I dare say, is more ancient than the use of hemp. Experience teaches us that men may have all these and many more weapons and be very expert in the use of them before any manner of government, except that of parents over their children, is to be seen among them; it is likewise very well known that savages furnished with no better arms, when they are strong enough in number, will venture to attack and even hunt after the fiercest wild beasts, lions and tigers not excepted. Another thing is to be considered that likewise favours our species and relates to the nature of the creatures of which in temperate climates man has reason to stand in bodily fear of.

Hor. Wolves and wild boars?

Cleo. Yes. That great numbers of our species have been devoured by the first is uncontested; but they most naturally go in quest of sheep and poultry, and as long as they can get carrion or anything to fill their bellies with, they seldom hunt after men or other large animals; which is the reason that in the summer our species, as to personal insults, have not much to fear from them. It is certain likewise that savage swine will hunt after men, and many of their maws have been crammed with human flesh; but they naturally feed on acorns, chestnuts, beech-mast, and other vegetables; and they are only carnivorous upon occasion and through necessity, when they can get nothing else; in great frosts, when the country is bare and everything covered with snow. It is evident, then, that human creatures are not in any great and immediate danger from either of these species of beasts but in hard winters, which happen but seldom in temperate climates. But as they are our perpetual enemies by spoiling and devouring everything that may serve for the sustenance of man, it is highly necessary that we should not only be always upon our guard against them, but likewise never cease to assist one another in routing and destroying them.

Hor. I plainly see that mankind might subsist and survive to multiply and get the mastery over all other creatures that should oppose them, and as this could never have been brought about unless men had assisted one another against savage beasts, it is possible that the necessity men were in of joining and uniting together was the first step toward society. Thus far I am willing to allow you to have proved your main point; but to ascribe all this to Providence, otherwise than that nothing is done without the Divine permission, seems inconsistent with the ideas we have of a perfectly good and merciful Being. It is possible that all poisonous animals may have something in them that is beneficial to men; and I will not dispute with you whether the most venomous of all the serpents which Lucan has made mention of* did not contain some antidote or other fine medicine still undiscovered; but when I look upon the vast variety of ravenous and blood-thirsty creatures that are not only superior to us in strength but likewise visibly armed by nature, as it were on purpose for our destruction; when, I say, I look upon these, I can find out no use for them nor what they could be designed for, unless it be to punish us: but I can much less conceive that the Divine Wisdom should have made them the means without which men could not have been civilized. How many thousands of our species must have been devoured in the conflicts with them!

Cleo. Ten troops of wolves with fifty in each would make a terrible havoc in a long winter among a million of our species with their hands tied behind them; but among half that number, one

---

*in *Pharsalia,* VI, 677 ff. and IX, 700-838.

pestilence has been known to slaughter more than so many wolves could have eaten in the same time, notwithstanding the great resistance that was made against it by approved of medicines and able physicians. It is owing to the principle of pride we are born with, and the high value we all, for the sake of one, have for our species, that men imagine the whole universe to be principally made for their use; and this error makes them commit a thousand extravagancies and have pitiful and most unworthy notions of God and his works. It is not greater cruelty or more unnatural in a wolf to eat a piece of man than it is in a man to eat part of a lamb or a chicken. What or how many purposes wild beasts were made for is not for us to determine; but that they were made we know; and that some of them must have been very calamitous to every infant nation and settlement of men is almost as certain; this you was fully persuaded of, and thought, moreover, that they must have been such an obstacle to the very subsistence of our species as was insurmountable. In answer to this difficulty which you started, I showed you from the different instincts and peculiar tendencies of animals that in nature a manifest provision was made for our species, by which, notwithstanding the rage and power of the fiercest beasts, we should make a shift, naked and defenceless, to escape their fury so as to be able to maintain ourselves and multiply our kind till by our numbers and arms acquired by our own industry, we could put to flight or destroy all savage beasts without exception, whatever spot of the globe we might have a mind to cultivate and settle on. The necessary blessings we receive from the sun are obvious to a child; and it is demonstrable that without it none of the living creatures that are now upon the earth could subsist. But if it were of no other use, being eight hundred thousand times bigger than the earth at least, one thousandth part of it would do our business as well, if it was but nearer to us in proportion. From this consideration alone I am persuaded that the sun was made to enlighten and cherish other bodies besides this planet of ours. Fire and water were designed for innumerable purposes; and among the uses that are made of them some are immensely different from others. But whilst we receive the benefit of these and are only intent on ourselves, it is highly probable that there are thousands of things, and perhaps our own machines among them, that in the vast system of the universe are now serving some very wise ends, which we shall never know. According to that plan of this globe, I mean the scheme of government in relation to the living creatures that inhabit the earth, the destruction of animals is as necessary as the generation of them.

Hor. I have learned that from the Fable of the Bees, and I believe what I have read there to be very true, that if any one species was to be exempt from death, it would in time crush all the rest to pieces, though the first were sheep and the latter all lions; but that the Supreme Being should have introduced society at the expense of so many lives of our species, I cannot believe, when it might have been done much better in a milder way.

Cleo. We are speaking of what probably was done and not of what might have been done. There is no question but the same Power that made whales might have made us seventy feet high and given us strength in proportion. But since the plan of this globe requires, and you think it necessary yourself, that in every species some should die almost as fast as others are born, why should you take away any of the means of dying?

Hor. Are there not diseases enough, physicians and apothecaries, as well as wars by sea and land that may take off more than the redundancy of our species?

Cleo. They may, it is true; but in fact they are not always sufficient to do this; and in populous nations we see that war, wild beasts, hanging, drowning, and an hundred casualties together, with sickness and all its attendants, are hardly a match for one invisible faculty of ours, which is the instinct men have to preserve their species. Everything is easy to the Deity; but to speak after an human manner, it is evident that in forming this earth and everything that is in it, no less wisdom or solicitude was required in contriving the various ways and means to get rid and destroy animals than seems to have been employed in producing them; and it is as demonstrable that our bodies were made on purpose not to last beyond such a period as it is that some houses are built with a design not to stand longer than such a term of years. But it is death itself to which our aversion by nature is universal; as to the manner of dying, men differ in their opinions; and I never heard of one yet that was generally liked of.

Hor. But nobody chooses a cruel one. What an unspeakable and infinitely excruciating torment must it be to be torn to pieces and eat* alive by a savage beast!

Cleo. Not greater, I can assure you, than are daily occasioned by the gout in the stomach and the stone in the bladder.

Hor. Which way can you give me this assurance; how can you prove it?

Cleo. From our fabric itself, the frame of human bodies, that cannot admit of any torment infinitely excruciating. The degrees of pain as well as of pleasure in this life are limited and exactly proportioned to everyone's strength; whatever exceeds that takes away the senses; and whoever has once fainted away with the extremity of any torture knows the full extent of what here he can suffer if he remembers what he felt. The real mischief which wild beasts have done to our species and the calamities they have brought upon it are not to be compared to the cruel usage and the multiplicity of mortal injuries which men have received from one another. Set before your eyes a robust warrior that, having lost a limb in battle, is afterwards trampled upon by twenty horses; and tell me, pray, whether you think that lying thus helpless with most of his ribs broke and a fractured skull, in the agony of death for several hours, he suffers less than if a lion has dispatched him?

Hor. They are both very bad.

Cleo. In the choice of things we are more often directed by the caprice of fashions and the custom of the age than we are by solid reason or our own understanding. There is no greater comfort in dying of a dropsy and in being eaten by worms than there is in being drowned at sea and becoming the prey of fishes. But in our narrow way of thinking, there is something that subverts and corrupts our judgment; how else could persons of known elegancy in their taste prefer rotting and stinking in a loathsome sepulchre to their being burnt in the open air to inoffensive ashes?

Hor. I freely own that I have an aversion to everything that is shocking and unnatural.

Cleo. What you call shocking I do not know; but nothing is more common to nature or more agreeable to her ordinary course than that creatures should live upon one another. The whole system of animated beings on the earth seems to be built upon this; and

---

eaten; pronounced *et.*

there is not one species that we know of that has not another that feeds upon it, either alive or dead; and most kind of fish are forced to live upon fish. That this in the last mentioned was not an omission or neglect is evident from the large provisions nature has made for it, far exceeding anything she has done for other animals.

Hor. You mean the prodigious quantity of roe they spawn.

Cleo. Yes, and that the eggs contained in them receive not their fecundity until they are excluded; by which means the female may be filled with as many of them as her belly can hold, and the eggs themselves may be more closely crowded together than would be consistent with the admission of any substance from the male; without this, one fish could not bring forth yearly such a prodigious shoal.

Hor. But might not the *aura seminalis* of the male be subtle enough to penetrate the whole cluster of eggs and influence every one of them without taking up any room, as it does in fowls and other oviparous animals?

Cleo. The ostrich excepted in the first place; in the second there are no other oviparous animals in which the eggs are so closely compacted together as they are in fish. But suppose the prolific power should pervade the whole mass of them; if all the eggs which some of the females are crammed with were to be impregnated whilst they are within the fish, it is impossible but the *aura seminalis,* the prolific spirit of the male, though it took up no room itself, would, as it does in all other creatures, dilate and more or less distend every egg; and the least expansion of so many individuals would swell the whole roe to a bulk that would require a much greater space than the cavity that now contains them. Is not here a contrivance beyond imagination fine, to provide for the continuance of a species, though every individual of it should be born with an instinct to destroy it!

Hor. What you speak of is only true at sea in a considerable part of Europe at least; for in fresh water most kinds of fish do not feed on their own species, and yet they spawn in the same manner and are as full of roe as all the rest; among them the only great destroyer with us is the pike.

Cleo. And he is a very ravenous one. We see in ponds that, where pikes are suffered to be, no other fish shall ever increase in number. But in rivers and all waters near any land, there are amphibious fowls and many sorts of them that live mostly upon fish. Of these water-fowls in many places are prodigious quantities. Besides these there are otters, beavers, and many other creatures that live upon fish. In brooks and shallow waters, the hearn [heron] and bittern will have their share. What is taken off by them perhaps is but little; but the young fry and the spawn that one pair of swans are able to consume in one year would very well serve to stock a considerable river. So they are but eat, it is no matter what eats them, either their own species or another. What I would prove is that nature produces no extraordinary numbers of any species but she has contrived means answerable to destroy them. The variety of insects in the several parts of the world would be incredible to anyone that has not examined into this matter; and the different beauties to be observed in them is infinite. But neither the beauty nor the variety of them are more surprising than the industry of nature in the multiplicity of her contrivances to kill them; and if the care and vigilance of all other animals in destroying them were to cease at once, in two years time the greatest part of the earth which is ours now would be theirs, and in many countries insects would be the only inhabitants.

Hor. I have heard that whales live upon nothing else; that must make a fine consumption.

Cleo. That is the general opinion, I suppose, because they never find any fish in them and because there are vast multitudes of insects in those seas hovering on the surface of the water. This creature likewise helps to corroborate my assertion that in the numbers produced of every species, the greatest regard is had to the consumption of them. This prodigious animal being too big to be swallowed, nature in it has quite altered the economy observed in all other fish; for they are viviparous, engender like other viviparous animals, and have never above two or three young ones at a time. For the continuance of every species among such an infinite variety of creatures as this globe yields, it was highly necessary that the provision for their destruction should not be less ample than that which was made for the generation of them; and therefore the solicitude of nature in procuring death and the consumption of animals is visibly superior to the care she takes to feed and preserve them.

Hor. Prove that, pray.

Cleo. Millions of her creatures are starved every year and doomed to perish for want of sustenance; but whenever any die, there is always plenty of mouths to devour them. But then again she gives all she has; nothing is so fine or elaborate as that she grudges it for food; nor is anything more extensive or impartial than her bounty; she thinks nothing too good for the meanest of her broods, and all creatures are equally welcome to everything they can find to eat. How curious is the workmanship in the structure of a common fly; how inimitable are the celerity of his wings and the quickness of all his motions in hot weather! Should a Pythagorean, that was likewise a good master in mechanics, by the help of a microscope pry into every minute part of this changeable creature and duly consider the elegancy of its machinery, would he not think it great pity that thousands of millions of animated beings, so nicely wrought and admirably finished, should every day be devoured by little birds and spiders, of which we stand in so little need? Nay, do not you think yourself that things would have been managed full as well if the quantity of flies had been less and there had been no spiders at all?

Hor. I remember the fable of the Acorn and the Pumpkin* too well to answer you; I do not trouble my head about it.

Cleo. Yet you found fault with the means which I supposed Providence had made use of to make men associate, I mean the common danger they were in from wild beasts, though you owned the probability of its having been the first motive of their uniting.

Hor. I cannot believe that Providence should have no greater regard to our species than it has to flies and the spawn of fish, or that nature has ever sported with the fate of human creatures as she does with the lives of insects, and been as wantonly lavish of the first as she seems to be of the latter. I wonder how you can reconcile this to religion, you that are such a stickler for Christianity.

---

*A fable by Mandeville, derived from *Le Gland et la Citrouille* by La Fontaine: a man who questions the wisdom of nature in allowing large pumpkins to grow on small creeping vines, while tiny acorns are supported by huge oaks, receives his answer when, sitting beneath an oak, he is struck by a falling acorn. He observes that nature knew what she was doing when she refused to hang pumpkins on an oak, *i.e.,* "Whatever is, is Right."

Cleo. Religion has nothing to do with it. But we are so full of our own species and the excellency of it that we have no leisure seriously to consider the system of this earth, I mean the plan on which the economy of it is built in relation to the living creatures that are in and upon it.

Hor. I do not speak as to our species but in respect to the Deity; has religion nothing to do with it that you make God the author of so much cruelty and malice?

Cleo. It is impossible you should speak otherwise than in relation to our species when you make use of those expressions which can only signify to us the intentions things were done with or the sentiments human creatures have of them; and nothing can be called cruel or malicious in regard to him who did it unless his thoughts and designs were such in doing it. All actions in nature, abstractly considered, are equally indifferent; and whatever it may be to individual creatures, to die is not a greater evil to this earth or the whole universe than it is to be born.

Hor. This is making the First Cause of things not an intelligent being.

Cleo. Why so? Can you not conceive an intelligent and even a most wise being that is not only exempt from but likewise incapable of entertaining any malice or cruelty?

Hor. Such a being could not commit or order things that are malicious and cruel.

Cleo. Neither does God. But this will carry us into a dispute about the origin of evil; and from thence we must inevitably fall on free-will and predestination, which, as I have told you before, is an inexplicable mystery I will never meddle with. But I never said nor thought anything irreverent to the Deity; on the contrary, the idea I have of the Supreme Being is as transcendently great as my capacity is able to form one of what is incomprehensible; and I could as soon believe that he could cease to exist as that he should be the author of any real evil. But I should be glad to hear the method after which you think society might have been much better introduced. Pray, acquaint me with that milder way you spoke of.

Hor. You have thoroughly convinced me that the natural love which it is pretended we have for our species is not greater than what many other animals have for theirs; but if nature had actually given us an affection for one another as sincere and conspicuous as that which parents are seen to have for their children whilst they are helpless, men would have joined together by choice; and nothing could have hindered them from associating, whether their numbers had been great or small and themselves either ignorant or knowing.

Cleo. O mentes hominum cæcas! O Pectora cæca!*

Hor. You may exclaim as much as you please; I am persuaded that this would have united men in firmer bonds of friendship than any common danger from wild beasts could have tied them with; but what fault can you find with it, and what mischief could have befallen us from mutual affection?

Cleo. It would have been inconsistent with the scheme, the plan after which, it is evident, Providence has been pleased to order and dispose of things in the universe. If such an affection had been planted in man by instinct, there never could have been any fatal quarrels among them nor mortal hatreds; men could never have been cruel to one another; in short, there could have been no wars of any duration, and no considerable numbers of our species could ever have been killed by one another's malice.

Hor. You would make a rare state physician, in prescribing war, cruelty and malice for the welfare and maintenance of civil society.

Cleo. Pray, do not misrepresent me. I have done no such thing; but if you believe the world is governed by Providence at all, you must believe likewise that the Deity makes use of means to bring about, perform, and execute his will and pleasure. As for example, to have war kindled there must be first misunderstandings and quarrels between the subjects of different nations and dissensions among the respective princes, rulers, or governors of them; it is evident that the mind of man is the general mint where the means of this sort must be coined; from whence I conclude that if Providence had ordered matters after that mild way which you think would have been the best, very little of human blood could have been spilt, if any at all.

Hor. Where would have been the inconveniency of that?

---

*Lucretius, *De Rerum Natura*, II, 14.: O blind minds of men! O blind hearts!

Cleo. You could not have had that variety of living creatures there is now; nay, there would not have been room for man himself and his sustenance; our species alone would have overstocked the earth if there had been no wars and the common course of Providence had not been more interrupted than it has been. Might I not justly say then that this is quite contrary and destructive to the scheme on which it is plain this earth was built? This is a consideration which you will never give its due weight. I have once already put you in mind of it that you yourself have allowed the destruction of animals to be as necessary as the generation of them. There is as much wisdom to be seen in the contrivances how numbers of living creatures might always be taken off and destroyed to make room for those that continually succeed them as there is in making all the different sorts of them, every one, preserve their own species. What do you think is the reason that there is but one way for us to come into the world?

Hor. Because that one is sufficient.

Cleo. Then from a parity of reason we ought to think that there are several ways to go out of the world, because one would not have been sufficient. Now, if for the support and maintenance of that variety of creatures which are here, that they should die is a *postulatum* as necessary as it is that they should be born; and you cut off or obstruct the means of dying and actually stop up one of the great gates through which we see multitudes go to death; do you not oppose the scheme? nay, do you mar it less than if you hindered generation? If there never had been war, and no other means of dying besides the ordinary ones, this globe could not have borne, or at least not maintained, the tenth part of the people that would have been in it. By war, I do not mean only such as one nation has had against another, but civil as well as foreign quarrels, general massacres, private murders, poison, sword, and all hostile force by which men, notwithstanding their pretence of love to their species, have endeavoured to take away one another's lives throughout the world from the time that Cain slew Abel to this day.

Hor. I do not believe that a quarter of all these mischiefs are upon record; but what may be known from history would make a prodigious number of men, much greater, I dare say, than ever was on earth at one time. But what would you infer from this?

They would not have been immortal; and if they had not died in war, they must soon after have been slain by diseases. When a man of threescore is killed by a bullet in the field, it is odds that he would not have lived four years longer, though he had stayed at home.

Cleo. There are soldiers of threescore perhaps in all armies, but men generally go to the war when they are young; and when four or five thousand are lost in battle, you will find the greatest number to have been under five-and-thirty; consider now, that many men do not marry till after that age who get ten or a dozen children.

Hor. If all that die by the hands of another were to get a dozen children before they die—

Cleo. There is no occasion for that; I suppose nothing that is either extravagant or improbable, but that all such as have been wilfully destroyed by means of their species should have lived and taken their chance with the rest; that everything should have befallen them that has befallen those that have not been killed that way; and the same likewise to their posterity; and that all of them should have been subject to all the casualties as well as diseases, doctors, apothecaries, and other accidents that take away man's life and shorten his days, war and violence from one another only excepted.

Hor. But if the earth had been too full of inhabitants, might not Providence have sent pestilences and diseases oftener? More children might have died when they were young, or more women might have proved barren.

Cleo. I do not know whether your mild way would have been more generally pleasing, but you entertain notions of the Deity that are unworthy of him. Men might certainly have been born with the instinct you speak of, but if this had been the Creator's pleasure, there must have been another economy, and things on earth from the beginning would have been ordered in a manner quite different from what they are now. But to make a scheme first and afterwards to mend it when it proves defective is the business of finite wisdom; it belongs to human prudence alone to mend faults, to correct and redress what was done amiss before, and to alter the measures which experience teaches men were ill concerted; but the knowledge of God was consummate from eternity. Infinite Wisdom is not liable to errors or mistakes; therefore all his works are universally good, and everything is made exactly as he would have it; the firmness and stability of his laws and councils are everlasting, and therefore his resolutions are as unalterable as his decrees are eternal. It is not a quarter of an hour ago that you named wars among the necessary means to carry off the redundancy of our species; how come you now to think them useless? I can demonstrate to you that nature in the production of our species has amply provided against the losses of our sex occasioned by wars by repairing them visibly, where they are sustained, in as palpable a manner as she has provided for the great destruction that is made of fish by their devouring one another.

Hor. How is that, pray?

Cleo. By sending more males into the world than females. You will easily allow me that our sex bears the brunt of all the toils and hazards that are undergone by sea and land; and that by this means a far greater number of men must be destroyed than there is of women; now if we see, as certainly we do, that of the infants yearly born, the number of males is always considerably superior to that of the females, is it not manifest that nature has made a provision for great multitudes, which, if they were not destroyed, would be not only superfluous but of pernicious consequence in great nations?

Hor. That superiority in the number of males born is wonderful indeed; I remember the account that has been published concerning it as it was taken from the bills of births and burials in the city and suburbs.

Cleo. For fourscore years; in which the number of females born was constantly much inferior to that of the males, sometimes by many hundreds; and that this provision of nature to supply the havoc that is made of men by wars and navigation is still greater than could be imagined from that difference only, will soon appear, if we consider that women, in the first place, are liable to all diseases within a trifle that are incident to men; and that, in the second, they are subject to many disorders and calamities on account of their sex, which great numbers die of and which men are wholly exempt from.

Hor. This could not well be the effect of chance; but it spoils the consequence which you drew from my affectionate scheme in case there had been no wars; for your fear that our species would have increased beyond all bounds was entirely built upon the supposition that those who have died in war should not have wanted women if they had lived; which, from this superiority in the number of males, it is evident, they should and must have wanted.

Cleo. What you observe is true; but my chief aim was to show you how disagreeable the alteration you required would have been every way to the rest of the scheme, by which it is manifest things are governed at present. For if the provision had been made on the other side, and nature, in the production of our species, had continually taken care to repair the loss of women that die of calamities not incident to men, then certainly there would have been women for all the men that have been destroyed by their own species, if they had lived; and the earth without war, as I have said, would have been over-stocked; or, if nature had ever been the same as she is now, that is, if more males had been born than females and more females had died of diseases than males, the world would constantly have had a great superfluity of men if there never had been any wars; and this disproportion between their number and that of the women would have caused innumerable mischiefs that are now prevented by no other natural causes than the small value men set upon their species and their dissensions with one another.

Hor. I can see no other mischief this would produce than that the number of males which die without ever having tried matrimony would be greater than it is now; and whether that would be a real evil or not is a very disputable point.

Cleo. Do not you think that this perpetual scarcity of women and superfluity of men would make great uneasiness in all societies, how well soever people might love one another; and that the value, the price, of women would be so enhanced by it that none but men in tolerable good circumstances would be able to purchase them? This alone would make us another world; and mankind could never have known that most necessary and now inexhaustible spring from which all nations where slaves are not allowed of are constantly supplied with willing hands for all the drudgery of hard and dirty labour; I mean the children of the poor, the greatest and most extensive of all temporal blessings that accrue from society, on which all the comforts of life in the civilized state have their unavoidable dependence. There are many other things from which it is plain that such a real love of man for his species would have been altogether inconsistent with the present scheme; the world must have been destitute of all that industry that is owing to envy and emulation; no society could have been easy with being a flourishing people at the expence of their neighbours or enduring to be counted a formidable nation. All men would have been levellers*; government would have been unnecessary; and there could have been no great bustle in the world. Look into the men of greatest renown and the most celebrated achievements of antiquity, and everything that has been cried up and admired in past ages by the fashionable part of mankind; if the same labours were to be performed over again, which qualification, which help of nature do you think would be the most proper means to have them executed: that instinct of real affection you required without ambition or the love of glory, or a staunch principle of pride and selfishness, acting under pretence to, and assuming the resemblance of, that affection? Consider, I beseech you, that no men governed by this instinct would require services of any of their species which they would not be ready to perform for others; and you will easily see that its being universal would quite alter the scene of society from what it is now. Such an instinct might be very suitable to another scheme different from this, in another world; where, instead of fickleness and a restless desire after changes and novelty, there was observed an universal steadiness, continually preserved by a serene spirit of contentment among other creatures of different appetites from ours, that had frugality without avarice and generosity without pride; and whose solicitude after happiness in a future state was as active and apparent in life as our pursuits are after the enjoyments of this present. But as to the world we live in, examine into the various ways of earthly greatness and all the engines that are made use of to attain to the felicity of carnal men, and you will find that the instinct you speak of must have destroyed the principles, and prevented the very existence, of that pomp and glory to which human societies have been, and are still, raised by worldly wisdom.

---

*levellers—extreme egalitarians.

Hor. I give up my affectionate scheme; you have convinced me that there could not have been that stir and variety, nor, upon the whole, that beauty, in the world, which there have been if all men had been naturally humble, good, and virtuous. I believe that wars of all sorts, as well as diseases, are natural means to hinder mankind from increasing too fast; but that wild beasts should likewise have been designed to thin our species I cannot conceive; for they can only serve this end when men are but few and their numbers should be increased instead of lessened; and afterwards, if they were made for that purpose, when men are strong enough, they would not answer it.

Cleo. I never said that wild beasts was designed to thin out species. I have showed that many things were made to serve a variety of different purposes; that in the scheme of this earth many things must have been considered that man has nothing to do with; and that it is ridiculous to think that the universe was made for our sake. I have said likewise that as all our knowledge comes *a posteriori* it is imprudent to reason otherwise than from facts. That there are wild beasts and that there are savage men is certain; and that where there are but few of the latter, the first must always be very troublesome and often fatal to them is as certain; and when I reflect on the passions all men are born with and their incapacity whilst they are untaught, I can find no cause or motive which is so likely to unite them together and make them espouse the same interest, as that common danger they must always be in from wild beasts in uncultivated countries, whilst they live in small families that all shift for themselves without government or dependance upon one another. This first step to society I believe to be an effect which that same cause, the common danger so often mentioned, will never fail to produce upon our species in such circumstances; what other and how many purposes wild beasts might have been designed for besides, I do not pretend to determine, as I have told you before.

Hor. But whatever other purposes wild beasts were designed for, it still follows from your opinion that the uniting of savages in common defence must have been one; which to me seems clashing with our idea of the Divine Goodness.

Cleo. So will everything seem to do which we call natural evil, if you ascribe human passions to the Deity and measure Infinite

Wisdom by the standard of our most shallow capacity; you have been at this twice already; I thought I had answered it. I would not make God the author of evil any more than yourself; but I am likewise persuaded that nothing could come by chance in respect to the Supreme Being; and, therefore, unless you imagine the world not to be governed by Providence, you must believe that wars and all the calamities we can suffer from man or beast, as well as plagues and all other diseases, are under a wise direction that is unfathomable. As there can be no effect without a cause, so nothing can be said to happen by chance, but in respect to him who is ignorant of the cause of it. I can make this evident to you in an obvious and familiar example. To a man who knows nothing of the tennis-court, the skips and rebounds of the ball seem to be all fortuitous, as he is not able to guess at the several different directions it will receive before it comes to the ground; so, as soon as it has hit the place to which it was plainly directed at first, it is chance to him where it will fall; whereas, the experienced player, knowing perfectly well the journey the ball will make, goes directly to the place if he is not there already, where it will certainly come within his reach. Nothing seems to be more the effect of chance than a cast of the dice; yet they obey the laws of gravity and motion in general as much as anything else; and from the impressions that are given them, it is impossible they should fall otherwise than they do; but the various directions which they shall receive in the whole course of the throw being entirely unknown and the rapidity with which they change their situation being such that our slow apprehension cannot trace them, what the cast will be is a mystery to human understanding at fair play. But if the same variety of directions was given to two cubes of ten feet each, which a pair of dice receive, as well from one another as the box, the caster's fingers that cover it, and the table they are flung upon, from the time they are taken up until they lie still, the same effect would follow; and if the quantity of motion, the force that is imparted to the box and dice was exactly known, and the motion itself was so much retarded in the performance that what is done in three or four seconds should take up an hour's time, it would be easy to find out the reason of every throw, and men might learn with certainty to foretell which side of the cube would be uppermost. It is evident, then, that the words fortuitous and casual have no other meaning than what depends upon our want of knowledge, foresight, and penetration; the reflection on which will show us by what an infinity of degrees all human capacity falls short of that universal *intuitus* with which the Supreme Being beholds at once everything without exception, whether to us it be visible or invisible, past, present, or to come.

Hor. I yield; you have solved every difficulty I have been able to raise; and I must confess that your supposition concerning the first motive that would make savages associate is neither clashing with good sense nor any idea we ought to have of the Divine attributes; but, on the contrary, in answering my objections, you have demonstrated the probability of your conjecture and rendered the wisdom and power of providence in the scheme of this earth, both as to the contrivance and the execution of it, more conspicuous and palpable to me than anything I ever heard or read had done before.

Cleo. I am glad you are satisfied, though far from arrogating to myself so much merit as your civility would compliment me with.

Hor. It is very clear to me now that, as it is appointed for all men to die, so it is necessary there should be means to compass this end; that from the number of those means, or causes of death, it is impossible to exclude either the malice of men, or the rage of wild beasts and all noxious animals; and that if they had been actually designed by nature and contrived for that purpose, we should have no more reason justly to complain of them than we have to find fault with death itself or that frightful train of diseases which are daily and hourly the manifest occasion of it.

Cleo. They are all equally included in the curse which after the fall was deservedly pronounced against the whole earth; and if they be real evils, they are to be looked upon as the consequence of sin and a condign punishment which the transgression of our first parents has drawn and entailed upon all their posterity. I am fully persuaded that all the nations in the world and every individual of our species, civilized or savage, had their origin from Seth, Cham, or Japhet*; and as experience has taught us that the greatest

---

Seth—apparently a mistake for *Shem; Cham*—*Ham*, as spelled in the Vulgate (*"Sem, Cham et Iapheth"*).

empires have their periods, and the best governed states and king-doms may come to ruin, so it is certain that the politest people being scattered and distressed may soon degenerate, and some of them by accidents and misfortunes, from knowing and well-taught ancestors, be reduced at last to savages of the first and lowest class.

Hor. If what you are fully persuaded of be true, the other is self-evident from the savages that are still subsisting.

Cleo. You once seemed to insinuate that all the danger men were in from wild beasts would entirely cease as soon as they were civilized and lived in large and well-ordered societies, but by this you may see that our species will never be wholly exempt from that danger, because mankind will always be liable to be reduced to savages; for, as this calamity has actually befallen vast multi-tudes that were the undoubted descendants of Noah, so the greatest prince upon earth that has children cannot be sure that the same disaster will never happen to any of his posterity. Wild beasts may be entirely extirpated in some countries that are duly cultivated, but they will multiply in others that are wholly neglected; and great numbers of them range now and are masters in many places where they had been rooted and kept out before. I shall always believe that every species of living creatures in and upon this globe, without exception, continues to be, as it was at first, under the care of that same Providence that thought fit to produce it. You have had a great deal of patience, but I would not tire it. This first step towards society, now we have mastered it, is a good resting place, and so we will leave off for today.

Hor. With all my heart. I have made you talk a great deal, but I long to hear the rest as soon as you are at leisure.

Cleo. I am obliged to dine at Windsor tomorrow. If you are not otherwise engaged, I can carry you where the honour of your company will be highly esteemed. My coach shall be ready at nine; you know you are in my way.

Hor. A fine opportunity, indeed, of three or four hours chat.

Cleo. I shall be all alone without you.

Hor. I am your man, and shall expect you.

Cleo. Adieu.

* * * *

DIALOGUE

BETWEEN

HORATIO AND CLEOMENES

HORATIO

NOW WE ARE OFF the stones, pray let us lose no time; I expect a great deal of pleasure from what I am to hear further.

Cleo. The second step to society is the danger men are in from one another: for which we are beholden to that staunch principle of pride and ambition that all men are born with. Different families may endeavour to live together and be ready to join in common danger, but they are all of little use to one another when there is no common enemy to oppose. If we consider that strength, agility, and courage would in such a state be the most valuable qualifications, and that many families could not live long together, but some, actuated by the principle I named, would strive for superiority: this must breed quarrels in which the most weak and fearful will, for their own safety, always join with him of whom they have the best opinion.

Hor. This would naturally divide multitudes into bands and companies that would all have their different leaders, and of which the strongest and most valiant would always swallow up the weakest and most fearful.

Cleo. What you say agrees exactly with the accounts we have of the uncivilized nations that are still subsisting in the world, and thus men may live miserably many ages.

Hor. The very first generation that was brought up under the tuition of parents would be governable, and would not every succeeding generation grow wiser than the foregoing?

Cleo. Without doubt they would increase in knowledge and cunning: time and experience would have the same effect upon them as it has upon others, and in the particular things to which they applied themselves they would become as expert and ingenious as the most civilized nations. But their unruly passions and the discords occasioned by contentions would be continually spoiling their improvements, destroying their inventions, and frustrating their designs.

Hor. But would not their sufferings in time bring them acquainted with the causes of their disagreement, and would not that knowledge put them upon making contracts not to injure one another?

Cleo. Very probably they would, but among such ill-bred and uncultivated people no man would keep a contract longer than that interest lasted which made him submit to it.

Hor. But might not religion, the fear of an invisible cause, be made serviceable to them, as to the keeping of their contracts?

Cleo. It might, without dispute; and would, before many generations passed away. But religion could do no more among them than it does among civilized nations where the Divine vengeance is seldom trusted to only, and oaths themselves are thought to be of little service where there is no human power to enforce the obligation and punish perjury.

Hor. But do you not think that the same ambition that made a man aspire to be a leader would make him likewise desirous of being obeyed in civil matters by the numbers he led?

Cleo. I do; and moreover that, notwithstanding this unsettled and precarious way communities would live in, after three or four generations human nature would be looked into and begin to be understood. Leaders would find out, that the more strife and discord there was amongst the people they headed, the less use they could make of them: this would put them upon various ways of curbing mankind; they would forbid killing and striking one another; the taking away by force the wives or children of others in the same community; they would invent penalties, and very early find out that nobody ought to be a judge in his own cause, and that old men, generally speaking, knew more than young.

Hor. When once they have prohibitions and penalties, I should think all the difficulty surmounted; and I wonder why you said that thus they might live miserably for many ages.

Cleo. There is one thing of great moment which has not been named yet, and until that comes to pass, no considerable numbers can ever be made happy. What signify the strongest contracts when we have nothing to show for them, and what dependence can we have upon oral tradition in matters that require exactness, especially whilst the language that is spoken is yet very imperfect? Verbal reports are liable to a thousand cavils and disputes that are prevented by records, which everybody knows to be unerring witnesses; and from the many attempts that are made to wrest and distort the sense of even written laws, we may judge how impracticable the administration of justice must be among all societies that are destitute of them. Therefore the third and last step to society is the invention of letters. No multitudes can live peaceably without government; no government can subsist without laws; and no laws can be effectual long, unless they are wrote down; the consideration of this is alone sufficient to give us great insight into the nature of man.

* * * *

Hor. . . . then which way could any language ever come into the world from two savages?

Cleo. By slow degrees, as all other arts and sciences have done, and length of time; agriculture, physic, astronomy, architecture, painting, &c. From what we see in children that are backward with their tongues, we have reason to think that a wild pair would make themselves intelligible to each other by signs and gestures before they would attempt it by sounds; but when they lived together for many years, it is very probable that for the things they were most conversant with they would find out sounds to stir up in each other the ideas of such things when they were out of sight. These sounds they would communicate to their young ones, and the longer they lived together the greater variety of sounds they would invent, as well for actions as the things themselves; they would find that the volubility of tongue and flexibility of voice were much greater in their young ones than they could remember it ever to have been in themselves. It is impossible but some of these young ones would either by accident or design make use of this superior aptitude of the organs at one time or other, which every generation would still improve upon; and this must have been the origin of all languages, and speech itself, that were not taught by inspiration. I believe, moreover, that after language (I mean such as is of human invention) was come to a great degree of perfection, and even when people had distinct words for every action in life as well as everything they meddled or conversed with, signs and gestures still continued to be made for a great while to accompany speech, because both are intended for the same purpose.

Hor. The design of speech is to make our thoughts known to others.

Cleo. I do not think so.

Hor. What! do not men speak to be understood?

Cleo. In one sense they do; but there is a double meaning in those words, which I believe you did not intend: if by man's speaking to be understood you mean, that when men speak, they desire that the purport of the sounds they utter should be known and apprehended by others, I answer in the affirmitive: but if you mean by it, that men speak in order that their thoughts may be known and their sentiments laid open and seen through by others, which likewise may be meant by speaking to be understood, I answer in the negative. The first sign or sound that ever man made, born of a woman, was made in behalf, and intended for the use, of him who made it; and I am of the opinion that the first design of speech was to persuade others, either to give credit to what the speaking person would have them believe; or else to act or suffer such things as he would compel them to act or suffer, if they were entirely in his power.

*   *   *   *

Hor. . . . . What time, how many ages do you think it would require to have a well-civilized nation from such a savage pair as yours?

Cleo. That is very uncertain, and I believe it impossible to determine any thing about it. From what has been said, it is manifest that the family descending from such a stock would be crumbled to pieces, reunited, and dispersed again several times before the whole of any part of it could be advanced to any degree of politeness. The best forms of government are subject to revolutions, and a great many things must concur to keep a society of men together till they become a civilized nation.

Hor. Is not a vast deal owing, in the raising of a nation, to the difference there is in the spirit and genius of people?

Cleo. Nothing but what depends upon climates, which is soon over-balanced by skilful government. Courage and cowardice, in all bodies of men, depend entirely upon exercise and discipline. Arts and sciences seldom come before riches, and both flow in faster or slower according to the capacity of the governors, the situation of the people, and the opportunities they have of improvements; but the first is the chief: to preserve peace and tranquillity among multitudes of different views and make them all labour for one interest is a great task, and nothing in human affairs requires greater knowledge than the art of governing.

Hor. According to your system, it should be little more than guarding against human nature.

Cleo. But it is a great while before that nature can be rightly understood, and it is the work of ages to find out the true use of the passions, and to raise a politician that can make every frailty of the members add strength to the whole body, and by dextrous management turn private Vices into public Benefits.

Hor. It must be a great advantage to an age when many extraordinary persons are born in it.

Cleo. It is not genius so much as experience that helps men to good laws: Solon, Lycurgus, Socrates, and Plato all travelled for their knowledge, which they communicated to others. The wisest laws of human invention are generally owing to the evasions of bad men whose cunning had eluded the force of former ordinances that had been made with less caution.

Hor. I fancy that the invention of iron and working the ore into a metal must contribute very much to the completing of society, because men can have no tools nor agriculture without it.

Cleo. Iron is certainly very useful, but shells and flints and hardening of wood by fire are substitutes that men make a shift with, if they can but have peace, live in quiet, and enjoy the fruits of their labour. Could you ever have believed that a man without hands could have shaved himself, wrote good characters, and made use of a needle and thread with his feet? Yet this we have seen. It is said by some men of reputation that the Americans in Mexico and Peru have all the signs of an infant world, because when the Europeans first came among them, they wanted a great many things that seem to be of easy invention. But considering that they had nobody to borrow from and no iron at all, it is amazing which way they could arrive at the perfection we found them in. First, it is impossible to know how long multitudes may have been troublesome to one another before the invention of letters came among them and they had any written laws. Secondly, from the many chasms in history we know by experience that the accounts of transactions and times in which letters are known may be entirely lost. Wars and human discord may destroy the most civilized nations only by dispersing them, and general devastations spare arts and sciences no more than they do cities and palaces. That all men are born with a strong desire and no capacity at all to govern has occasioned an infinity of good and evil. Invasions have made strange alterations in the world. Sometimes large empires are divided into several parts and produce new kingdoms and principalities; at others, great conquerors in few years bring different nations under one dominion. From the decay of the Roman empire alone we may learn that arts and sciences are more perishable, much sooner lost, than buildings or inscriptions; and that a deluge of ignorance may overspread countries without their ceasing to be inhabited.

Hor. But what is it at last that raises opulent cities and powerful nations from the smallest beginnings?

Cleo. Providence.

Hor. But Providence makes use of means that are visible; I want to know the engines it is performed with.

Cleo. All the ground work that is required to aggrandize nations, you have seen in the Fable of the Bees. All sound politics and the whole art of governing are entirely built upon the knowledge of human nature. The great business in general of a politician is to promote and, if he can, reward all good and useful actions on the one hand, and on the other, to punish or at least discourage everything that is destructive or hurtful to society. To name particulars would be an endless task. Anger, lust, and pride may be the causes of innumerable mischiefs that are all carefully to be guarded against: but setting them aside, the regulations only that are required to defeat and prevent all the machinations and contrivances that avarice and envy may put man upon, to the detriment of his neighbour, are almost infinite. Would you be convinced of these truths, do but employ yourself for a month or two in surveying and minutely examining into every art and science, every trade, handicraft and occupation, that are professed and followed in such a city as London; and all the laws, prohibitions, ordinances and restrictions that have been found absolutely necessary to hinder both private men and bodies corporate, in so many different stations, first from interfering with the public peace and welfare; secondly, from openly wronging and secretly overreaching, or any other way injuring one another: if you will give yourself this trouble, you will find the number of clauses and provisos to govern a large flourishing city well to be prodigious beyond imagination; and yet every one of them tending to the same purpose, the curbing, restraining, and disappointing the inordinate passions and hurtful frailties of man. You will find, moreover, which is still more to be admired, the greater part of the articles in this vast multitude of regulations, when well understood, to be the result of consummate wisdom.

Hor. How could these things exist, if there had not been men of very bright parts and uncommon talents?

Cleo. Among the things I hint at, there are very few that are the work of one man or of one generation; the greatest part of them are the product, the joint labour, of several ages. Remember what in our third conversation I told you, concerning the arts of shipbuilding and politeness. The wisdom I speak of is not the offspring of a fine understanding or intense thinking, but of sound and deliberate judgment acquired from a long experience in business and a multiplicity of observations. By this sort of wisdom, and length of time, it may be brought about that there shall be no greater difficulty in governing a large city than (pardon the lowness of the simile) there is in weaving of stockings.

Hor. Very low indeed.

Cleo. Yet I know nothing to which the laws and established economy of a well-ordered city may be more justly compared than the knitting-frame. The machine, at first view, is intricate and unintelligible; yet the effects of it are exact and beautiful, and in what is produced by it there is a surprising regularity: but the beauty and exactness in the manufacture are principally, if not altogether, owing to the happiness of the invention, the contrivance of the engine. For the greatest artist at it can furnish us with no better work than may be made by almost any scoundrel after half a year's practice.

Hor. Though your comparison be low, I must own that it very well illustrates your meaning.

Cleo. Whilst you spoke, I have thought of another which is better. It is common now to have clocks that are made to play several tunes with great exactness: the study and labour, as well as trouble of disappointments which, in doing and undoing, such a contrivance must necessarily have cost from the beginning to the end, are not to be thought of without astonishment. There is something analogous to this in the government of a flourishing city that has lasted uninterrupted for several ages; there is no part of the wholesome regulations belonging to it, even the most trifling and minute, about which great pains and consideration have not been employed, as well as length of time; and if you will look into the history and antiquity of any such city, you will find that the changes, repeals, additions and amendments that have been made in and to the laws and ordinances by which it is ruled, are in number prodigious, but that when once they are brought to as much perfection as art and human wisdom can carry them, the whole machine may be made to play of itself with as little skill as is required to wind up a clock; and the government of a large city once put into good order, the magistrates only following their noses, will continue to go right for a while though there was not a wise man in it, provided that the care of Providence was to watch over it in the same manner as it did before. . . .

* * * *

Hor. Here is the castle before us.

Cleo. Which I suppose you are not sorry for.

Hor. Indeed I am, and would have been glad to have heard you speak of kings and other sovereigns with the same candour, as well as freedom, with which you have treated prime ministers, and their envious adversaries. When I see a man entirely impartial, I shall always do him that justice as to think that if he is not in the right in what he says, at least he aims at truth. The more I examine your sentiments by what I see in the world, the more I am obliged to come into them; and all this morning I have said nothing in opposition to you, but to be better informed, and to give you an opportunity to explain yourself more amply. I am your convert, and shall henceforth look upon the Fable of the Bees very differently from what I did; for though, in the Characteristics, the language and the diction are better, the system of man's sociableness is more lovely and more plausible, and things are set off with more art and learning; yet in the other there is certainly more truth, and nature is more faithfully copied in it almost everywhere.

Cleo. I wish you would read them both once more, and, after that, I believe you will say that you never saw two authors who seem to have wrote with more different views. My friend the author of the Fable, to engage and keep his readers in good humour, seems to be very merry, and to do something else, whilst he detects the corruption of our nature; and having shown man to himself in various lights, he points indirectly at the necessity, not only of revelation and believing, but likewise of the practice of Christianity manifestly to be seen in men's lives.

Hor. I have not observed that. Which way has he done it indirectly?

Cleo. By exposing, on the one hand, the vanity of the world, and the most polite enjoyments of it; and, on the other, the insufficiency of human reason and heathen virtue to procure real felicity: for I cannot see what other meaning a man could have by doing this in a Christian country, and among people that all pretend to seek after happiness.

Hor. And what say you of Lord Shaftesbury?

Cleo. First, I agree with you that he was a man of erudition, and a very polite writer; he has displayed a copious imagination, and a fine turn of thinking, in courtly language and nervous expressions. But, as on the one hand, it must be confessed, that his sentiments on liberty and humanity are noble and sublime, and that there is nothing trite or vulgar in the Characteristics; so, on the other, it cannot be denied, that the ideas he had formed of the goodness and excellency of our nature were as romantic and chimerical as they are beautiful and amiable; that he laboured hard to unite two contraries that can never be reconciled together, innocence of manners, and worldly greatness; that to compass this end, he favoured deism, and, under pretence of lashing priestcraft and superstition, attacked the Bible itself; and, lastly, that by ridiculing many passages of Holy Writ, he seems to have endeavoured to sap the foundation of all revealed religion, with design of establishing Heathen virtue on the ruins of Christianity.

F I N I S

CAPRICORN TITLES

G. P. PUTNAM'S SONS

210 Madison Avenue ● New York 16, N. Y